The Hatherleigh Guide

to

Psychiatric Disorders

The Hatherleigh Guides series

1. Psychiatric Disorders
2. Psychotherapy
3. Managing Depression
4. Issues in Modern Therapy
5. Child and Adolescent Therapy
6. Marriage and Family Therapy
7. Substance Abuse I
8. Substance Abuse II
9. Career Counseling
10. Ethics in Therapy

The Hatherleigh Guide
to
Psychiatric Disorders

Hatherleigh Press • New York

The Hatherleigh Guide to Psychiatric Disorders

Cover photo: Christopher Flach, PhD
Production Editor: Joya Lonsdale
Indexer: Angela Washington-Blair, PhD
Cover Designer: Gary Szczecina

A Division of The Hatherleigh Company, Ltd.
420 East 51st Street, New York, NY 10022

This book is printed on acid-free paper.

Compiled under the auspices of the editorial boards of *Directions in Mental Health Counseling, Directions in Clinical Psychology,* and *Directions in Rehabilitation Counseling.*

Library of Congress Cataloging-in-Publication Data

The Hatherleigh Guide to Psychiatric Disorders

Includes bibliographical references and index.
ISBN 1-886330-05-0

First Edition: January 1996

10 9 8 7 6 5 4 3 2 1

About the photograph and the photographer

Kendra, 1995
A young woman yearning to escape the darkness of depression. The natural tones and range of light suggest not only her pain and anguish; they reveal the beauty and hope she possesses within herself.

Christopher Flach, PhD, is a psychologist in private practice in southern California. An avid photographer for more than 20 years, his favorite subjects include people and nature. He has studied photography with Ansel Adams, and his work has been on display in public galleries and in private collections.

Table of Contents

Illustrations

Introduction

The Hatherleigh Guide to Psychiatric Disorders contains a unique group of practical articles by outstanding clinicians about behavioral and psychopathologic disorders. We encounter some of these disorders, such as panic disorders and phobias, frequently in practice; others, such as dissociative identity disorder, we may have never seen—or at least may not have been aware of seeing.

In my more than 40 years of practice, I personally have never seen a patient with dissociative identity disorder (formerly called multiple personality disorder). Several years ago, however, I did receive a note from a former patient, a 34-year-old woman with depression and concomitant anxiety. She claimed to have multiple personalities and that I had missed the diagnosis. I tried to contact her, but never heard from her again. Perhaps she was correct. Unfortunately, though, I'll never know. But now that I have access to Dr. Richard Kluft's chapter, "The Diagnosis and Treatment of Dissociative Identity Disorder," the chances of my making that kind of mistake in the future are greatly diminished.

There are quite a few surprises in these pages. Did you know that psychodynamic psychotherapy and even traditional psychoanalysis are quite ineffective in treating obsessive-compulsive disorder? Dr. Thomas Insel provides us with new information about psychotherapeutic and psychopharmacologic approaches to this disorder that seem to be genuinely effective. In his chapter on "The Criminal Personality," Dr. Stanton E. Samenow describes the true criminal as a person who cannot be understood within the framework of our traditional psychological concepts. Contrary to some peoples' opinions, the criminal cannot be rehabilitated. The criminal personality can manifest as an overwhelming dissatisfaction with responsible living, a penchant for calculated prevarication, and extremely amoral and unrealistic expectations of the world. As Dr. Samenow emphasizes, persons with this personality type must be taught to change the way they *think*, a goal that can be extremely difficult to achieve.

There's a touch of the gambler in all of us. But when gambling is tied to narcissistic needs, as Dr. Richard McCormick demonstrates, it can progress to a debilitating addictive disorder—with the anxiety that accompanies risk, the rush of excitement that comes with winning, the dejection that comes with losing. The intense pressure to further the cycle usually leads to seriously disrupted interpersonal relationships and, often, to personal bankruptcy. Pathological gambling is a challenging disorder to recognize, especially when it is not blatant. Furthermore, as would be the case with any patient population, we must work diligently and compassionately with compulsive gamblers to break them out of their vicious, self-destructive pattern of behavior.

There is also a touch of posttraumatic stress disorder in our lives, not necessarily in its full-blown form, but certainly to the extent that no life is lived without any profoundly disturbing experiences. In 1950, I was in a boating accident off the coast of Cuba. I floated for 14 hours—much of it in pitch-black darkness—sitting in the shell of the boat, which was filled with water up to my waist. I knew that the distance to shore was too far to swim and the sea was full of sharks. When the sun came up the next morning, I was thrilled to see that I was still approximately 1 mile from land; the current must have pulled me along parallel to the island. An old freighter, "Lehigh Portland Cement" painted in large white letters on its side, was moving steadily toward me. In half an hour, I was aboard, drinking coffee and chewing on a rather hard biscuit, safe. That's all that mattered to me: I was alive. The terror of the night was something to be quickly forgotten. I never spoke to anyone about how I felt when I was convinced of my imminent death. I certainly did not consider myself as being at risk for posttraumatic stress disorder.

Today's concepts and knowledge about posttraumatic stress disorder, as cogently described in Dr. Thomas W. Miller's chapter, simply did not exist. It would be another 30 years before I really understood that the insomnia, anxiety, and depressive feelings that I experienced for several years after my harrowing experience warranted a diagnosis of PTSD. More important, had I known more about the complex clinical nuances of PTSD, I could have taken some fairly simple steps to resolve the emotional turmoil that the accident had quite logically induced.

If you are involved in therapy with patients with borderline personality disorder, Dr. Glen Gabbard's insightful chapter on this topic should be considered required reading. A large portion of the psychotherapeutic literature suggests that there is only *one way* to treat these patients, although experts differ as to which particular approach each would recommend for a given BPD patient. The fact is that there are numerous types of borderline patients; accordingly, they require different psychotherapeutic approaches. Dr. Gabbard explains what these psychotherapeutic strategies are and how they can be appropriately employed in your practice.

Economic and political changes in the health care field in the past few years have already had a major impact on how medical services are provided. The effect on how psychiatric and psychological services are provided has been especially profound—and arguably quite disturbing. Once-famous private psychiatric hospitals have closed their doors. Remuneration for psychotherapy has been significantly reduced. Those of us treating the millions of patients in the mental health system often must seek approval for what we propose to do every step of the way. Inevitably, patients and their families will have to assume much more responsibility for their own wellbeing. Three important chapters address this issue: "Parent Training for Children with Attention-Deficit/Hyperactivity Disorder," by Dr. Robert F. Newby; "Teaching Self-Help Strategies to Manic Clients," by Mary Ellen Copeland; and "Self-Management Approaches for Seriously Mentally Ill Persons," by Drs. Alex Kopelowicz and Robert Paul Liberman.

The future of mental health service delivery is already upon us—not just in terms of organizational changes, but also in terms of new psychological and pharmacotherapeutic treatment approaches. I believe you'll find that *The Hatherleigh Guide to Psychiatric Disorders* represents an invaluable contribution to our efforts to remain well-informed and up-to-date.

Frederic Flach, MD
New York

Dr. Flach is Adjunct Associate Professor of Psychiatry, Cornell University Medical College, New York; and Attending Psychiatrist at Payne Whitney Clinic of the New York Hospital and St. Vincent's Hospital and Medical Center, New York.

1

An Update on Posttraumatic Stress Disorder

Thomas W. Miller, PhD, ABPP

Dr. Miller is Chief of Psychology Services at the Department of Psychiatry, University of Kentucky Medical Center, Lexington, KY.

KEY POINTS

- This chapter examines prominent theories and controversies related to stressful life events and their impact on health and adjustment.
- The issues and implications arising from trends in diagnosis and treatment of stress-related disorders are discussed.
- Victims of posttraumatic stress disorder (PTSD) have been identified as those experiencing combat; prisoners of war; torture victims; police officers; victims of crime, other assaults, and natural disasters; and persons experiencing divorce, the death or injury of a significant other, near-fatal illnesses, family violence, and rape and/or other sexual abuse.
- Comprehensive assessment of life stress events involves a number of basic goals, including: identification of experiences and symptoms; consideration of the presence of coexisting psychological disorders; and specificity, with respect to the most recent diagnostic and statistical evaluation criteria.
- Future clinical investigations into PTSD must focus not only on the science of stressful life events, but also on the interaction among psychological variables and the variety of genetic, metabolic, and biochemical aspects of life that contribute to our adaptation to stressful life events.

INTRODUCTION

Clinical and epidemiologic studies have supported the belief that human beings exposed to stressful life events are vulnerable to the symptomatology consistent with posttraumatic stress disorder (PTSD). Examined in this chapter are prominent theories and controversies related to stressful life events and their impact on health and adjustment. Also discussed are the issues and implications arising from trends in diagnosis and treatment of stress-related disorders.

Victims of traumatic stress have been identified as those experiencing combat (Davidson, Kudler, Saunders, & Smith, 1990; Hryvniak & Rosse, 1989; Miller & Basoglu, 1992; Miller, Martin, & Spiro, 1989; Roszell, McFall, & Malas, 1991; Rundell, Ursano, Holloway, & Silberman, 1989; Sierles, Chen, Messing, Besyner, & Taylor, 1986), prisoners of war (Engdahl, Speed, Eberly, & Schwartz, 1991; Speed, Engdahl, Schwartz & Eberly, 1989), torture victims (Allodi, 1991; Miller, 1992), police officers (Saathoff & Buckman, 1990), victims of crime and other assaults (Jacobson, Koehler, & Jones-Brown, 1987; Kilpatrick et al., 1985; Sonnenberg, 1988) and victims of natural disasters (McFarlane, 1986), as well as persons experiencing divorce, the death of a significant other, near-fatal illnesses, injuries to a significant other, family violence (Wilson, Smith, & Johnson, 1985) and rape and/or other sexual abuse (Browne & Finkelhor, 1986; Gise & Paddison, 1988; Green, Wilson, & Lindy, 1985; Jacobson et al., 1987; Miller & Veltkamp, 1988; Reiker & Carmen, 1986; Rose, 1986; Veltkamp, Miller, Kearl, Barlow, Elliott, & Bright, 1992).

HISTORICAL REVIEW

The impact of stressful life experiences on adaptation has been the focus of several theorists (Miller, 1989). In the seventeenth century, Descartes argued that the mind, as constituted by thoughts and emotions, was separate from the body, whereas

Spinoza contended that a person's thoughts and emotions were integrated with bodily functions. By the nineteenth century, Pavlov argued that the functions of the brain should be investigated with the same empirical vigor characterized by contemporary European investigations of physiologic functioning. Some theorists believe a constitutional predisposition may explain poor adaptation to stressful life experiences.

This view was countered by Freud and Breuer, who argued that unconscious psychological processes played a role in how a person responded to stress, and that traumatization contributed to the formulation of anxiety and stress-related disorders. They contended that any study of responses to stressful life events would have to involve a careful analysis of both the mind's internal milieu and thought processes as well as the emotional responsivity of the body to such stresses.

The twentieth century brought new hypotheses and more complete conceptualizations. In Horowitz's (1977) conceptual view of stress, traumatizing events destroy a person's perception of reality, necessitating a reformulation of the internal scheme of functioning. Horowitz further suggests that survivors of traumatic stress will experience symptoms in identifiable stages, especially persons who delay assimilating the event. He states that the immediate reaction may be emotional disruption, followed by denial and numbing of feelings. The person may then experience periods of intrusive ideas or images and "attacks of emotion" (p. 8) and/or compulsive behaviors, which alternate with continued denial and numbing. All phases serve to protect the survivor from the implications of fully assimilating the information.

Janoff-Bulman (1985) elaborates on this theory, more specifically stating that stressful events force the recognition and examination of assumptions about personal invulnerability ("It can't happen to me") and the belief that the world is meaningful and comprehensible (p. 18). When such events cannot be incorporated into existing assumptions, the old views are challenged and disequilibrium results; being "out of balance" is characterized by intense stress and anxiety.

Green (1990) outlines eight separate dimensions of stressful events:

- Feeling a threat to life or bodily integrity, characterized by the experiences of victims of man-made disasters or crime

- Incurring severe physical harm or injury, such as that experienced by crime and rape victims, persons exposed to combat, or people wounded in terrible accidents or natural disasters

- Receiving intentional injury or harm, exemplified by rape, torture, combat, or family violence

- Being exposed to the grotesque, which might be found in airplane crashes, technological accidents, and Vietnam-style combat

- Violently or suddenly losing a loved one

- Witnessing, or learning of, violence to a loved one (e.g., a child being injured, kidnapped, or abused, or the rape or mugging of a significant other)

- Learning of one's exposure to a toxic agent. In this case, the potential impact that the information conveys is the stressor [as with nuclear accidents or acquired immunodeficiency syndrome (AIDS)]

- Causing death or harm to another person, particularly when doing so is an integral part of one's role (i.e., in combat or as a member of law enforcement)

Green suggests that the stress process consists of the environmental change (the event), the person's perception and appraisal of the event, and his or her psychological reaction. Green and colleagues (1985) identify environmental factors and individual characteristics that determine the appraisal and influence the total processing of the event.

DEFINING PTSD

Horowitz (1977) has defined traumatic stress as the response to events that violate a person's sense of personal vulnerability and safety. Figley (1985) added that trauma is "an emotional state of discomfort and stress resulting from memories of an extraordinary, catastrophic experience which shatters the survivor's sense of invulnerability" (p. xviii); a traumatic stress reaction is "a set of conscious and unconscious activities and emotions associated with dealing with the stressors of the catastrophe and its immediate aftermath" (p. xix). Thus, in Figley's view, PTSD comprises clinical indicators of the problems connected to the trauma and is represented by posttraumatic stress reactions.

According to the fourth edition of the *Diagnostic and Statistical Manual of Mental Disorders* (DSM-IV) (American Psychiatric Association, 1994), the essential feature of PTSD is the development of characteristic symptoms wherein the person has been exposed to a traumatic event in which both of the following have been present:

- The person has experienced, witnessed, or been confronted with an event or events that involve actual or threatened death or serious injury, or a threat to the physical integrity of oneself or others.

- The person's response involved intense fear, helplessness, or horror. This definition of PTSD has sparked a considerable debate over how the stressor is defined and conceptualized. A comparison of DSM-III-R and DSM-IV criteria for PTSD is offered in Table 1.1.

Breslau and Davis (1987) state that stressors are defined

Table 1.1
Comparison of DSM Criteria for Posttraumatic Stress Disorder (DSM-III-R and DSM-IV)

DSM-III-R	DSM-IV
1. Experience of an event outside the range of usual human experience	Exposure to a traumatic event in which *both* of the following have been present: 1. The person has experienced, witnessed, or been confronted with an event or events that involve actual or threatened death or serious injury, or a threat to the physical integrity of oneself or others 2. The person's response involved intense fear, helplessness, or horror
2. Reexperiencing of the trauma through intrusive recollections, dreams, flashbacks, or exposure	The traumatic event is persistently reexperienced in at least one of the following ways: 1. Recurrent and intrusive distressing recollections of the event 2. Recurrent distressing dreams of the event 3. Acting or feeling as if the traumatic event were recurring 4. Intense psychological distress at exposure to internal or external cues that symbolize or resemble an aspect of the traumatic event 5. Physiologic reactivity upon exposure to internal or external cues that symbolize or resemble an aspect of the traumatic event

DSM-III-R	DSM-IV
3. Numbing of responsiveness, detachment, estrangement, constricted affect	Persistent avoidance of stimuli associated with the trauma and numbing of general responsiveness (not present before the trauma)
4. Symptoms of increased arousal a. Sleep disturbance b. Irritability or outbursts of anger c. Difficulty concentrating d. Hypervigilance e. Exaggerated startle response f. Physiologic reactivity	Persistent symptoms of increased arousal (not present before the trauma), as indicated by at least two of the following: 1. Difficulty falling or staying asleep 2. Irritability or outbursts of anger 3. Difficulty concentrating 4. Hypervigilance 5. Exaggerated startle response

Source: American Psychiatric Association. (1994). *Diagnostic and statistical manual of mental disorders* (4th ed.). Washington DC: Author. Copyright 1994 American Psychiatric Association. Reprinted with permission.

only by their magnitude, exert a cumulative effect, are conditional on social and individual factors, and occur in a unilateral, cause-and-effect fashion. However, Lindy, Green and Grace (1987), as well as Ursano (1987), disagree. Ursano argues that the DSM-IV definition does not negate the quality of the stressor as a factor—it is simply not addressed. The quantity of a stressor is not the same as its type or class, both of which require environmental interaction by definition. Lindy and colleagues concur, saying that the concept of the stressor must be multidimensional and include personal, environmental, and event-processing factors for its fullest comprehension.

Keane (1985) concurs that a strictly environmental definition of the stressor oversimplifies a genuinely complex topic. Lindy and colleagues (1987) comment that the flexibility in the "stressor" definition has been useful, leading to research that might not otherwise have been performed, had the definition been restrictive. In other words, stressors not necessarily outside the range of human experience may cause traumatic stress responses in some persons, and experiences outside that range do not necessarily cause such responses in all persons.

Horowitz, Weiss, and Marmar (1987) agree that differentiating ordinary and extraordinary stressors is difficult, but they do not think this diminishes the usefulness of the PTSD diagnosis. Robins (1990) believes that whether the stressor is "inside" or "outside" of the range of usual human experience depends on where one lives, one's age, and how one spends one's time. For instance, being diagnosed with a fatal disease before the age of 40 may be more "outside" the range of usual experience than being diagnosed in one's 60s. Despite this debate, as Keane (1985) notes, clinicians need a coherent way to use the term *traumatic stress* in order to communicate effectively with their clients.

ASSESSMENT OF LIFE STRESS

Comprehensive assessment of life stress events involves a number of basic goals, including: the identification of experiences and symptoms, consideration of the presence of coexisting psychological disorders, and specificity with respect to the most recent diagnostic and statistical evaluation criteria. Such approaches often include structured clinical interviews as well as psychometric and behavioral assessment strategies. A discussion of some of the multiaxial measures currently utilized in assessing life stress events follows.

Structured Clinical Interview for DSM-III-R:

The structured clinical interview for DSM-III-R (Spitzer & Williams, 1987) is an instrument that provides operational criteria for assessing the 17 symptoms of PTSD within the criterion categories of reexperiencing, numbing avoidance, and physiologic arousal. The SCID instructs the clinician to ask specific questions, the answers to which determine whether a patient satisfies the diagnostic criteria for major Axis I disorders. The number of symptoms positively endorsed is summed to arrive at an index of PTSD symptom severity.

PTSD Subscale of the MMPI and MMPI-2:

The Minnesota Multiphasic Personality Inventory (MMPI) and Minnesota Multiphasic Personality Inventory-2 (MMPI-2) (Hathaway & McKinley, 1967) are two standardized measures used in the assessment of psychopathology and the study of traumatization and stress. The PTSD subscale of the MMPI consists of 49 items from the MMPI found to distinguish between patients with mixed psychiatric diagnoses but no PTSD and patients with a PTSD diagnosis. A minimum subscale score of 30 indicates the presence of PTSD. The correct classification of patients with PTSD and without PTSD has ranged from 66% to 82% in a variety of studies.

Mississippi Scale for Combat-Related PTSD:

The Mississippi Scale for Combat-Related PTSD (Keane et al., 1988) is a 35-item Likert scale questionnaire originally developed to assess DSM-III symptoms and various associated features in Vietnam veterans who have been exposed to combat. The Mississippi Scale has high internal consistency ($\alpha = 0.94$). A score above 106 has been shown to have high sensitivity (93%) and specificity (89%) in distinguishing combat veterans with PTSD from (a) psychiatric patients who never engaged in military combat and (b) nonpatient veteran populations. Subsequent validation studies of the Mississippi Scale have found similarly high levels of sensitivity and specificity in discriminating patients with PTSD from various controls without PTSD. The factor structure for this instrument is stable, and the six factors could be labeled as: reexperiencing the traumatic events, affective interpersonal problems, depression, memory and concentration problems, aggression, and sleep disturbance.

The Civilian Mississippi Scale:

This 39-item inventory is based on the Mississippi Scale for Combat-Related PTSD and adapted to civilian experiences independent of combat or wartime. It also can be applied to natural disasters and other types of traumatized experience. The factor structure for this instrument attempts to measure symptomatology consistent with traumatic stress, including sleep disturbance, memory and concentration difficulties, depression, interpersonal problems, affective disturbance, and reexperiencing the traumatic event.

The Mississippi Scale–Hostage Version:

This 39-item inventory is adapted from the original Mississippi Scale for Combat-Related PTSD. It assesses DSM-III-R criteria, including symptoms and associated features of victims of hostage-taking experiences. As with the Civilian Mississippi Scale, it is geared specifically for the assessment of post-hostage adaptation, focusing on difficulties in memory and concentration, aggression, sleep disturbance, interpersonal difficulties, and reexperiencing the trauma.

Allodi Trauma Scale:

The Allodi Trauma Scale (Allodi, 1985) is a semistructured interview schedule developed to document traumatization related to torture experiences. This 41-item questionnaire assesses traumatic experiences associated with political persecution, imprisonment, as well as disappearance and death of persons and entire families. It includes seven parts: (a) nonviolent persecution, (b) arrest history, (c) physical torture, (d) deprivation during imprisonment, (e) sensory manipulation, (f) psychological torture and ill treatment, and (g) violence to family members. This instrument yields a subtotal for each section as well as a total score that measures the victim's total trauma/torture experience.

Harvard Trauma Questionnaire:

The Harvard Trauma Questionnaire (HTQ) (Mollica, Wyshak, de Marneffe, Khuon, & Lavelle, 1987) is designed to measure the traumatic events and syndromes of people who have survived torture and other trauma of mass violence. Modeled after the successfully validated Hopkins Symptom Checklist 25 for anxiety and depression, it is given in three Indochinese languages as well as in English. The initial validation of the HTQ has revealed inter-rater reliability of 0.93. Preliminary analysis suggests that highly symptomatic respondents have the best test-retest concordance.

The HTQ is comprised of three sections. The first section includes 17 specific trauma events that are historically accurate for assessing the Indochinese refugee experience, such as starvation and the death of family members. The second section consists of an open-ended question that asks the respondent to describe the most terrifying events in his or her life. The third section elicits 30 symptoms related to the torture/trauma experience. Sixteen of these symptoms are derived from the DSM-III-R criteria for PTSD.

Vietnam Experiences Questionnaire:

The Vietnam Experiences Questionnaire (VEQ) (Miller & Buchbinder, 1982) is a 70-item measure that has been factor-analyzed into six distinct scale descriptions. Scales include: disturbance in interpersonal relationships; sleep disturbance; hypersensitivity; psychotic symptomatology; perceived capacity for violence; and motivational disturbances. The VEQ assesses the impact of stressful life events using symptoms associated with PTSD, as well as items similar to the critical items of the MMPI. Although the VEQ was developed primarily for use with veterans from the Vietnam War, its applicability to other populations who have been traumatized through combat or war-type experiences is recognized.

The Boston Clinical Interview for PTSD:

The Boston Clinical Interview for PTSD (Gerardi & Wolfe, 1989) is a structured, 122-item, clinical interview that includes demographic information and background, a family diagram and premilitary history, legal problems prior to military service, substance abuse, and evaluation of stressful experiences or significant losses prior to military experience. Other sections focus on military history, carefully evaluating specific stressful life events and patterns of coping; postmilitary experience and adjustment, including postmilitary stressful experiences or significant losses; family and social relationships; and psychiatric treatment history, including prescribed medications and a log of hospitalizations. A medical history section and a section addressing veterans' perceived problem areas requiring treatment and clinical observation are included as well.

Clinician-Administered PTSD Scale:

The Clinician-Administered PTSD scale (CAPS) (Blake, Weathers, & Nagy, 1990) is a structured clinical interview designed to assess the 17 symptoms for PTSD outlined in DSM-III-R. The CAPS provides a methodology for evaluation of the frequency and intensity of symptoms, as well as the distinguishing characteristics of each symptom, the impact of the symptoms on the patient's social and occupational functioning, the overall severity of the symptom complex, and the patient's global improvement since baseline and validity ratings were obtained. The time frame for each symptom measured is 1 month. A frequency rating of 1 or greater and an intensity rating of 2 or greater reflect significant problems with a particular symptom and, as such, should be considered a symptom endorsement.

FACTORS AFFECTING RESPONSE TO TRAUMATIC STRESS

Factors that influence the severity of responses to traumatic stress and the etiology of comorbidity merit close examination. Reiker and Carmen (1986) emphasize the context as an important influence on how a traumatic event is experienced and suggest that a person's life context (social climate) may prevent victims of sexual abuse from being able to acknowledge abuse and the feelings associated with it.

The same events (especially those outside the range of usual human experience) do not always generate stress disorders (implying that individual differences interact with the stressor in different ways). Keane (1985) says that personal control, personal resources, and social support are all moderating factors in how stress is experienced. A person-environment interaction has also been suggested by Wilson and colleagues (1985). The response to a severe stressor is a function of a person's psychosocial development and developmental state. Sonnenberg (1988) notes that it is still not clear whether preexisting personality characteristics make a person more vulnerable to develop severe responses to stress or whether the nature of the trauma produces the dysfunction.

Types of Stressors and Comorbidity:

The specificity of interactions is based on the type of stressor. Allodi (1991) proposes that the degree of posttraumatic symptomatology in torture victims is related to the severity of the trauma and specific fears of persecution. He adds that the impact of the trauma is also mediated by individual personality characteristics. Again, personality characteristics predictive of different types of responses to trauma are not readily defined.

For the victims of the Australian bush fire, for example, the amount of personal and property loss affected the risk of developing any type of psychiatric illness (McFarlane, 1986).

Speed and associates (1989) found that several variables, such as family history of alcoholism or mental illness, prior personal psychiatric history, unusual childhood trauma, and age at capture were not associated with whether a prisoner of war developed PTSD. However, of those soldiers who did develop PTSD, all of these variables were related to the severity of PTSD symptoms. In addition, severe weight loss and torture were strong predictors of PTSD symptom severity.

Among trauma survivors, Wilson and associates (1985) found that severe stress was experienced when the event involved "loss" versus "no-loss," even if the "no-loss" condition included other types of trauma. Interaction influences are also pertinent when examining traumatic stress and comorbidity. The traditional view of comorbidity in survivors of rape is that the trauma exacerbates preexisting psychopathology (Rose, 1986). Green and colleagues (1985) agree that this is a common view and state that DSM-III-R suggests that preexisting psychopathology predisposes a person to PTSD despite the lack of confirming, empirical evidence. Because the evaluation of PTSD is usually made shortly after the traumatic event, Robins (1990) states that comorbidity "will almost always have preceded PTSD's onset" (p. 1676).

Ursano (1987) has taken a more moderate position, maintaining that preexisting psychopathology is not necessary or sufficient for a psychiatric diagnosis following trauma; however, this does not mean that it may be unimportant. Reiker and Carmen (1986), who worked with psychiatric patients with histories of sexual abuse, hold that responses to trauma are mediated by psychosocial context as well as a person's psychological composition. They suggest that victims of sexual abuse who become psychiatric patients use defense mechanisms (such as repression and dissociation) to protect themselves from feelings and memories that might be overwhelming. In their view, the patient "decontextualizes" or cognitively disconnects himself or herself from the context. In effect, these survival strategies become the core of the mental disorder, with the most extreme example being the person with dissociative identity disorder (multiple personality disorder). In this case, the development of psychopathology in the survivor of sexual abuse is not a simple cause-and-effect end result; rather, the decision to seek professional help involves interactions between personality characteristics, the nature of the abuse, and the context in which it occurs.

The Relationship Among Psychopathologies:

Although disagreement over the etiology of PTSD persists, Davidson and colleagues (1990) found that most veterans in their sample first developed PTSD rather than mental disorders. Of 36 veterans with comorbidity, the psychopathology was present before PTSD in only four cases. They suggest that depression activates PTSD symptoms in older veterans; they also hypothesized that there may be a closer genetic relationship between PTSD and anxiety than between PTSD and depression.

Davidson and colleagues (1990) offer similar findings in another study. As a general rule, PTSD was reported as occurring first, followed by anxiety and depressive disorders. However, in this sample, when PTSD was comorbid with alcoholism, the alcoholism usually preceded PTSD in Vietnam veterans but did not develop until an average of several years later in World War II veterans. (They suggest that the excessive alcohol consumption constituted self-medication for the PTSD symptoms by the older group.) Rundell and colleagues (1989) also examined PTSD and alcoholism in a veteran population. They agree that if the alcoholism develops after the trauma, it is likely to be a self-medication strategy—the effects of alcohol possibly suppressing nightmares and decreasing autonomic arousal.

Keane and Wolfe (1990) examined depression, substance abuse, and antisocial personality disorder in relationship to PTSD in veterans. They hypothesize that a person with these diagnoses may be at greater risk for developing PTSD when exposed to stressors; another explanation was that such disorders develop as a function of PTSD symptoms and represent a person's attempt to cope with the distress of the symptoms.

For veterans who had been prisoners of war, Roszell and associates (1991) found that the experience of witnessing or participating in torture increased the comorbidity of PTSD and alcohol abuse or depression. They also found that other anxiety disorders may be found with PTSD if the person was exposed to high-risk and/or terrifying acts. Moreover, they suggest that when depression is codiagnosed with PTSD, the symptoms of PTSD may cause the depression.

Page, Engdahl, and Miller (1991) view this relationship somewhat differently; they hold that when depression in prisoners of war is associated with chronic PTSD and serves as its precursor, it makes resolving PTSD more difficult.

Psychopathology As a Catalyst:

Other theorists (Bean-Bayog, 1988; Shaner & Eth, 1989) explain how a specific psychopathology may cause traumatic stress responses. The traditional view posits that stress and anxiety predispose to, and are associated with, schizophrenia (Shaner & Eth, 1989). According to this perspective, the experience of schizophrenia is terrifying, and psychotic reactions may cause PTSD in some patients with schizophrenia. If a traumatic stressor is outside the range of usual human experience and would be distressing to most everyone, then psychotic symptoms, such as delusions and hallucinations, may indeed be traumatic stressors.

Alcoholism may also be a traumatic stressor (Bean-Bayog, 1988). How a person feels about and reacts to alcoholism as it develops—and, more specifically, to the loss of control associated with alcoholism—may be traumatic. Events possibly linked with a loss of control are behaviors that engender shame and guilt, which lead to lowered self-esteem. When an alcoholic person is unable to control his or her drinking, he or she may also be subject to life-threatening and psychologically threatening situations (e.g., car accidents; blackouts; chronic threats to self-esteem and personal integrity; loss of relationships; jeopardized financial, occupational, and legal status; and damaged health). Cognitive impairment may interfere with a person's ability to respond to any or all of these events.

Psychological functioning is also affected by the mood- and mind-altering properties of alcohol. Bean-Bayog (1988) likens the alcoholic's loss of control to the experience of a stroke victim—an attack on the integrity of the personality. The behavioral components are exacerbated by how a person perceives being out of control and by repeatedly experiencing related events.

CASE STUDY

In the remote village of Spitak, Armenia, a 12-year-old girl named Anastasia lives in a tent adjacent to the house she once lived in before it was destroyed by an earthquake. She lost her mother, father, and younger brother due to the devastation. She stays with extended family and continues to have recurrent, intrusive, and distressing recollections of the natural disaster some 6 months after the earthquake.

Before the earthquake, Anastasia was described as happy and outgoing. She made friends easily and felt close to her family. Since the earthquake, she describes herself as "a different person." She is often irritable and sad. During a psychiatric interview at a district clinic, she had difficulty discussing the losses she had experienced during the earthquake. When she was able to express her thoughts, her focus was on the loss of her family members and her friends as a result of the earthquake; she also spoke of the intensification of symptoms with exposure to noise or vibrations. She discussed attempts to avoid the thoughts and feelings associated with the earthquake as well as situations that aroused recall. Since the earthquake, Anastasia has developed increased feelings of detachment from others and has found that she no longer has the ability to feel joy.

She talks of fears of darkness. Also, she experiences difficulty in falling asleep, and, later, staying asleep. While lying on her cot, she often thinks of how her parents and brother died in the earthquake. When a train comes through her town, the vibrations and sounds remind her of the traumatization she experienced during the earthquake. The train passing through Spitak never fails to trigger the recurrent, intrusive, and distressing thoughts of the earthquake experience.

ANALYSIS

In discussing this case, we must address several important elements, including the impact of living in a society and culture that does not permit movement and change from province to province. Anastasia clearly has experienced an event that is outside the range of usual human experience and that would likely be markedly distressing for almost any person. The earthquake that resulted in more than 20,000 deaths, two thirds of whom were children and adolescents, is a constant reminder of Anastasia's own vulnerability. The area is highly prone to earthquakes and continues to be a serious threat to her life, yet she is forced to live with her extended family in a tent adjacent to the home that was destroyed during the earthquake.

The loss of her parents, brother, and close friends also serves as a constant reminder to her, as does the sudden destruction of her home and community. She reports "recurrent, intrusive, and distressing" recollections of the event that affect her sleep pattern and sometimes lead to sudden acts and feelings as if the traumatic event were recurring. The train that moves through the countryside on a daily basis reminds her—both by sound and vibration—of what was experienced at the time of the earthquake.

It has been difficult for Anastasia to avoid the thoughts and feelings associated with this disaster because she has no way of relocating from what has now been recognized as the epicenter of the earthquake. She shows markedly diminished interest in the important activities of her life, feels detached and estranged from others, and is careful not to make or attempt to make new friendships for fear that another earthquake will take these friends from her.

Difficulty in sleeping, fear of the dark, and intensification of symptoms upon exposure to both noise and vibrations (as well as physiologic reactivity on reexposure to experiences that may symbolize or resemble the earthquake) indicate a syndrome consistent with delayed stress syndrome. The provisional diagnosis is posttraumatic stress disorder. In addition, there is uncomplicated bereavement in this case, with signs and symptoms of depression noted as a normal reaction to such a loss. It is culturally significant that the ongoing bereavement in this Armenian village has lasted for an extended period.

TREATMENT ISSUES AND IMPLICATIONS

Treatment of patients with PTSD has received considerable attention in the clinical literature. Models ranging from psychoanalytic to cognitive-behavioral to pharmacotherapeutic (and the various modifications of each) have been clearly expounded (Walker, 1989). Approaches to the treatment of PTSD must be sensitive to the processing and accommodation of traumatic and stressful life experiences.

Although a variety of cognitive-behavioral techniques may address the immediate aspects of anxiety-inducing experiences, and although more analytically oriented therapeutic interventions are effective in the exploration of intrapsychic motives and beliefs, a combination of short-term pharmacotherapy and appropriate psychotherapeutic techniques may be the most beneficial for processing traumatizing experiences in patients with PTSD.

DeJong (1985) suggests the following objectives in the treatment of trauma victims:

- Identify the traumatized person. Some victims complain directly about the trauma, whereas others exhibit various vague physical and emotional symptoms.

- Address acute medical problems, including physical injury. Be prepared to make a referral to a physician if necessary.

- Obtain and record an accurate history of the trauma.

- Manage acute emotional problems resulting from the trauma itself. Mixed feelings of anger, guilt, and frustration often exacerbate these problems.

- Safeguard the victim against further trauma. Formulate treatment plan and follow-up plans for the victim's medical and psychological needs.

- Comply with all legal requirements.

Clinical research by Friedman (1991) suggests that the multisymptomatic presentation noted in patients with PTSD can make choosing the appropriate forms of intervention somewhat difficult. However, growing evidence indicates that medication may alleviate the symptoms associated with PTSD early on in treatment and that pharmacotherapy alone is rarely sufficient to provide complete remission of the disorder. Miller and Feibelman (1987) note that symptom relief provided by medication facilitates a patient's participation in individual behavior and group-oriented psychotherapies; moreover, drug-mediated attenuation of intrusive or hyperarousal symptoms improves the benefits of psychotherapy for relevant concerns (e.g., grief, guilt, intimacy, and the psychological pain associated with PTSD). They also observed that catastrophic exposure to trauma is often followed by stable biological alterations in the sympathetic nervous system, neuroendocrine system, and sleep/dream cycle. These alterations appear to be unique to PTSD and distinguish it from both major depression and panic disorder (Friedman, 1991).

Types of Therapeutic Interventions:

A multiplicity of therapeutic interventions is available for patients who have experienced PTSD. Cognitive and behavioral therapies that have proved efficacious often use techniques such as systematic desensitization, thought-stopping, and response prevention. Insight-oriented therapists rely more on relationships, rapport, and the patient's understanding of the cognitive and emotional consequences of trauma. Although cognitive-behavioral methodologies may provide important coping strategies to deal with symptomatology, the need for long-term psychotherapeutic counseling is not uncommon. This often allows the patient to work through intrapsychic conflicts that may emerge over time as a result of the recurring impact of the life stress event.

Psychopharmacologic approaches have provided some improvement and adaptation for patients but usually are used in combination with other psychotherapeutic models. Increasing evidence suggests that the efficacy of clomipramine (Anafranil) in obsessive-compulsive disorder (OCD) may be advantageous in treating the obsessive-compulsive features of delayed stress. Dosages of clomipramine typically begin at 25 mg or less a day and gradually increase to 250 mg a day (DuPont, 1995). However, because clomipramine produces more untoward effects than the newer selective serotonin reuptake inhibitors (SSRIs), it generally is not the first medication prescribed for OCD. First-line medications for the treatment of OCD include: fluoxetine (Prozac), in dosages up to 80 mg a day; fluvoxamine (Luvox), 300 mg a day; and sertraline (Zoloft), 200 mg a day (DuPont, 1995). Clinical psychologists should also be cognizant of the fact that some of their PTSD clients may be prescribed a benzodiazepine to help reduce dysfunction associated with concomitant anxiety; 0.25 mg a day of alprazolam (Xanax) as needed (up to six tablets per day) is a typical pharmacotherapeutic indication for such persons.

The Realm Of Future Research:

Although significant strides have been made in both the diagnosis and treatment of PTSD in adults, a considerable need still exists for studying the impact of delayed stress, with specific attention focused on the following:

- Systematic documentation of group-specific events that cause trauma in children and adults and the cognitive and behavioral processing of events
- Standardized assessment protocols specifically designed for the diagnosis of PTSD, with special emphasis placed on group and individual differences, including culturally unique methods of processing trauma and stress
- Treatment outcome studies as well as studies addressing gender and age differences by the category of traumatic stressful life event
- Comparability studies that address neurobiologic markers and the personality, cultural, and environmental differences among persons who do (and do not) experience traumatizing and stressful life events
- External psychosocial factors, including the presence of parental substance abuse, foster placement, parental divorce and separation, financial hardship, and neglect
- Exposure of adults and children who experience traumatizing events to various coping styles, including the coping styles of television and cartoon models

Furthermore, growing evidence suggests that stressful life events and perceived stress are closely associated with changes in immune function. Although psychological stress is often described as suppressing immune response, the implications of stress-induced immunologic changes for susceptibility to disease continue to be an area of growing scientific interest.

Considerable effort must be exerted in developing both theoretical and research perspectives to help us better understand the impact of traumatic stress on children and adults. The clinical assessment and treatment interventions provided for patients with PTSD must explore the impact of stressful life events within the context of analyzing the interaction of the traumatized person with the environment; the nature and course of the disorder; and the environment in which the person lives, including the victim's support systems. The professional community has clearly recognized that stressful life events must be addressed from the perspective of not only the external stimulus but also its relationship to the psychobiology of the patient. The interaction between the person and his or her environment is unique in every situation, and the response pattern of each person will be influenced by the nature of the physical and psychosocial environments in which he or she functions.

SUMMARY

The growing understanding of psychological stress is conceptualized as a response to environmental events considered to be traumatic. Our current measures may also reflect personality characteristics that are independent of environmental factors and contribute to the adaptation process. Self-esteem and locus of control, two personality characteristics strongly associated with and challenged by stress, continue to be important variables in our growing understanding of the impact of stressful life events on health. The relationship between stress and susceptibility to illness may be determined in studies that incorporate control for important demographic and biologic characteristics and that further examine broadly defined indices of stress, controlled exposure to traumatization, and the use of relatively large samples.

Future clinical investigations must focus not only on the science of life stress events, but also on the interaction among psychological variables and the variety of genetic, metabolic, and biochemical aspects of life that contribute to our adaptation to stressful life events.

REFERENCES

Allodi, F. (1985). Physical and psychiatric effects of torture: Canadian study. In E. Stover & E. O. Nightingale (Eds.), *The breaking of bodies and minds: Torture, psychiatric abuses and the health professions* (pp. 66–78). New York: W. H. Freeman & Co.

Allodi, F. (1991). Assessment and treatment of torture victims: A critical review. *Journal of Nervous and Mental Disease, 179*, 411.

American Psychiatric Association (1994). *Diagnostic and statistical manual of mental disorders* (4th ed.). Washington, DC: Author.

Bean-Bayog, M. (1988). Alcohol and drug abuse: Alcoholism as a cause of psychopathology. *Hospital and Community Psychiatry, 39*, 352–354.

Blake, W., Weathers, P., & Nagy, R. (1990). *Clinician Administered PTSD Scale (CAPS)*. Boston: National Center for PTSD, Behavioral Sciences Division.

Breslau, N., & Davis, C. (1987). Posttraumatic stress disorder: The stressor criterion. *Journal of Nervous and Mental Disease, 175*, 255–264.

Browne, A., & Finkelhor, D. (1986). Impact of child sexual abuse: A review of the research. *Psychological Bulletin, 99*, 66–77.

Davidson, J., Kudler, H., Saunders, W., & Smith, R. (1990). Symptoms and morbidity patterns in World War II and Vietnam veterans with posttraumatic stress disorder. *Comprehensive Psychiatry, 142,* 90–93.

DeJong, A. R. (1985). The medical evaluation of sexual abuse in children. *Hospital and Community Psychiatry, 36,* 503–509.

DuPont, R. H. (1995). Treating obsessive-compulsive disorder. *Directions in Psychiatry, 15*(4), 4.

Engdahl, F., Speed, N., Eberly, R., & Schwartz, J. (1991). Comorbidity of psychiatric disorders and personality profiles of American World War II prisoners of war. *Journal of Nervous and Mental Disease, 179,* 181–187.

Figley, C. (1985). Introduction. In C. Figley (Ed.), *Trauma and its wake* (pp. xvii–xxvi). New York: Brunner/Mazel.

Friedman, M. (1991, July). *Neurological alterations associated with posttraumatic stress disorder* (Teleconference report). National Center for PTSD, Clinical Laboratory and Education Division, White River Junction, Vermont.

Gerardi, R., & Wolfe, J. (1989). *Boston clinical interview for PTSD.* Boston: National Center for PTSD, Behavioral Sciences Division.

Gise, L., & Paddison, P. (1988). Rape, sexual abuse, and its victims. *Psychiatric Clinics of North America, 11*(4), 629–648.

Green, B. (1990). Defining trauma: Terminology and generic stress dimensions. *Journal of Applied Social Psychology, 20,* 1632–1642.

Green, B., Wilson, J., & Lindy, J. (1985). Conceptualizing posttraumatic stress disorder: A psychosocial framework. In C. Figley (Ed.), *Trauma and its wake* (pp. 53–69). New York: Brunner/Mazel.

Hathaway, S. R., & McKinley, J. C. (1967). *Minnesota Multiphasic Personality Inventory: Manual for administration and scoring.* New York: Psychological Corporation.

Horowitz, M. (1977). *Stress response syndromes and brief psychotherapy* (Strecker Monograph Series No. 14). Philadelphia: Pennsylvania Hospital.

Horowitz, M., Weiss, D., & Marmar, C. (1987). Diagnosis of posttraumatic stress disorder (Commentary). *Journal of Nervous and Mental Disease, 175*, 267–268.

Hryvniak, M., & Rosse, R. (1989). Concurrent psychiatric illness in inpatients with posttraumatic stress disorder. *Military Medicine, 154*, 399–401.

Jacobson, A., Koehler, J., & Jones-Brown, C. (1987). The failure of routine assessment to detect histories of assault experiences by psychiatric patients. *Hospital and Community Psychiatry, 38*, 386–389.

Janoff-Bulman, R. (1985). The aftermath of victimization: Rebuilding shattered assumptions. In C. Figley (Ed.), *Trauma and its wake* (pp. 15-35). New York: Brunner/Mazel.

Keane, T. (1985). Defining traumatic stress: Some comments on the current terminological confusion. *Behavior Therapy, 16*, 419–423.

Keane, T. M., Caddell, J. M., & Taylor, K. L. (1988). Mississippi Scale for Combat-Related Posttraumatic Stress Disorder: Three studies in reliability and validity. *Journal of Consulting and Clinical Psychology, 56*(1), 85–90.

Keane, T., & Wolfe, J. (1990). Comorbidity in posttraumatic stress disorder: An analysis of community and clinical studies. *Journal of Applied Social Psychology, 20*, 1776–1788.

Kilpatrick, D., Best, C., Veronen, L., Amick, A., Villeponteaux, L., & Ruff, G. (1985). Mental health correlates of criminal victimization: A random community survey. *Journal of Consulting and Clinical Psychology, 53*, 866–873.

Lindy, J., Greene, B., & Grace, M. (1987). The stressor criterion and posttraumatic stress disorder: Commentary. *Journal of Nervous and Mental Disease, 175*, 269–272.

McFarlane, A. (1986). Posttraumatic morbidity of a disaster: A study of cases presenting for psychiatric treatment. *Journal of Nervous and Mental Disease, 174*, 4–13.

Miller, T. W. (1989). Conceptual and theoretical problems in measuring life stress. In T. W. Miller (Ed.), *Stressful life events*. Madison, CT: International Universities Press, Inc.

Miller, T. W. (1992). Long-term effects of torture in former POW's. In M. Basoglu (Ed.), *Torture and its consequences*. Cambridge, England: Cambridge University Press, Inc.

Miller, T. W., & Basoglu, M. (1992). Posttraumatic stress disorder: The impact of life stress events on adjustment. *Integrative Psychiatry, 44*, 209-217.

Miller, T. W., & Buchbinder, J. (1982). *Vietnam Experiences Questionnaire (VEQ): An experimental measure for assessing stress in veterans*. Lexington, KY: Department of Psychiatry, College of Medicine, University of Kentucky.

Miller, T. W., & Feibelman, N. D. (1987). Obsessional thought disturbance in a gainfully employed traumatic stress disorder patient. *Journal of Occupational Health Nursing, 35*(2), 69–73.

Miller, T. W., Martin, W., & Spiro, K. (1989). Traumatic stress disorder: Diagnostic and clinical issues in former prisoners of war. *Comprehensive Psychiatry, 30*(2), 139–148.

Miller, T. W., & Veltkamp, L. J. (1988). Effects of multigenerational sexual abuse in rural America. *International Journal of Family Psychiatry, 9*(3), 259-275.

Mollica, R. F., Wyshak, G., de Marneffe, D., Khuon, F., & Lavelle, J. (1987). Indochinese versions of the Hopkins Symptom Checklist 25: A screening instrument for the psychiatric care of refugees. *American Journal of Psychiatry, 144*(4), 497–500.

Page, W. W., Engdahl, B., & Miller, T. W. (1991). Age, education, maltreatment and social predictors of chronic depression in former prisoners of war. *Social Psychiatry and Psychiatric Epidemiology, 38*(9), 178-182.

Reiker, P., & Carmen, E. (1986). The victim to patient process: The disconfirmation and transformation of abuse. *American Journal of Orthopsychiatry, 56*, 360–370.

Robins, L. (1990). Steps toward evaluating posttraumatic stress reaction as a psychiatric disorder. *Journal of Applied Social Psychology, 20*, 1674–1677.

Rose, D. (1986). 'Worse than death': Psychodynamics of rape victims and the need for psychotherapy. *American Journal of Psychiatry, 143*, 817–824.

Roszell, D., McFall, M., & Malas, K. (1991). Frequency of symptoms and concurrent psychiatric disorder in Vietnam veterans with chronic PTSD. *Hospital and Community Psychiatry, 42*, 293–296.

Rundell, J., Ursano, R., Holloway, H., & Silberman, E. (1989). Psychiatric responses to trauma. *Hospital and Community Psychiatry, 40*, 68–74.

Saathoff, G., & Buckman, J. (1990). Diagnostic results of psychiatric evaluations with state police officers. *Hospital and Community Psychiatry, 41*, 429–432.

Shaner, A., & Eth, S. (1989). Can schizophrenia cause posttraumatic stress disorder? *American Journal of Psychiatry, 43*, 588–597.

Sierles, R., Chen, J., Messing, M., Besyner, J., & Taylor, M. (1986). Concurrent psychiatric illness in non-Hispanic outpatients diagnosed as having posttraumatic stress disorder. *Journal of Nervous and Mental Disease, 174*, 171–173.

Sonnenberg, S. (1988). Victims of violence and posttraumatic stress disorder. *Psychiatric Clinics of North America, 11*, 581–590.

Speed, N., Engdahl, B., Schwartz, J., & Eberly, R. (1989). Posttraumatic stress disorder as a consequence of the POW experience. *Journal of Nervous and Mental Disease, 177*, 147–153.

Spitzer, R. J., & Williams, J. B. W. (1987). *Structured Clinical Interview for DSM-III (SCID 3/15/83)*. New York: Biometrics Research Department, New York State Psychiatric Institute.

Ursano, R. (1987). Posttraumatic stress disorder: The stressor criterion (Commentary). *Journal of Nervous and Mental Disease, 175*, 273–275.

Veltkamp, L. J., Miller, T. W., Kearl, G. W., Barlow Elliott, L., Bright, K. (1992). Interdisciplinary treatment of abused families in Kentucky. *Journal of the Kentucky Medical Association, 90*, 232–239.

Walker, J. I. (1989). Chemotherapy of traumatic war stress. In T. W. Miller (Ed.), *Stressful life events*. Madison, CT: International Universities Press, Inc.

Wilson, J., Smith, W., & Johnson, S. (1985). A comparative analysis of PTSD among various survivor groups. In C. Figley (Ed.), *Trauma and its wake* (pp. 142–172). New York: Brunner/Mazel.

2

Obsessive-Compulsive Disorder: New Findings

Thomas R. Insel, MD

Dr. Insel is Director, Yerkes Primate Center, and Professor of Psychiatry, Emory University School of Medicine, Atlanta, GA.

KEY POINTS

- Obsessions are cognitive symptoms; compulsions are ritualistic behaviors.
- Both obsessions and compulsions are present in a variety of conditions, including mood disorders, schizophrenia, anorexia nervosa, and Tourette's syndrome, as well as in normal mental functioning.
- Patients with Obsessive-Compulsive Disorder (OCD) typically present with one or more of the following four symptoms: washing, checking, pure obsession, and primary obsessional slowness. OCD is usually a chronic disorder.
- OCD has an unjustified reputation of being a "rare" disorder; although the prevalence of OCD has been estimated at about 1% in a given treatment population, the actual prevalence is probably considerably higher—perhaps 1%-2% in the general population—because patients with the disorder are generally quite secretive.
- Whether the cause of OCD is ultimately determined to be genetic, neurologic, or biochemical, it is generally best treated in a multimodal fashion, utilizing behavioral and pharmacologic approaches.

INTRODUCTION

Obsessions and compulsions are present in a variety of psychopathologic conditions including mood disorders, schizophrenia, anorexia nervosa, and Tourette's syndrome, as well as in normal mental functioning. A unique syndrome for which obsessions or compulsions are the primary symptoms and the major source of disability has been recognized for more than three centuries. That condition, which we now call obsessive-compulsive disorder (OCD), was previously known as scruples, religious melancholy, or obsessional neurosis. Although the disorder has changed very little over the centuries, explanations for its cause have ranged from religious to psychosexual, in keeping with the prevailing intellectual theories. Contemporary advances in genetics, neuropharmacology, and neuropsychology have increasingly dominated our search for the etiology of psychiatric illnesses. Accordingly, the new findings in OCD reflect a neurobiological basis. The usefulness of that approach may ultimately depend less on determining an etiology and more on providing new therapies for this mysterious disorder.

DIAGNOSIS

Obsessions are cognitive symptoms; compulsions are ritualistic behaviors. The most recent attempt to define criteria for the syndrome is shown in Table 2.1 (American Psychiatric Association, 1994).

The following points about the diagnosis of OCD deserve special emphasis. Unlike individuals with obsessive-compulsive character disorder, persons with OCD complain of egodystonic symptoms ("I know that it is stupid to be so concerned about trivial things, yet I have to check them again and again. It's like being on remote control."). OCD patients tend to be seen as people with compulsive characters who have decompensated. Although the names are similar and the two diagnoses share several defense mechanisms (e.g., reaction formation, undoing, and displacement) many patients with OCD do not have compulsive characters (Rachman & Hodgson, 1980). Indeed, those with OCD are more likely to manifest such premorbid traits as introversion and dependence rather than classic obsessionality. Rapoport (1988) and her colleagues have followed children with OCD prospectively to determine the relationship of "trait" and "state" obsessionality. Their data suggest that OCD children manifest few if any obsessional character traits prior to the onset of the disorder. Years later, after a long struggle with OCD, many of those children showed more of the rigidity, stubbornness, and emotional constriction usually associated with the obsessional character. Those traits may thus be secondary to the disorder rather than etiologically linked to OCD.

Unlike patients with major psychotic syndromes, those with OCD retain insight ("This thought about contamination is crazy, but I still have to wash my hands, and that's what bothers me so much."). That distinction, which may seem obvious in most patients, is integral to almost all definitions of the syndrome. Unfortunately, the presence of insight is equivocal for a substantial subgroup of patients. Those patients, who have been labeled either obsessive-compulsive psychotics or schizo-obsessives, appear either more bizarre or more disabled than those with the classic "neurotic" forms of the disorder (Insel & Akiskal, 1986). It is becoming increasingly clear that such patients belong within the spectrum of OCD, although they may be more resistant to treatment than most OCD patients.

Similar to phobic disorders, OCD is usually characterized by avoidant behavior. However, for the OCD patient, avoidance usually does not prevent anxiety. The anxiety associated with OCD is generally secondary to an inner compelling force or expectation rather than to an external cue, such as that associated with a phobia. Indeed, one useful distinction between OCD and a phobic disorder is that in the former, avoidance cannot succeed. Although the OCD patient may

Table 2.1
DIAGNOSTIC CRITERIA FOR OBSESSIVE COMPULSIVE DISORDER (DSM-IV)

A. Either obsessions or compulsions.

Obsessions, as defined by (1), (2), (3), and (4):

(1) recurrent and persistent thoughts, impulses, or images that are experienced, at some time during the disturbance, as intrusive and inappropriate and that cause marked anxiety or distress

(2) the thoughts, impulses, or images are not simply excessive worries about real-life problems

(3) the person attempts to ignore or suppress such thoughts, impulses, or images, or to neutralize them with some other thought or action

(4) the person recognizes that the obsessional thoughts, impulses, or images are a product of his or her own mind (not imposed from without as in thought insertion).

Compulsions, as defined by (1) and (2):

(1) repetitive behaviors (e.g., hand washing, ordering, checking) or mental acts (e.g., praying, counting, repeating words silently) that the person feels driven to perform in response to an obsession, or according to rules that must be applied rigidly

(2) the behaviors or mental acts are aimed at preventing or reducing distress or preventing some dreaded event or situation; however, these behaviors or mental acts either are not connected in a realistic way with what they are designed to neutralize or prevent or are clearly excessive

B. At some point during the course of the disorder, the person has recognized that the obsessions or compulsions are excessive or unreasonable. *Note: this does not apply to children.*

C. The obsessions or compulsions cause marked distress, are time consuming (take more than 1 hour a day), or significantly interfere with the person's normal routine, occupational (or academic) functioning, or usual social activities or relationships.

D. If another Axis I disorder is present, the content of the obsessions or the compulsions is not restricted to it (e.g., preoccupation with food in the presence of an Eating Disorder; hair pulling in the presence of Trichotillomania; concern with appearance in the presence of Body Dysmorphic Disorder; preoccupation with drugs in the presence of a Dysmorphic Disorder; preoccupation with drugs in the presence of a Substance Use Disorder; preoccupation with having a serious illness in the presence of Hypochondriasis; preoccupation with sexual urges or fantasies in the presence of a Paraphilia; or guilty ruminations in the presence of Major Depressive Disorder).

E. The disturbance is not due to the direct physiological effects of a substance (e.g., a drug of abuse, a medication) or a general medical condition.

Source: American Psychiatric Association. (1994). *Diagnostic and statistical manual of mental disorders* (4th ed.). Washington DC: Author. Copyright 1994 American Psychiatric Association. Reprinted with permission.

describe his or her symptoms as a germ or contamination phobia, the actual cue is either invisible, ubiquitous, or unavoidable.

SYMPTOM CLUSTERS

It is curious that of all the ways one might obsess or ritualize, patients with OCD present a relatively restricted repertoire of symptoms. Four of the most common syndromes are described below.

Washing:

Representing about 50% of most OCD samples (Foa & Kozak, 1995), washers are obsessed with dirt, contamination, germs, or bugs. They may spend several hours each day washing their hands or showering. Concerns with contamination most frequently revolve around urine, feces, vaginal secretions, or natural bodily processes that cannot be avoided. Washers may become incapacitated by their rituals and, if they avoid public rest rooms, may ultimately be unable to leave home. Resistance at times seems halfhearted. Although the patients states, "I know I am not really going to transmit cancer if I don't wash," one may find in him or her a truculent refusal to shake hands or to touch doorknobs. Occasionally, washers are not even certain why they are washing but express a vague presentiment that "something terrible will happen if I don't."

Checking:

A second presentation for OCD involves pathologic doubt accompanied by compulsive checking. Typically the "checker" fears the gas jets have been left on or that a bump in the road was a body; the doubts reveal a concern with violence. Although some uncertainty about carelessness, particularly carelessness that could lead to catastrophic consequences, is common to us all, for the obsessional the uncertainty takes on a gnawing, malignant quality. Checking, which is enough to resolve "normal" uncertainty, often only contributes to the obsessional's doubt. For instance, if after checking, a bump in the road does not appear to be a body, then the obsessional fears that the body may have been knocked into the bushes. Ultimately, by some inscrutable means, the patient resolves one particular doubt only to have it replaced by a new obsessional preoccupation. Rachman and Hodgson (1980) described compulsive checking as "preventive," because the fears are often future-oriented, in contrast to washing, which is "restorative." Resistance, which in this case is the attempt to refrain from checking, leads to difficulty in concentration and exhaustion from the never-ending assault of nagging uncertainties. Checkers live as if they are the guilty party perpetually in search of a crime, and, unsurprisingly, they frequently describe strict religious principles.

Pure Obsession:

A third clinical picture is that of the pure obsessional. Approximately 25% of patients with OCD are in this category (Akhtar et al., 1975). Repetitive, intrusive thoughts, usually sexual or aggressive and always reprehensible, may be associated with impulses (which have been called horrific temptations) or fearful images. When the obsession is an aggressive impulse, it is most often directed at the one person most valuable to the patient and thus becomes an indirect attack on the self. Occasionally, the thought may seem relatively neutral to the observer, but for the patient, the preoccupation invariably seems laden with guilt. Resistance, which may involve cognitive (e.g., counting or counter-thoughts) rather than behavioral rituals, may be more bothersome than the original intrusive thought. A patient who was afraid he would decapitate his younger brother struggled with that impulse by avoiding sharp objects, then avoiding his family, and ultimately avoiding letters of the alphabet contained in his brother's name. Each time he would encounter the word "ax" or his brother's initials, he went through an extensive mental "counter-ritual" to undo the image of decapitation.

Primary Obsessional Slowness:

The final presentation is the rare and disabling syndrome of primary obsessional slowness (Rachman, 1974). Although slowness is a consequence of most rituals, it occasionally becomes the predominant symptom. The patient may take an hour or more to brush his or her teeth or 2 hours to eat breakfast. One patient presented with stasis pigmentation of both ankles, a result of the 8 to 10 hours spent each day at the bathroom sink. Even though such patients may have extensive rituals and severe obsessional preoccupations, they manifest very little anxiety. For them, life grinds on at a remarkably low speed.

Those four presentations are clusters of symptoms, but not entirely independent syndromes. In many cases, washing and checking coexist. In addition, some adult patients who have pure obsessional complaints give a history of compulsive handwashing or compulsive checking during young adulthood. Thus, within individuals, the different symptom clusters may overlap or develop sequentially.

PREVALENCE

The traditional reputation of OCD as "rare" is probably not accurate. Although the administered prevalence (i.e., the number of OCD patients in a treatment population) is probably close to 1%, with some variance depending on the treatment center (Black, 1974), patients with the disorder are quite secretive, and, therefore, one might expect the actual prevalence to be considerably higher. The Epidemiologic Catchment Area study sponsored by the National Institute of Mental Health sought to establish the actual prevalence of several psychiatric disorders by administering the Diagnostic Interview Schedule in a door-to-door survey (Myers et al., 1984). Results suggest an astonishing 1.3%–2.0% of the general population meeting criteria for OCD. If that diagnostic method is validated and the results are replicated, OCD would appear to be more prevalent in the general population than in the psychiatric clinic. One might then wonder if that tiny fraction of obsessionals who become patients can truly be distinguished by their symptoms or if some other factor, such as family conflicts, depression, or a particular personality style might determine when obsessionals become psychiatric patients. Alternatively, many OCD patients may be misdiagnosed in the psychiatric setting.

Little evidence is available to determine significant cultural or national differences in the prevalence of OCD. Description of the disorder from Asian, European, African, and American clinicians suggest remarkable similarities, although the preponderance of the various symptom clusters differs across settings (Hunter & MacAlpine, 1963; Lo, 1967; Rasmussen & Tsuang, 1984).

OCD is also one of the few psychiatric illnesses that is found in children in a form nearly identical to its adult presentation. Perhaps the only distinguishing feature of the childhood form of OCD is that boys appear more affected than girls, with a male-female ratio of 3:1, whereas the sexes are equally represented in adult cohorts with the disorder (Rapoport, 1988). The overall prevalence of OCD may be slightly lower in children, although children have yet to be comprehensively surveyed. As many as one third of adults with OCD admit to onset of symptoms prior to age 18, often prior to puberty (Rasmussen & Tsuang, 1984).

GENETICS

Sophisticated adoption studies such as those used in research on schizophrenia and affective illness are not available for OCD. Studies of the families of obsessional patients have generally yielded a high incidence of obsessional "features" (noninterfering obsessional thoughts or behavior) but not of obsessional disorder *per se* (Insel, Hoover, & Murphey, 1983). A number of reports have described identical twins concordant for OCD. Although that might indicate a genetic component for the disorder, such data are always suspect to reporting bias, because discordant pairs are less likely to be reported. Systematic twin studies, while sparse, demonstrate high concordance rates in monozygotic twins, but only when the measure is obsessional features, not full-blown OCD (Carey & Gottesman, 1981). The picture that emerges from those studies is that some predisposition to obsessional behavior is inherited; however, consistent with the preliminary epidemiologic data, the development of the full disorder leading to treatment appears to be an uncommon event.

Pauls and colleagues (1986), in an important study of Tourette's syndrome, noted that OCD occurs in as many as 20% of the first-degree relatives of Tourette's patients, a figure considerably higher than the corresponding number of relatives of OCD patients. In that study, many of the Tourette's patients also had obsessional symptoms, but, surprisingly, the high rate of OCD in relatives was not limited to those index cases with obsessional symptoms. It appears then that the two disorders, or some subtype of the two disorders, share a common genetic predisposition. Pauls and associates are currently using the techniques of molecular genetics to determine if those pedigrees have a specific genetic abnormality. With such techniques, it may be possible to localize the part of the genome that is altered in people with the disorder and to define specific gene products that result from this alteration. First, however, it will be important to determine what "disorder" to look for—Tourette's, OCD, obsessional features, or some combination of the three.

OCD AND AFFECTIVE ILLNESS

More than most anxiety disorders, OCD shares many features of affective illness. Beyond the response to one subgroup of antidepressants, the selective serotonin reuptake inhibitors (SSRIs), studies of persons with OCD have revealed a number of neurobiologic abnormalities previously thought to be specific to patients with major depression, including an increased rate (25%–40%) of nonsuppression on the dexamethasone suppression test (DST), shortened rapid eye movement (REM) latency during electroencephalographic recording of sleep, and blunted plasma growth hormone response to intravenous administration of clonidine. Those neurobiologic findings are not limited to patients with OCD who have secondary depression, nor are they predictive of response to antidepressant treatment. They serve to remind us of what perceptive clinicians have known for the past century: obsessional symptoms are intimately linked to changes in affect. Not only are obsessions common in primary depressive illness, but major depressive episodes occur in at least 67% of OCD cases (Rasmussen Eisen, & Pato, 1993). Some chronically obsessional patients only present for treatment when they become acutely depressed. Moreover, even in obsessionals who are not overtly depressed, affective-like symptoms such as low self-esteem, guilt, exhaustion, and indecisiveness are prominent.

Obsessive-compulsive disorder might then seem a variant of affective illness, as suggested in the last century by Maudsley. However plausible that may seem in individual cases, group data are not entirely supportive of that notion. In contrast to affective illness, OCD tends to be more chronic, shows a younger age of onset, and has a lower ratio of female-to-male incidence.

NEUROPSYCHOLOGIC FINDINGS

Several leads suggest neuropsychologic dysfunction in OCD (Insel et al., 1983). Many cases of OCD appear to evolve as sequelae to encephalitis lethargica, a disease with well-documented neuropathologic lesions. Grimshaw reported a high incidence of premorbid neurologic illness in addition to encephalitis in his series of patients with OCD. One report suggests that patients with "atypical" symptoms have a high incidence of birth trauma. Obsessionalism is evident as an interictal trait in temporal lobe epileptics. And finally, discrete neurosurgical lesions have been shown selectively to reduce obsessional symptoms.

Despite such leads, no clear evidence of a specific neurologic dysfunction has been documented. There are conflicting reports of EEG abnormalities in patients with OCD, but even the most outspoken claims cite only nonspecific, nonlocalized findings such as increased slow-wave activity. Shagass and colleagues (1984) have reported an increased amplitude in one of the middle latency waves of the somatosensory-evoked response. Unlike other findings of electrophysiologic abnormalities, this finding is distinct to OCD. The pathoetiologic significance of that finding remains to be determined.

Recent results using new imaging techniques have been particularly intriguing. Some young adults with OCD appear to show atrophy of the caudate nucleus on volumetric CT scans (Rapoport, 1988). Positron emission tomography studies show increased metabolic activity in the orbital frontal cortex and caudate nucleus (Baxter et al., 1987). Current research is leading toward a hypothesis regarding abnormal frontal-striatal activity in at least some patients with OCD. Although it is not yet clear if the abnormalities reported are of etiologic significance, the therapeutic efficacy of surgically interrupting frontal-striatal pathways in OCD has been known for decades, so that pathway may represent an important focus for treatment (Kelly, 1980). In addition, both behavioral and pharmacologic treatments that reduce OCD symptoms have been shown to normalize the increased metabolic activity in this frontal-striatal circuit (Baxter et al., 1993).

REHABILITATIVE TREATMENT

Of all psychiatric conditions, OCD has generally been considered one of the most refractory to treatment. Patients with the disorder frequently present with symptoms seemingly laden with unconscious symbolism and dynamic meaning. However, psychodynamic treatments—particularly if they are loosely structured and nondirective—rarely reduce the symptoms. Behavioral approaches and pharmacologic treatments have recently been shown to offer considerable promise in OCD.

Behavioral Treatments:

Of the number of frequently used behavioral interventions, only in vivo exposure and response prevention have been repeatedly successful in OCD. Both techniques require a thorough knowledge of the patient's symptoms. In vivo exposure includes contact with the objects associated with discomfort, contamination, or fear. A patient with fears of contamination from urine will be exposed to public bathrooms and may ultimately touch a urine soaked cloth for 2 hours each day, until the dread of contamination subsides. In addition, the patient will not be permitted to wash, or at least not to wash excessively. That restriction of washing, which is called *response prevention*, appears particularly important for decreasing compulsive behavior. Indeed, careful studies by Steketee, Foa, and Grayson (1982) have demonstrated that for decreasing the combination of both obsessions and compulsions in one client, the two techniques should be used together.

The best patient for behavior therapy is the washer or checker with well-defined external cues, associated avoidance, and high motivation for change. The therapy is built around risk taking, with the patient pushing himself or herself to do the very things that have seemed so reprehensible. Not every OCD patient is right for in vivo exposure and response prevention. Those with depression and those with little resistance to their symptoms may not respond. In addition, patients with pure obsessions or those with primary obsessional slowness may not be appropriate for such treatment. Perhaps the major limitation of this form of behavior therapy, however, is the therapist. Behavioral techniques require a therapist with adequate training and time. During the early phases of this treatment, the therapist may spend 3 hours a day with each patient. Clearly, if the disorder is as common as currently believed, this treatment can help only a tiny fraction of those with OCD.

Although behavior treatment is intense and difficult, as many as 80% of those who undergo in vivo exposure and response prevention are much improved within a few weeks (Steketee et al., 1982). Follow-up studies reveal continued improvement at 1 year following treatment, although in many cases the need for behavioral homework or brief "refresher" sessions may be helpful. Most important, OCD patients who undertake behavior treatment rarely develop "substitute symptoms" or psychoses, although patients usually fear one or both of these adverse outcomes.

Pharmacologic Treatment:

For the patients who will not undertake behavioral therapy, who have significant depressive symptoms, or for whom avoidant behavior is not a major part of the symptom picture, medication may be especially useful. The pharmacologic treatment of OCD has recently become an intriguing area of research as well as a promising avenue of therapy (Zohar & Insel, 1987).

The major finding from studies in Europe, Canada, and the United States is that the antidepressants clomipramine, fluoxetine, and fluvoxamine reduce the symptoms of OCD, whereas a number of structurally related antidepressants such as desipramine (Norpramin, Pertofrane), amitriptyline (Elavil), and nortriptyline (Pamelor) have not been found to be effective. Among antidepressants, the antiobsessional drugs are distinguished by their potencies for blocking the neuronal reuptake of serotonin, which is the major route of metabolism of that neurotransmitter. Several lines of evidence link the drug's serotonergic and antiobsessional effects. Improvement during clomipramine treatment is correlated with decreases in the serotonin content of platelets and the serotonin metabolite, 5-hydroxyindoleacetic acid (5-HIAA), in cerebrospinal fluid.

Some studies have observed a correlation between an improvement in obsessional symptoms and the plasma level of clomipramine (but not its less-selective metabolite desmethylclomipramine). Reducing serotonin function following a treatment response can be associated with a worsening of obsessional (Benkelfat, 1989) or depressive (Barr et al., 1994) symptoms.

In addition to these findings implicating serotonin in the reduction of OCD symptoms, evidence demonstrates that OCD patients show altered sensitivity to certain serotonin-like drugs (Zohar et al., 1987). One such drug, metachlorophenylpiperazine, actually provokes severe obsessional symptoms in OCD patients at a dose that is without behavioral effects in healthy volunteers. This altered sensitivity is corrected by treatment with clomipramine (Zohar et al., 1988). Further evidence that serotonin may be involved in the pathophysiology of OCD comes from reports of increased levels of 5-HIAA in the cerebrospinal fluid of drug-free OCD patients (suggesting increased central metabolism or turnover of serotonin) and decreased levels of the serotonin uptake site in platelets from OCD patients (Zohar et al., 1987). It may be too early to integrate the emerging data into a single model. However, from a simplistic view, it is tempting to contrast OCD and its apparently increased 5-HIAA in cerebrospinal fluid with impulsive sociopathy—its phenomenologic opposite—which is associated with decreased cerebrospinal fluid 5-HIAA levels. Preclinical studies have demonstrated a role for brain serotonergic systems in the modulation of aggression (Valzelli, 1984). It should not be surprising that OCD, which is replete with guilt and aggressive thoughts, might also involve some alteration of serotonergic function. During the next decade, we should learn more about which of the brain's many serotonergic pathways are involved in OCD and how those pathways alter OCD symptoms.

In the meantime, the major focus will be finding the best pharmacologic treatment. Although we now have several strong leads tying serotonin to the pathophysiology and/or pharmacologic treatment of OCD, only a few antiobsessional drugs of greatest promise are as yet available. Some have suggested that clomipramine is the most effective medication for OCD, though selective serotonin reuptake inhibitors (SSRIs) like fluoxetine and fluvoxamine are also effective (Greist, 1994) with fewer side effects. However, individual clients may respond better to one specific agent.

In certain cases, several less specifically antiobsessional antidepressants such as imipramine (Tofranil) or the monoamine oxidase inhibitors such as tranylcypromine (Parnate) may be useful. In addition, the presence of Tourette's-like symptoms may indicate the need for augmenting the antiobsessional medication with a dopamine antagonist such as haloperidol (McDougle et al., 1994).

Whichever agent is used, our current experience suggests a prolonged trial (i.e., 6 weeks at full dosage) should be offered before assessing efficacy and that continuous treatment may be necessary if the medication is successful at reducing the target symptoms. This latter point deserves emphasis. None of the pharmacologic treatments are cures; patients continue to have some symptoms, but they appear less distressed and are usually able to return to work or school. Frequently, however, the symptoms revert to their original severity when the medication is stopped.

THERAPEUTIC RAPPORT

OCD is usually a chronic disorder. Whether its cause is ultimately genetic, neurologic, or biochemical, its treatment is likely to be multimodal, including behavioral and pharmacologic approaches. In addition, a good therapeutic rapport is necessary, if not sufficient, for treatment. In many cases, the opportunity to explore both the intrapersonal and interpersonal meanings of the disorder may be welcomed by the patient. Although such an exploration may not predictably reduce the symptoms of OCD, it may greatly help the patient adjust to any aspects of the disorder that do not respond to specific treatments and to build on strengths not affected by the disorder.

In OCD, perhaps more than in other psychiatric disorders, the correlation between the severity of the symptoms and the amount of disability is often very weak. Indeed, many people with years of extensive washing rituals seem to lead productive lives and only come for treatment when they develop a disabling depression. Conversely, as OCD receives more attention in the media, people with relatively mild compulsive symptoms who are disabled by severe character pathology are labeled as having OCD. In both cases, the disorder may be present, but OCD need not be the focus of therapy. In evaluating a patient for OCD, the interviewer should elicit the patient's past highest level of ego functioning as well as take a history of the various symptoms. Similarly, treatment must address the entire person rather than simply the obsessions and compulsions.

REFERENCES

Akhtar, S., et al. (1975). A phenomenological analysis of symptoms in obsessive-compulsive neurosis. *British Journal of Psychiatry, 127*, 342-348.

American Psychiatric Association (1994). *Diagnostic and statistical manual of mental disorders* (4th ed.), Washington DC: Author.

Barr, et al. (1994). Tryptophan depletion in patients with obsessive-compulsive disorder who respond to serotonin reuptake inhibitors. *Archives of General Psychiatry, 51*, 309-317.

Baxter, L. R., et al. (1987). Local cerebral glucose metabolic rates in obsessive-compulsive disorder. *Archives of General Psychiatry, 44,* 211-216.

Baxter, L. R., et al. (1993). Caudate glucose metabolic rate changes with both drug and behavior therapy for obsessive-compulsive disorder. *Archives of General Psychiatry, 49,* 681-689.

Benkelfat, et al. (1989). Clomipramine in obsessive-compulsive disorder: Further evidence of a serotonergic mechanism of action. *Archives of General Psychiatry, 46,* 22-28.

Black, A. (1974). The natural history of obsessional neurosis. In H. R. Beech (Ed.), *Obsessional states.* London: Methuen and Co.

Carey, G. & Gottesman I. I. (1981). Twin and family studies of anxiety, phobic, and obsessive disorders. In D. F. Klein & J. G. Rabkin (Eds.), *Anxiety: New research and changing concepts* (pp. 117-136). New York: Raven Press.

Foa, E. B. & Kozak, M. J. (1995). DSM-IV field trial: OCD. *American Journal of Psychiatry, 152,* 97-101.

Greist, J. H., et al. (1995) Efficacy and tolerability of serotonin transport inhibitors in OCD. *Archives of General Psychology, 52,* 53-60.

Hunter, R. & MacAlpine, I. (1963). *Three hundred years of psychiatry.* London: Oxford University Press.

Insel, T. R., & Akiskal, H. (1986). Obsessive-compulsive disorder with psychotic features: A phenomenologic analysis. *American Journal of Psychiatry, 143,* 1527-1533.

Insel, T. R., Hoover, C., & Murphy, D. L. (1983). Parents of patients with obsessive-compulsive disorder. *Psychological Medicine, 13,* 807-811.

Insel, T. R., et al. (1983). Neurological and neuropsychological studies of patients with obsessive compulsive disorder. *Biological Psychiatry, 18,* 741-751.

Kelley, D. (1980). *Anxiety and Emotions.* Springfield, IL: Charles C. Thomas Co.

Lo, W. (1967). A follow-up study of obsessional neurotics in Hong Kong Chinese. *British Journal of Psychiatry, 113,* 823-832.

McDougle, et al. (1994). Haloperidol addition in fluvoxamine-refractory obsessive-compulsive disorder: A double-blind, placebo-controlled study in patients with and without tics. *Archives of General Psychiatry, 51,* 302-308.

Myers, J. K., et al. (1984). Six-month prevalence of psychiatric disorders in three communities: 1980-1982. *Archives of General Psychiatry, 41,* 959-970.

Pauls, D. L., et al. (1986). Gilles de la Tourette's syndrome and obsessive-compulsive disorder. *Archives of General Psychiatry, 43,* 1180-1182.

Rachman, S. J. (1974). Primary obsessional slowness. *Behavior Research and Therapy, 11,* 463-471.

Rachman, S. J. & Hodgson R. J. (1980). *Obsessions and compulsions.* Englewood Cliffs, NJ: Prentice-Hall.

Rapoport, J. (1988). *Childhood obsessive-compulsive disorder.* Washington DC: American Psychiatric Press.

Rasmussen, S. A., Eisen, J. L., & Pato, M. T. (1993). Current issues in the pharmacologic management of OCD. *Journal of Clinical Psychiatry, 54* (6, suppl.), 4-9.

Rasmussen, S. A., & Tsuang, M. T. (1984). The epidemiology of obsessive-compulsive disorder. *Journal of Clinical Psychiatry, 45,* 450-457.

Shagass, C., et al. (1984). Distinctive somatosensory evoked potential features in obsessive-compulsive disorder. *Biological Psychiatry, 19,* 1507-1524.

Steketee, G. S., Foa, E. B., & Grayson, J. B. (1982). Recent advances in the behavioral treatment of obsessive-compulsives. *Archives of General Psychiatry, 39,* 1365-1371.

Valzelli, L. (1984). Psychobiology of aggression. *Biological Psychiatry,* 8, 311-325.

Zohar, J., & Insel, T. R. (1987). Obsessive-compulsive disorder: Psychobiological approaches to diagnosis, treatment, and pathophysiology. *Biological Psychiatry, 22,* 705-707.

Zohar, J., et al. (1987). Serotonergic responsivity in obsessive-compulsive disorder. *Archives of General Psychiatry,* 44, 946-951.

Zohar, J., et al. (1988). Serotonergic responsivity in obsessive-compulsive disorder: Effects of clomipramine treatment. *Archives of General Psychiatry, 45,* 167-172.

3

The Diagnosis and Treatment of Dissociative Identity Disorder

Richard P. Kluft, PhD, MD, FAPA

Dr. Kluft is Clinical Professor of Psychiatry, Temple University School of Medicine, and Senior Attending Psychiatrist and Director of the Dissociative Disorders Program, The Institute of Pennsylvania Hospital, Philadelphia.

KEY POINTS

- Dissociative identity disorder (DID), formerly known as multiple personality disorder (MPD), is a severe dissociative disorder involving a disturbance of both memory and identity.
- A DID client has two or more personalities, which often have names of their own; perceive and represent themselves as different in age, race, gender, and sexual orientation; claim origin from different families, cultures, and/or epochs; and have different values, beliefs, symptom pictures, and even handwriting.
- This chapter outlines the therapeutic stages of the treatment of DID, offers an overview of treatment issues, and discusses therapists' reactions to working with DID clients.
- Approaches to treating persons with DID include: psychoanalysis, cognitive and behavioral approaches, family intervention, amobarbital and/or videotaping, hypnotherapy, hospital treatment, treatment with medications, and postfusion therapy.
- The prognosis for DID clients is optimistic: long-term stable clinical integration is quite possible and relapse of treated dividedness occurs infrequently after the client has been integrated.

BACKGROUND

Dissociative identity disorder (DID), formerly known as *multiple personality disorder* (MPD) continues to be recognized, diagnosed, and treated with increasing frequency and has become the subject of considerable study and research. In recent years, five major journal issues have been dedicated to DID (Braun, 1983a, 1984d; Kluft, 1984e; Loewenstein, 1991b; Orne, 1984), and *Dissociation*, a journal specializing in the study of the dissociative disorders, has become the voice of this emerging field. Also, four scholarly bibliographies have been compiled (Boor & Coons, 1983; Damgaard, van Benschoten & Fagan, 1985; Goettman, Greaves & Coons, 1994). The International Society for the Study of Multiple Personality and Dissociation (renamed the International Society for the Study of Dissociation) was formed, and rapidly grew to more than 3,000 members.

It has become increasingly clear that the distribution of this condition is widespread at least in the United States, if not worldwide (Coons, Bowman, Kluft, & Milstein, 1991; van der Hart, 1993). Well-documented and thoughtful research studies, reviewed in Putnam (1984, 1991a, 1991b), explore the psychophysiological correlates of the personality states and the switch phenomenon. Follow-up studies of treatment results (Coons, 1986; Kluft, 1984b, 1986, 1994a, 1994b) have become available, and the discovery of children with DID has been documented (see Coons, 1985; Fagan & McMahon, 1984; Hornstein & Putnam, 1992; Hornstein & Tyson, 1991; Kluft, 1984d). A comprehensive exploration of the childhood experiences of these patients has been published (Kluft, 1985a), and their family constellations have been described (Kluft, Braun, & Sachs, 1985).

The natural history of DID is slowly being explored, and its presentations from childhood to senescence are simultaneously being illustrated (Kluft, 1985c, 1991a). In 1944, Taylor and Martin noted the literature contained approximately 100 cases of DID. In 1980, Bliss claimed that approximately 200 cases had been reported. Braun (1984a) observed there were approximately 1,000 contemporary cases of DID in treatment, and Kluft (1985b), who polled 70 students attending a course on DID, found they had encountered 267 previously unreported cases. A recent comprehensive review (Kluft, 1991b) reported several large series of contemporary DID patients, ranging from 50 to 355 subjects. More than a dozen special centers for the treatment of DID patients have developed. Recent studies have further clarified the epidemiology of DID, demonstrating that DID is a rather common psychiatric disorder (Boon & Draijer, 1993; Ross, 1991; Ross, Anderson, Fleisher, & Norton, 1991; Saxe et al., 1993).

Dissociative identity disorder has always been—and may well continue to be—a controversial entity: lay accounts that exploit DID for sensationalistic ends can make this condition appear a subject more fit for a soap opera than for science. The condition has been closely associated with a history of child abuse (Putnam, Guroff, Silberman, Balban, & Post, 1986; Ross, Norton, & Wozney, 1989; Schultz, Braun, & Kluft, 1989; Wilbur, 1984, 1985). Although the alarming prevalence of the mistreatment of children is slowly achieving long-overdue recognition, these patients' accounts can seem so repugnant, farfetched, or incredible as to become intolerable, thus promoting a defensive denial and derealization on the part of the clinician. The clinician's attitudes may then manifest as skepticism (Goodwin, 1985). Even experienced workers in the field report countertransference experiences of wishing to distance themselves from the client and disavow the possibility that what they are hearing is true.

Recently, much controversy has broken out on the reliability of memories of abuse recovered in the course of treatment. In this context, it is useful to bear in mind that abuse was documented in 95.3% of the dissociative youngsters described by Hornstein and Putnam (1992) and 95% of those treated by Coons (1994). Furthermore, Bliss (1984b) documented some allegations by twelve of thirteen DID patients. It is clear, however, that some of the allegations made by DID patients are inaccurate. Kluft (1994c) identified the need to examine with more care the process by which the relatively simple and usually documentable allegations of youthful DID patients can become suffused with fantasy and confabulation in some adult cases, and result in inaccurate and conflated allegations. Therefore, all allegations made should be heard sympathetically, but with an awareness that their ultimate accuracy cannot be established for certain without external corroboration, which is not usually forthcoming and which is difficult to obtain in many adult cases.

Notwithstanding the dearth of evidence for the iatrogenic creation of DID, many very prestigious authorities continue to believe that this is the true cause of most if not all cases (e.g., McHugh, 1993; Mersky, 1992). A more substantial problem is that of factitious or malingered DID, which is often difficult to discern in the clinical context (Coons & Milstein, 1994), and increasingly so in the forensic context as newer malingerers are able to avail themselves of an encyclopedic literature and many video and media presentations.

DEFINITION AND DESCRIPTION

Characteristics of DID:

DID is a severe dissociative disorder involving a disturbance of both memory and identity (Nemiah, 1981). Putnam and associates (1984) observed, "The existence of multiple amnestic episodes, together with the presence of alternating separate and distinct identities, distinguishes multiple personality disorder from all other psychiatric syndromes." They agree with Kluft (1985c) that stigmata suggestive of concurrent or alternative diagnoses are almost invariably present and note that if the features of DID are documented, it should be regarded as a superordinate diagnosis in which other manifestations are often encompassed (Putnam et al., 1984). This is a pragmatic clinical stance. There are compelling data showing that clients often do well with treatments that address their DID (Kluft, 1984f, 1986, 1993b), and disheartening data descriptive of clients whose DID was not recognized and treated, and who failed to respond to over a decade of "competent" but misdirected therapy (Kluft, 1982, 1984f, 1985c, 1993b).

The *Diagnostic and Statistical Manual of Mental Disorders* (DSM-IV) (American Psychiatric Association, 1994, p. 487) diagnostic criteria for DID are presented in Table 3.1.

Table 3.1
DIAGNOSTIC CRITERIA FOR DISSOCIATIVE IDENTITY DISORDER (DSM-IV)

A. The presence of two or more distinct identities or personality states (each with its own relatively enduring pattern of perceiving, relating to, and thinking about the environment and self).

B. At least two of these identities or personality states recurrently take control of the person's behavior.

C. Inability to recall important personal information that is too extensive to be explained by ordinary forgetfulness.

D. The disturbance is not due to the direct physiological effects of a substance (e.g., blackouts or chaotic behavior during Alcohol Intoxication) or a general medical condition (e.g., partial complex seizures). *Note: In children, the symptoms are not attributable to imaginary playmates or other imaginary fantasy play.*

Source: American Psychiatric Association. (1994). *Diagnostic and statistical manual of mental disorders* (4th ed.). Washington DC: Author. Copyright 1994 American Psychiatric Association. Reprinted with permission.

With regard to amnesia, DSM-IV notes that the gaps of personal memory may be frequent, both for remote and recent autobiographical events. The degree of awareness that the personalities have of each other can vary dramatically from one case to another.

> Individuals with this disorder experience frequent gaps in memory for personal history, both remote and recent. The amnesia is frequently asymmetrical. The more passive identities tend to have more constricted memories, whereas the more hostile, controlling, or "protector" identities have more complete memories. An identity that is not in control may nonetheless gain access to consciousness by producing auditory or visual hallucinations (e.g., a voice giving instructions). Evidence of amnesia may be uncovered by reports from others who have witnessed behavior that is disavowed by the individual or by the individual's own discoveries (e.g., finding items of clothing at home that an individual cannot remember having bought). There may be loss of memory not only for recurrent periods of time, but also for some extended period of childhood (American Psychiatric Association, 1994, pp. 484-485).

In clinical practice, an apparent absence of amnesia is not uncommon. Braun (1986) noted that one can see an apparent absence of amnesia that reflects one's personality having learned of—but not experienced—another's experiences, thus reporting knowledge as memory. I have repeatedly warned that one can "forget one forgot," and offer an account devoid of reference to amnesia.

Number of Personalities:

In the reported literature, DID has a 4:1 to 9:1 female predominance. Many argue males with DID encounter difficulty with the law and enter the criminal justice rather than the mental health system; hence, their pathology goes unrecognized. Most cases in the older literature appear to have involved dual or triple personalities (Taylor & Martin, 1944). Two series reported an average of 13.3 and 13.9 personalities (Kluft, 1984f); a third described a modal range of 8–13 (Kluft, 1984a); and 44.2% of a series of 70 had 11 or more (Kluft, 1991b). Very complex cases are not infrequent, and the successful treatment of clients with over 100 alters has been reported (Kluft, 1988b). The older literature seemed to report cases with a small number of discrepant and apparently opposite personalities, frequently the "retiring spinster" and the "flamboyant, promiscuous bar habitué" (American Psychiatric Association, 1980). One text suggested the most common alter was a persecutor in form (Beahrs, 1982). Actually, studies of large series challenge long-held preconceptions. The most frequent alter personalities are scared children, who embody the clients' experience of traumatic events (Kluft, 1984a; Putnam et al., 1986).

Differences Between Personalities:

The overt differences and separate self-concepts among personalities range from minimal divergence to extreme polarity. Personalities usually, but not inevitably, have names of their own and may perceive and represent themselves as different in age, race, gender, and sexual orientation. They often claim origin from a different family and, occasionally, from a different culture and/or epoch. Their values, beliefs, and symptom pictures may be different, and they may be preoccupied with relatively different issues and problems. In classic cases, alters may have separate wardrobes, possessions, pursuits, and interpersonal styles. Sometimes different alters have different jobs and social circles. Not uncommonly, different alters, assessed at different times, are given different diagnoses.

Personalities may show differences in handwriting, voice, vocabulary, speech pattern, accent, pitch, rhythm, and even preferred language. Their facial expressions may be different on a dramatic and consistent basis. When personalities have pursued different interests, acquired wardrobes and possessions that reflect their separate tastes, interacted with others extensively, and become invested in their separateness, their distinctness can be quite marked. Conversely, when they remain relatively bound to their original defensive purposes and attempt to remain hidden from detection, their differences may appear so bland as to call the diagnosis into question (Kluft, 1985c, 1991a).

Host, Presenting, and Original Personalities:

Several terms proposed by Braun (1986) are often used to describe specific phenomena. The *host personality* has executive control of the body the greatest amount of time during a given period. The *presenting personality* presents itself for therapy. The *original personality* is a theoretical construct that denotes the identity from which the first other personality splits off. Some consider these concepts crucial; others do not. No "type" of personality is invariably present.

The classic host personality is often, but not inevitably, the presenting personality that seeks treatment and is commonly depressed, anxious, somewhat neurasthenic, compulsively good, masochistic, and conscience stricken. It is usually constricted hedonically, and suffers both psychophysiological symptoms and time loss or distortion.

Purposes of Personalities:

The personalities usually come into existence to serve defensive purposes. Over time, they may come to acquire a high degree of secondary autonomy and narcissistic investment in separateness. Their perception of autonomy may approach an intensity Coons (1980, 1984) and Kluft (1984d) have termed "pseudo-delusional." In such instances, the others are so strongly experienced as separate, not-me, and ego alien that an alter may behave as if its actions are irrelevant to it. They may try to kill one another, refusing to concede that the death of one dooms all, or they may experience the body as an object and a possession of another alter, and, with consummate "trance logic" (Orne, 1959), use the body to attack the body and proclaim that the personality to which they attribute the body has been punished or mutilated while they remain untouched.

Child-like personalities are quite common—often several exist within a DID client. Some are fearful, some recall and encapsulate traumatic memories, some seek love and approval, and still others may preserve the idealized potential for happiness, growth, and the healthy expression of feelings that traumatization has distorted in others.

Protectors, helpers, friends, and advisers, occasionally assuming the serene rational stance Allison (1974) described in *inner self helpers,* also are encountered. As might be expected, they may take the form of idealized figures, friends, playmates, kind relatives, positive aspects of ambivalently perceived objects, or culturally sanctioned images of benevolence or caring.

Personalities that are based on identifications with aggressors or constructed upon culturally sanctioned images of malevolent intent often become internal persecutors, involved in intropunitive behaviors. Their voices often are perceived as hallucinations, sometimes with command intensity pressuring the client toward self-harm.

Some personalities are guardians of memories and secrets. Some serve as memory traces for the common overall experience. Others may be impervious to pain and usually develop out of autohypnotic efforts to block out suffering. Still others may express forbidden impulses, serve as avengers, defend or apologize for abusers, undo by incorporation/identification the loss or feared loss of significant others, or serve very specialized functions. In some clients, many personalities' structures are quite frail and seem to represent a friable self-structure connected to a traumatic episode. Such alters often vanish after abreaction.

DIAGNOSING DID

Signs of DID:

Some of the findings alluded to above have proved highly useful as signs to suggest careful scrutiny for DID. Condensing lists by Greaves (1980), Kluft (1984a, 1991b), and Putnam et al. (1986), they are:

1. Prior treatment failure
2. Three or more prior diagnoses
3. Concurrent psychological and somatic symptoms
4. Fluctuating symptoms and level of function
5. Severe headaches
6. Time distortion or time lapses
7. Being told of disremembered behaviors
8. Others' noting observable changes
9. Discovery of productions, objects, or handwriting in one's possession that one cannot account for or recognize
10. The hearing of voices (more than 80% experienced as within the head), experienced as separate, urging toward some good or bad activity

11. The use of "we" in a collective sense
12. The elicitability of other alters through hypnosis and/or amobarbital (Amytal)
13. A history of child abuse
14. An inability to recall childhood events from the years 6 to 11

Item 11 is widely cited, but some believe it occurs only with initial co-consciousness or after barriers are broached in treatment. Item 12 is subject to cautions. The clinician who is unaware of normative ego state phenomena or hidden observer findings (Hilgard, 1987) is likely to mistake easily elicited and nonpathological phenomena as a bona fide dissociative disorder.

Interview Inquiries:

The clinician must be alert to brief evidences of forgetfulness and fluctuations of voice, speech, and movement characteristics within the interview, as well as overt dissociation into alters and positive responses on suggestive items. A surprising number of DID clients avert or partially cover their faces and lower their voices to minimize the clinician's detection of such evidences. Although Goodwin (1982) has noted similar behaviors in victims of childhood and adult sexual abuse, these signs are not yet generally recognized as suggestive of DID as well. Sometimes clients suspected of DID reveal themselves if assigned to write a diary 30 minutes a day: alters intrude, and different writing is noted. I have yet to find a client with currently active DID who does not dissociate if the interview is extended to 4 hours, but the technique is rarely pragmatic.

One of the strengths of Steinberg's (1993) Structured Clinical Interview for the Diagnosis of DSM-IV Dissociative Disorder (SCID-D) is that its very length (often 2–3 hours) weakens dissociative defenses.

Inquiry about traumatic experiences common in DID histories can be raised later in a nonleading manner, but often they are denied by or inaccessible to the presenting personality. Unless recent, distressing, and ego-dystonic dissociation has occurred, direct inquiry about amnesia is often met with denial or unwitting confabulation. Many clients are too mortified to report they have regained awareness in strange places, or have engaged in activities they consider out of character and/or reprehensible.

Therefore, indirect inquiry, such as asking about unexplained objects, possessions, productions, and writing is less threatening, as is asking about unexplained relationships and/or changes in relationships. Ask if people unknown to the client address him or her as if they were known to the client, and/or by a different name. Ask if people ever act as if their relationship to the client had been influenced by factors of which the client was unaware. Also ask about the presence of inexplicable skills and knowledge—or the absence of expected ones. Irregular school and/or work performance is common. Often dissociative experiences of childhood are reported undefensively.

Checklists for suspecting the presence of childhood DID have been published (e.g., Fagan & McMahon, 1984; Kluft, 1984d; Putnam, Helmers, & Trickett, 1993). Most DID clients were noted to be "in a trance" or considered liars as children, usually because they disavowed behavior others observed. Inquiry about imaginary companionship in childhood is advised on theoretical grounds, but clinical findings thus far are equivocal.

Diagnostic Tools:

Recently, a number of useful diagnostic tools have been developed and are achieving increasing use. Bernstein and Putnam's Dissociative Experience Scale (DES) (1986) has been used in many studies conducted in numerous countries, and translated into over a dozen languages. A screening instrument, responses to which can be easily dissimulated, the DES is extremely useful in assessment. Initially, studies pursued scores of 20 or more with structured instruments. Lately, researchers have had a tendency to use 30, because one of seven clients with this score or above will have DID, while only one in 100 with a lower score will (Carlson et al., 1993). As useful as this is in general, by the time a patient reaches a consultant, it may be assumed their condition has been hard to diagnose and may be somewhat dissimulated. Under these circumstances, cut-off scores are usually less relevant than pursuit of particular items that are endorsed or not endorsed.

Two structured interviews are currently available: Ross's (1989) Dissociative Disorders Interview Schedule (DDIS) and Steinberg's (1993) Structured Clinical Interview for the Diagnosis of DSM-IV Dissociative Disorder (SCID-D). Both are sensitive (picking up 90% or more of gold standard DID patients), reliable, and valid. The DDIS will find false positives in approximately 5% of patients. The DDIS is a 236-item, yes or no question schedule that takes 45-75 minutes to administer. The SCID-D is actually semistructured with allowances for interviewer discretion, and while it yields extremely rich material, it may take 2-3 hours to administer in some cases.

Loewenstein's (1991b) special mental status for dissociative phenomena has been a significant contribution as well. It allows clinicians to assess dissociative phenomenology with facility in a conversational interview.

Hypnosis:

It is not unusual for signs suggestive of DID to manifest in a client or for the diagnostic issue to be unresolved pending direct contact with an alter, despite ample historical and suggestive data. Likewise, the diagnosis may seem firm from ancillary sources, yet the clinician has had no direct contact with an alter. Under such circumstances (if prompt resolution is necessary), the clinician may consider the use of hypnosis. Braun (1984d) states, "I withhold the use of hypnosis until I have exhausted other means," but he does not advocate an indefinite delay. A number of papers opine that the risks of inducing DID by such an approach are highly overstated (Braun, 1984b; Gruenewald, 1984; Kluft, 1982, 1989a).

For this reason, judicious hypnotic inquiry can play a valuable role in clarifying the diagnostic situation. Such inquiry should not be undertaken by the inexperienced or by those unaware of normative ego state phenomena that may be misinterpreted as DID (Kluft, 1982). Also, it should not be pursued unless the clinician is adequately trained in hypnosis, has sufficient time to deal with the emergence of an alter personality, and has studied techniques by which the original constellation can be restored (Braun, 1984e; Kluft, 1982). It is necessary to return executive control of the body to the personality that entered the office. Under forensic circumstances, it is inadvisable to explore a client for DID with hypnosis without numerous special safeguards and precautions.

It is imperative to bear in mind that the use of hypnosis may be held to have tainted the hypnotized person as a witness. The use of hypnosis without attending to such considerations may deprive a person of the right to bear witness to his or her own misfortunes, and has been held to be malpractice.

Sharing the Diagnosis:

The diagnosis must be shared in a common-sense fashion with the client, who otherwise will be mystified by the clinician's inquiries and procedures. Explanations must be pragmatic, clarifying, and devoid of implicit suggestions that the client, in terror and/or confusion, may seize upon as implicit or explicit advice or invitations to demonstrate certain phenomena. The usual responses are surprise, denial, or a transient sense of relief. Agitation may well follow the first session in which an alter emerges spontaneously or via hypnosis. The clinician must be accessible to the client during these difficult days. Even if the sessions have been taped, the client's presenting personality may well deny the diagnosis (Braun, 1984e). It suggests the intensity of the inner pain that the client has erected dissociative defenses to contain and presages the vicissitudes of the therapeutic process (Kluft, 1984b).

COEXISTING SYNDROMES

Bear in mind that many Axis I and Axis II entities may coexist with DID without explaining it. Coryell (1983) and Kluft (1984b) described the coexistence of affective disorder and DID. Kluft felt that the diagnoses were autonomous, but Coryell wondered if, at times, DID was an epiphenomenon of affective illness. Many have discussed DID as a borderline variant (Benner & Joscelyne, 1984; Buck, 1983; Clary, Burstin, & Carpenter, 1984), as a narcissistic disorder (Gruenewald, 1977), or have correlated it with the Briquet syndrome (Bliss, 1980).

Borderline Personality Disorder:

Authors who have studied large series of clients have found that the findings from single cases or small series do not hold up well when making generalizations. For example, the most extensive exploration of the relationship between borderline personality disorder (BPD) and DID, conducted by Horevitz and Braun (1984), found 70% of the DID clients also qualified for a BPD designation. Comparison of their sample with that of Kluft (1982), whose clients in general had higher ego strength, led them to conclude the presence of BPD was correlated with the clients' overall level of dysfunction, not with their DID *per se*. They surmised that DID is separate and distinct from—but may coexist with—BPD.

Depression:

More than 90% of DID clients show signs of depression.

Uncommonly, dissociative episodes can occur in depression (Ackner, 1954), and the disorders may coexist. Many DID clients have been considered to be bipolar, or "rapid cyclers" at times during their clinical career. Placebo-like responses to medication make an apparent cessation of dissociative signs upon initiating medication an unreliable indicator (Kluft, 1984b; Loewenstein, 1991a). I have been impressed that the use of hypnosis to attempt to access alters and discuss the alternations that are perceived as mood swings can resolve the differential promptly in most cases. If alters are encountered, a trial of DID therapy is indicated; if not, a pharmacologic regimen should be tried. Rechecking and crossover are possible if clinical considerations so dictate.

Schizophrenia:

Many DID clients in my series were once diagnosed as schizophrenic. Rosenbaum (1980) suggests this is a common phenomenon. Indeed, the hallucinations of alters' voices and presences, the alters' quasi-delusional sense of separateness, and their experience of being influenced by other entities and forces overlap with schizophrenic signs (Bliss, 1984a; Kluft, 1985b, 1987a, 1991a). DID clients may have brief psychotic episodes (Coons, 1984), and schizophrenics may have fugues (Ackner, 1954).

Coons (1984) and Kluft (1983) concur it is useful to look for Bleuler's primary symptoms as a guide. A person with DID may become withdrawn, but the other features are not found. Most schizophrenics' hallucinations are experienced as outside the head; most hallucinations in DID are perceived as coming from within. Unlike the schizophrenic, the DID client preserves reality testing and usually, once preliminary anxieties are resolved, establishes good rapport.

Epilepsy:

Temporal lobe epilepsy has been offered as a concomitant,

a differential diagnosis, and an etiology of DID (Schenk & Bear, 1981). Coons (1984) correctly points out that most of the temporal lobe clients in frequently cited articles (Mesulam, 1981; Schenk & Bear, 1981) did not have DID by DSM-III criteria and that clients' descriptions of alters often were not documented by the observation of dissociated personalities.

Certainly fugues, presumably organic, occur in 78% of temporal lobe epileptics (Coons, 1984). During such states a person may wander, appear perplexed, and engage in complex stereotypic behavior. The person usually experiences complete amnesia. Hypnosis or amobarbital as well as intense observation are useful in those cases where neither routine clinical assessment nor electroencephalography prove helpful. In one case, a hospital nurse observed a "seizure" episode and was able to engage an alter, then in control, in dialogue.

Malingering:

Malingering is often considered in the differential diagnosis of DID, especially when a client's circumstances rather than his or her psychology would make the production of the symptoms of DID useful. A considerable number of DID clients run afoul of the law; antisocial behaviors by alters are far from rare. Thus, it is not unexpected that the augmentation of DID or partial malingering of a DID picture by a legitimate DID client who is also a malefactor can be encountered.

When a person is suspected of malingering DID, it becomes critical to be aware when a forensic issue is involved and distinguish between the role of evaluator and therapist. The problem has been addressed at length in discussion of the Hillside Strangler Case (Orne, 1984). In practice, most malingering of DID is crude and reveals itself by inconsistency and preoccupation with stressful circumstances that the person with DID is feigned to avoid (Kluft, 1987b), although today's malingerer may profit from the availability of more information about DID and may concoct a more refined display than the malingerers of a decade ago. This is especially more likely if the person in question has had significant exposure to genuine DID patients. Therefore, careful observation and corroboration from external sources become important. Malingering may be sustained under hypnosis and amobarbital. In my experience, persons who feign DID follow lay sources, "overstate their case," and do not maintain the consistency of their alters in areas unrelated to the motivation for their malingering. Differential diagnosis in this difficult area remains quite problematic.

TREATMENT OF DID

This is an exciting but confusing epoch in the history of the treatment of dissociative identity disorder. On one hand, an increasing number of DID clients are being identified and are seeking psychotherapeutic help. On the other, despite the upsurge in the number of clients diagnosed as suffering from DID, many important questions remain unsolved. The first outcome studies are quite recent (Coons, 1986; Kluft, 1982, 1984e, 1986); controlled studies are not available. Many articles offer advice generalized from single cases or from small or unspecified data bases.

A number of authors have recently offered cautious estimations. Putnam (1989, 1993) has noted the heterogeneity of DID cohorts and indicated that a certain percentage of DID patients were untreatable. Kluft (1993b, 1994a, 1994d) emphasized that several groups of DID patients have different treatment courses and prognoses. Kluft found an excellent prognosis group that improved relatively rapidly, a "low trajectory" group whose treatments were slow, arduous, and of uncertain outcome, and a diverse "middle trajectory group." It was not unusual for a middle or low trajectory patient to move toward a good or "high" trajectory after therapeutic breakthroughs. In general, the more extreme the allegations of abuse and the more the allegations diverge from more mundane forms of mistreatment, the more difficult and prolonged the treatment.

Despite these encouraging observations, many continue to question whether the condition should be treated intensively or discouraged with benign neglect. Concern has been expressed that naïve and credulous therapists may suggest or create the condition in basically histrionic (Thigpen & Cleckley, 1984) or schizophrenic (Kline, 1984) individuals, or even enter a *folie à deux* with their clients (Victor, 1975).

Arguments to the contrary have been offered (Fink, 1991; Gruenewald, 1984; Kluft, 1982, 1985a). In 21 years, I have seen over 2,500 DID clients diagnosed by more than 1,800 separate clinicians in consultation and referral. In my experience, referral sources have been circumspect rather than zealous in their approach to DID, and I have seen little evidence to support the notion that iatrogenic factors are significant concerns.

Although no controlled trials compare the fates of DID clients in active-treatment, placebo-like-treatment, and no-treatment cohorts, some recent data from a long-term follow-up study bear on the controversy. Of those patients who declined treatment of their DID or who entered treatments in which their DID was acknowledged, all continued to have clinical DID on follow-up 2–8 years later. In addition, patients who entered treatments in which their DID was acknowledged but not addressed directly achieved integration in only 2%–3% of cases. Conversely, clients reassessed after treatment to integration for DID have been found to retain their gains rather well (Kluft, 1984f, 1986, 1993b).

TREATMENT ISSUES

The treatment of DID is a subset of the treatment of the traumatized. As such, it should follow the principles of post-traumatic therapies in being triphasic. Herman (1992) demonstrated that work with the traumatized begins with a phase of safety, during which the patient is helped to be safe and is strengthened prior to approaching painful materials. In a second phase, that of remembrance and mourning, painful experiences are metabolized and their consequences grieved. Finally, in a phase of reconnection, the patient reintegrates his or her self, reestablishes or improves relationships, and once again becomes a member of his or her social group and society. This overall orientation is a useful context when one considers the treatment of DID.

Treatment Goals:

In general, the tasks of therapy are the same as those in any intense change-oriented approach but are pursued, in this case, in one who lacks a unified personality. This precludes the possibility of an ongoing unified and available observing ego and implies the disruption of certain ego strengths and functions that are usually autonomous, such as memory. The personalities may have different perceptions, recollections, problems, priorities, goals, and degrees of involvement with—and commitment to—the therapy and one another. Therefore, it usually becomes essential to replace this dividedness with agreement to work toward certain common goals and to achieve unity of purpose and motivation for treatment success. Work toward such cooperation and the possible integration of the several personalities distinguishes the treatment of DID from other types of treatment (Kluft, 1984d, 1984e, 1984f, 1991b). Although some therapists (Beahrs, 1982; Watkins & Watkins, 1988) argue multiplicity should be transformed from a symptom into a skill rather than be ablated, most consider integration preferable.

In this chapter, the terms *unification, integration,* and *fusion* are used synonymously and are understood to connote the spontaneous or facilitated coming together of personalities after adequate therapy has helped the client see, abreact, and work through the reasons for being of each separate alter. Consequently, therapy serves to erode the barriers between the alters and allow mutual acceptance, empathy, and identification. It does not indicate the dominance of one alter, the creation of a new "healthy" alter, or a premature compression or suppression of alters into the appearance of a resolution (Kluft, 1984e).

A General Outline of Treatment:

Virtually every aspect of treatment is dependent on the strength of the therapeutic alliance, which must be cultivated with each individual alter. In the face of severe psychopathology, painful material, crises, difficult transferences, and the likelihood that—at least early in treatment—the alters may have grossly divergent perceptions of the clinician and test him or her rigorously, the client's commitment to the task of therapy and collaborative cooperation is critical. This emphasis is implicit in a general treatment plan outlined by Braun (1980, 1984c), Kluft (1991b), Putnam (1989) and Ross (1989), which has sufficient universality to be applied in most therapy formats.

Following is a synthesis of the works of these authors and my own work (from Kluft, 1991b). The stages, which often overlap and/or are simultaneously ongoing, are:

1. *Establishing the psychotherapy* involves the creation of an atmosphere of safety in which the security of the treatment frame is confirmed, the therapeutic alliance achieves a preliminary form, and the patient is oriented to the nature of the treatment that will occur.

2. *Preliminary interventions* entail accessing alters, contracting against self-harm and other dysfunctional behaviors, fostering communication across the alters, enhancing the therapeutic alliance, building coping expertise, and offering whatever symptomatic relief is possible.

3. *History gathering and mapping* involves learning more about the alters, their purported origins, and their

interactions as both a system of self and as an inner world of the personalities. Therapy begins to address the particular alters' difficulties and their interactive difficulties.

4. *Metabolism of the trauma* refers to working with and resolving the patient's traumatic experiences. Modern therapists attempt to learn what material is to be dealt with before plunging into such endeavors, use techniques that allow the painful material to be approached slowly and gradually, and pace the treatment to protect the patient against decompensation. For an introduction to such considerations, see Fine (1991) and Kluft (1988b, 1989b, 1993a).

5. *Moving toward integration-resolution* involves enhancing cooperation and communication across the alters and working through recovered material across the alters, leading to more mutual awareness, identification, and empathy. Alters may begin to blend, to blur their once more discrete features, and/or fade in prominence.

6. *Integration-Resolution* "consists of the patient's coming to a new and more solid stance toward his or her self and the world. A smooth collaboration among the alters will constitute a resolution; their blending into a unity is an integration" (Kluft, 1991b, p. 179).

7. *Learning new coping skills* entails mastering the management of circumstances previously handled by dissociative defenses. From the perspective of unity, many major relationships and decisions may require reconsideration and renegotiation.

8. *Solidification of gains and working through* involves relearning how to live in the world and how to understand and approach relationships more productively. Addressing residual characterologic difficulties and addressing the past as it appears in the transference may be central as well.

9. *Follow-up* allows for sequential reassessment of the patient's gains and the emergence of previously overlooked or relapsing dissociative elements. Tapering rather than terminating contact is recommended on the basis of research findings on relapse identification (Kluft, 1986).

THE COURSE AND CHARACTERISTICS OF TREATMENT

It is difficult to conceive of a more demanding and painful treatment, and those who must undertake it have many inherent vulnerabilities (Kluft, 1983, 1984c, 1984e). Dissociation and dividedness make insight difficult to attain. Deprived of a continuous memory, and switching in response to both inner and outer pressures and stressors, the patient finds that self-observation and learning from experience are compromised. Alters may alienate support systems as their disruptive and inconsistent behaviors and their memory problems may make them appear unreliable at best. Traumatized families may openly reject the client and/or disavow everything the client has alleged.

The alters' switching and battles for dominance can create an apparently unending series of crises. Alters who identify with aggressors or traumatizers may try to suppress those who want to cooperate with therapy, or punish those they dislike by inflicting injury upon the body. Battles between alters may result in hallucinations and quasipsychotic symptoms (Kluft,

1983, 1984d, 1984e, 1987a, 1991a). Some alters may suddenly withdraw the client from therapy.

Painful memories may emerge as hallucinations, nightmares, or passive influence experiences. In order to complete the therapy, longstanding repressions must be undone, and dissociative defenses and switching must be abandoned and replaced. The alters also must give up their narcissistic investments in separateness, abandon aspirations for total control, and "empathize, compromise, identify, and ultimately coalesce with personalities they had long avoided, opposed and rejected" (Kluft, 1984e).

In view of the magnitude of the changes required and the difficulty of the materials that must be worked through, therapy may prove arduous for client and therapist alike. Ideally, a minimum of two sessions a week is desirable, with the opportunity for prolonged sessions to work on upsetting materials and the understanding that crisis intervention sessions may be needed. Telephone accessibility is desirable, but firm, nonpunitive limit-setting is very much in order to prevent unwarranted intrusiveness. The pace of therapy must be modulated to allow the client respite from incessant exposure to traumatic materials (Fine, 1991; Kluft, 1989b, 1993a). Some clients, once their amnestic barriers are eroded, will be in states of "chronic crisis" for long periods of time.

THERAPISTS' REACTIONS TO WORKING WITH DID CLIENTS

Working to cure DID can be arduous and demanding. Most therapists feel rather changed by the experience and believe their overall skills have been improved by meeting the challenge of working with this complex psychopathology. A smaller number feel traumatized. Initial reactions of excitement, fascination, overinvestment, and interest in documenting the panoply of pathology are often followed by bewilderment, exasperation, and a sense of being drained. Many feel overwhelmed by the painful material, the high incidence of crises, the need to bring to bear a variety of clinical skills in rapid succession and/or novel combinations, and the skepticism of usually supportive colleagues. Many counselors, sensitive to their clients' isolation and the rigors of therapy, find it difficult both to be accessible and to remain able to set reasonable and nonpunitive limits. They discover clients consume substantial amounts of their professional and personal time.

Often the therapist is distressed to find preferred techniques ineffective and cherished theories disconfirmed. As a result, the therapist may become exasperated with some alters' failure to cooperate with or value the goals of the therapy. The therapist may also become exasperated with their incessant testing of his or her trustworthiness and good will.

Empathic tendencies are sorely taxed. It is difficult to feel along with the separate personalities, and to remain in touch with the "red thread" of a session across dissociative defenses and personality switches. Furthermore, the material of therapy is often painful and difficult to accept on an empathic level. Four reaction patterns are common among therapists (Wilbur & Kluft, 1989). The therapist may:

- Retreat from painful affect and material into a cognitive stance and undertake an intellectualized therapy in which he or she plays detective, becoming a defensive skeptic or an obsessional worrier over "what is real"

- Abandon a conventional stance and undertake providing an actively nurturing corrective emotional experience

- Move beyond empathy to counteridentification, often with excessive advocacy

- Move toward masochistic self-endangerment and/or self-sacrifice on the client's behalf

These four patterns, however they are rationalized, may serve the therapist's countertransference needs more than the goals of the treatment. An extensive discussion of countertransference in work with DID patients can be found in Loewenstein (1993) and Kluft (1994b).

Therapists who work smoothly with DID clients set firm but nonrejecting boundaries and sensible but nonpunitive limits. They safeguard their practice and private lives. They know therapy may be prolonged; therefore, they avoid placing unreasonable pressures upon themselves, the clients, or treatment. They are wary of accepting a DID client they do not find likeable, because they know that their relationship with the client may become quite intense and complex and go on for many years. As a group, successful DID therapists are flexible and ready to learn from their clients and colleagues.

MODALITIES OF TREATMENT

Psychoanalytic Approaches:

Psychoanalytic approaches to DID have been discussed by Brenner (1994), Kluft (in press-a), Lampl-de Groot (1981), Lasky (1978), Marmer (1980a, 1991), Reis (1958), and Wilbur (1986). It seems clear that some clients with DID who have the ego strength to undertake analysis, who are not alloplastic, whose personalities are cooperative, and who are completely accessible without hypnosis can be treated with analysis. However, they constitute a small minority of DID clients. Some have undergone analysis without the diagnosis being suspected; others, also undiagnosed, have had their analyses interrupted by regressive phenomena not recognized as manifestations of the DID condition (Kluft, 1987b). While psychoanalytic understanding is often considered desirable in work with DID (Kluft, 1987b, in press-b; Wilbur, 1984), formal psychoanalysis should be reserved for a small number of cases.

Psychoanalytic psychotherapy, with or without facilitation

by hypnosis, is widely recommended. Bowers and colleagues (1971) offered several useful precepts, Wilbur (1984, 1986) described her approaches, and Marmer (1980b) discussed working with the dreams of dissociating clients. Kluft's articles (1982, 1984e, 1984f, 1991b) on treatment described aspects of work in psychoanalytic psychotherapy facilitated by hypnosis, but their emphasis was on the hypnosis and crisis management aspects rather than the application of psychodynamic precepts. Kluft (1984c, 1984d, 1984e) described the problems and impairment of ego functions suffered by DID clients by virtue of their dividedness, and have shown how they render the application of a purely interpretive psychoanalytic paradigm problematic. An overview of psychoanalytic psychotherapy for DID has been compiled (Kluft, in press-b).

Cognitive and Behavioral Approaches:

Behavioral treatments have been described by Kohlenberg (1973), Price and Hess (1979), and most elegantly by Klonoff and Janata (1984). No doubt, behavioral regimens can make dramatic transient impacts on DID's manifest pathology, but there is no extant case report of a behavioral regimen resulting in a successful long-term cure. The report of a successful cognitive behavioral treatment of DID (Caddy, 1985) is potentially misleading in that the therapy involved the use of many interventions associated with other types of therapy in addition to its use of these modalities. Klonoff and Janata found that unless the underlying issues were resolved, relapse occurred. Many workers think behavioral approaches inadvertently replicate childhood traumas in which clients' pain was not responded to or in which they were psychologically and/or physically confined or bound rather than allowed freedom. In fact, many clients experience them as punitive. The behavioral therapy of DID *per se* currently must be regarded as ancillary rather than primary. Cognitive therapy has proved useful, demonstrated primarily in the work of Fine (1991, 1992).

Family Intervention:

Family interventions have been reported by Beale (1978), Benjamin and Benjamin (1992), Davis and Osherson (1977), Kluft, Braun, and Sachs (1985), and Levenson and Berry (1983). Summing up their research, although DID is all too often an aftermath of family pathology, family therapy is rarely successful as a primary treatment modality. However, it often can be a valuable adjunct (Kluft et al., 1985).

Empirically, treatment of an adult DID client with a traumatizing family of origin frequently does no more than result in retraumatization. However, family interventions may be essential to treat or stabilize a child or early adolescent with DID (Hornstein & Tyson, 1991; Kluft, 1984d). Family work may allow relationships to be saved and strengthened and may protect the children from incorporating or being drawn in to some aspects of the DID psychopathology.

In general, the concerned others in the DID client's family may require considerable education and support. In difficult and crisis-filled cases, their support of the therapy and the therapist's support of them can be critical to the outcome of the treatment. Recent publications have addressed the primary treatment issues and preferred interventions in work with the spouses of DID clients (Panos, Panos, & Allred, 1990; Sachs, Frischholz, & Wood, 1991).

Group Treatment:

Group treatment of DID can prove difficult. Caul (1984), who summarized the problems such clients experience in and impose upon heterogeneous groups, found unintegrated DID clients may incapacitate the group's productivity, as the materials and experiences they share may overwhelm the group members. DID clients often are exquisitely sensitive and become engulfed in others' issues, and they are prone to dissociate in and/or run from sessions. They work more successfully in task-oriented or project-oriented groups that focus on occupational therapy, music therapy, movement therapy, or art therapy (Kluft, 1984c).

Some anecdotally describe their successful inclusion in groups with a shared experience, such as incestuous relationships, rape, or alcoholism. Caul (1984) proposed a model for undertaking an internal group therapy among the alters. Homogeneous groups of DID clients are becoming common as more are identified. Such groups can be quite helpful as adjuncts to individual psychotherapy if structured and focused on here-and-now issues, as opposed to dealing with past traumata in detail. In the absence of such precautions, these groups can become chaotic and unmanageable (Caul, Sachs, & Braun, 1986; Coons & Bradley, 1985).

Amobarbital and/ or Videotaping:

Workers have described the facilitation of treatment with amobarbital (Amytal) and/or videotaped interviews. Hall, Le Cann, and Schoolar (1975) describe treating a client by retrieving material in amobarbital interviews that were videotaped and then used in treatment; de Vito (1993) reported in detail a patient who benefited from a series of drug-facilitated interviews. Caul (1984) has described taping hypnotically facilitated sessions and offered cautions about the timing of playing back such sessions to the client. Although the personalities of some clients tolerate videotaped confrontation with evidence and alters from which they were profoundly dissociated, many people are overwhelmed by such data or re-repress it. Such approaches are best considered on a case-by-case basis. Caul seems to advocate a version of what hypnotherapists refer to as "permissive amnesia"; that is, the client can see the tape when ready (an analogy to the suggestion the client will remember a traumatic event when he or she is ready to do so).

Hypnotherapy:

Hypnotherapeutic interventions have an established role in

the contemporary treatment of DID, despite the controversy that surrounds their use. On one hand, a large number of clinicians have helped a good many DID clients with such interventions. On the other, many prominent and eloquent individuals have raised concerns that hypnosis can concretize, exacerbate, or even create DID.

Often the debate becomes arcane to those unfamiliar with the literature of hypnosis and the specialized concerns of forensic hypnosis, in which workers struggle to guard against the induction of confabulated or false memories that are perceived as concrete reality, and, if so reported, can impede the judicial process (Orne, 1979). Judicious hypnotherapeutic interventions, thoughtfully integrated into a well-planned psychotherapy, individualized to a particular client, and oriented toward integration, can be extremely productive and helpful, and ill-advised hypnotic work, like any other inappropriate steps, may well miscarry (Kluft, 1982, 1991b; Wilbur & Kluft, 1989). The use of hypnosis has been described and documented by Allison (1974), Bowers et al. (1971), Brandsma and Ludwig (1984), Braun (1980, 1984d, 1984e), Caul (1984), Erickson and Kubie (1939), Gruenewald (1971), Horevitz (1983), Howland (1975), Kluft (1982, 1983, 1984e, 1984f, 1992a, 1992b), and Spiegel (1991), among others.

Reparenting:

Some clinicians advocate the provision of a very tangible corrective emotional experience, under the rubric of reparenting. They seek to create experiences within treatment that nurture the client through a more positive recapitulation of various developmental issues and to provide more positive introjects. My experience shows that successful treatment does not necessitate such measures, and such efforts often become therapeutic misadventures. Reparenting is not advised, and most authorities consider it contraindicated and potentially dangerous.

Hospital Treatment:

A dissociative identity disorder client may require hospitalization for self-destructive episodes, severe dysphoria, fugues, or alters' inappropriate behaviors. Sometimes a structured environment is advisable for difficult phases of treatment. If the hospital staff accepts the diagnosis and is supportive of the treatment, most patients with DID can be managed adequately. Failing these conditions, a DID client's admission can be traumatizing to the client and hospital alike. A DID client rarely splits a staff into various groups; on the contrary, a staff splits itself by allowing individual divergent views about this controversial condition to influence professional behavior. DID clients, especially the first few admitted to a unit, can be so overwhelming as to threaten the sense of competence of that particular milieu. The staff's sense of helplessness vis-à-vis the client can engender resentment of both the client and the admitting practitioner. The therapist should help the staff in matter-of-fact problem-solving, explain his or her therapeutic approach, and be available by telephone.

The following guidelines emerge from clinical experience:

1. Request a private room, which offers the client a place of refuge and diminishes crises.

2. Treat all alters with equal respect and address the client as he or she wishes in one to one contacts. Insisting on a uniformity of name or personality presence provokes crises or suppresses necessary data. However, insist that the patient respond to his or her legal name in public and group settings.

3. Make it clear that the staff is not expected to recognize each alter. Alters must identify themselves to staff members if they find such acknowledgment important.

4. Anticipate likely crises with staff; emphasize your availability.

5. Explain ward rules personally, having requested all alters to listen, and insist on reasonable compliance. If problems emerge, offer warm and firm responses and eschew punitive measures.

6. Because such clients often have trouble with verbal group therapy, encourage art, movement, or occupational therapy groups.

7. Encourage a cooperative therapeutic thrust despite staff members' disagreement about DID; emphasize the need to maintain a competent therapeutic environment for the client.

8. Help the client focus on the goals of the admission rather than succumb to a preoccupation with minor mishaps and problems on the unit.

9. Clarify to the client each staff member's role, and emphasize that all members will not work in the same way. For example, it is not unusual for clients whose therapists elicit and work intensively with various alters to misperceive staff as unconcerned if they do not follow suit, even though it usually would be inappropriate if they did so (Kluft, 1984c, 1991b).

Medications:

It is generally agreed that medication does not influence the core psychopathology of DID but may palliate symptomatic distress or impact upon a coexisting drug-responsive condition or target symptom (Kluft, 1984c; Loewenstein, 1991a). Many clients are treated successfully without medication.

Kluft (1984c) observed 6 clients with DID and major depression and found that treating either disorder as primary failed to impact on the other. However, Coryell (1983) reported a single case in which he conceptualized DID as an epiphenomenon of depression.

Most DID clients manifest depression, anxiety, panic attacks, and phobias; some show transient (hysterical) psychoses. However, pharmacotherapy for such symptoms may yield responses so rapid, transient, inconsistent across alters, and/or persistent despite the discontinuation of the medication, that the clinician cannot be sure that an active drug intervention—rather than a placebo-like response—has occurred. Alters within a single client are known to show different responses to a single medication (Braun, 1983b; Kluft, 1984c). Loewenstein (1991a) provides an authoritative overview of psychopharmacologic approaches to DID, and is quite conservative in his estimation of the efficacy of medications. Partial, rather than complete, relief of target systems is most common.

With rare exceptions, medication should not be prescribed for a particular personality. Symptoms restricted to one or a few alters are usually more responsive to psychotherapy, especially when facilitated by hypnosis. With the occasional exception of minor tranquilizers the use of medications is most likely to be circumspect and productive when the target symptoms are shared by all or almost all of the personalities.

Hypnotic and sedative drugs are often prescribed for sleep disturbance. Many clients fail to respond initially or after transient success; many try to escape from dysphoria with surreptitious overdosage. Most DID clients suffer sleep disruption when alters are in conflict and/or painful material is emerging. Often one must adopt a compromise regimen that provides "a modicum of relief and a minimum of risk" (Kluft, 1984c).

Minor tranquilizers are useful, but tolerance can be expected, and occasional abuse is encountered. High doses often become a necessary transient compromise if anxiety becomes disorganizing or incapacitating. In the absence of coexisting mania or agitation in affective disorder, or for transient use with severe headaches, major tranquilizers should be used with caution and generally avoided. A wealth of anecdotal reports describe serious adverse effects, and no documented proof of their beneficial impact has been published. Their major use in DID is for sedation when minor tranquilizers fail or abuse/tolerance has become a problem.

Many DID clients have depressive symptoms, and a trial of antidepressants may be warranted. In cases without classic depression, results are often equivocal. Prescription must be circumspect, since many clients may ingest prescribed medication in suicide attempts. Monoamine oxidase inhibitor (MAOI) drugs give the client the opportunity for self-destructive abuse but may help atypical depressions in reliable clients. Those with coexistent bipolar disorders and DID may have the former disorder relieved by lithium. Two articles suggested a connection between DID and seizure disorders (Mesulam, 1981; Schenk & Bear, 1981). Notwithstanding that the clients cited had, overall, equivocal responses to anticonvulsants, many clinicians have instituted such regimens. I have now seen over 100 classic DID clients others had placed on anticonvulsants without observing a single unequivocal response.

Loewenstein, Hornstein, and Farber (1988) demonstrated that clonazepam (Klonopin) can offer substantial relief to approximately half the DID clients that suffer posttraumatic symptom complexes. Braun (1990) described the use of large doses of propranolol (Inderal) to reduce dysphoric and uncontrolled switching, but this regimen remains experimental and must be used cautiously.

Postfusion Therapy:

Those who leave treatment after achieving apparent unity usually relapse within 2–24 months. Further therapy is indicated to work through issues, prevent rerepression of traumatic memories, and facilitate the development of nondissociative coping strategies and defenses. Clients often wish and are encouraged by concerned others to "put it all behind [them]," forgive and forget, and make up for their time of compromise or incapacitation. In fact, a newly integrated DID client is a vulnerable neophyte who has just achieved the unity with which most clients enter treatment. Moritoria about major life decisions are useful, as is anticipatory socialization in potentially difficult situations. The emergence of realistic goal-setting, accurate perception of others, increased anxiety tolerance, and gratifying sublimations augur well, as does a willingness to work through painful issues in the transference. Avoidance-coping styles and defenses require confrontation. Because partial relapse and the discovery of other alters are both possible, the integration *per se* should not be regarded as sacrosanct. An integration's failure is no more than an indication that its occurrence was premature (Kluft, 1982, 1984e).

Many clients remain in treatment nearly as long after integration as they were when trying to achieve fusion. A detailed exploration of postfusion therapy is available (Kluft, 1988a).

Follow-up Studies:

Case reports and a study of the natural history of DID suggest that untreated DID clients do not enjoy spontaneous remission, but instead many (70%–80%) appear to shift to a one-alter predominant mode with relatively infrequent or covert intrusions of others as they progress into middle age and senescence (Ellenberger, 1970; Kluft, 1985a; Rosenbaum, 1980). Most case reports do not describe complete or successful therapies. Many that appear successful have no firm fusion criteria and unclear follow-up and offer confusing conceptualizations, such as describing integrations in which other alters are still occasionally noted.

Using operational fusion criteria, Kluft (1982, 1984e, 1986) followed a cohort of intensively treated DID clients and periodically studied the stability of their unification. The 33 clients averaged 13.9 personalities (ranging from 2 to as many as 86) and 21.6 months from diagnosis to apparent integration. Reassessed a minimum of 27 months after apparent fusion (2 years after fulfilling fusion criteria), 31 (94%) had not relapsed into behavioral DID and 25 (75.8%) showed neither residual nor recurrent dissociative phenomena. No genuine full relapse was noted. Of the two with DID, one had feigned integration and the other had a brief reactivation of 1 of 32 previously integrated alters when her spouse was found to be terminally ill. Six had alters who had not assumed executive control and were classified as intrapsychic. Of those, two had new entities: one formed upon a lover's death, the other upon the client's return to college. Three clients showed layering phenomena, groups of preexisting alters who had been long suppressed but were beginning to emerge as other alters were solidly integrated. The other relapse events were partial relapses of previous alters under stress, but those alters remained intrapsychic. Object loss, rejection, or the threat of those experiences triggered 75% of the relapse events. Three remain in treatment for the newly discovered layers of alters, and all are approaching integration. One individual worked years to initiate a relapse autohypnotically and only recently returned for treatment.

The author's more recent (Kluft, 1993b, unpublished data) follow-ups of cohorts integrated for 5, 10, and 15 years indicate that long-term stable clinical integration of dissociative identity disorder clients is quite possible and that relapse of treated dividedness occurs infrequently after long-term integration; however, occasional alters overlooked in initial therapies may still be encountered on occasion. In sum, the prognosis is optimistic for those who are offered intensive treatment and are motivated to accept it.

REFERENCES

Ackner, B. (1954). Depersonalization II: Clinical syndromes. *Journal of Mental Science, 100,* 854-872.

Allison, R. B. (1974). A new treatment approach for multiple personality. *American Journal and Clinical Hypnosis, 17,* 15-32.

American Psychiatric Association. (1980). *Diagnostic and statistical manual of mental disorders* (3rd ed.), Washington, DC: Author.

American Psychiatric Association. (1987). *Diagnostic and statistical manual of mental disorders* (3rd ed. rev.), Washington, DC: Author.

American Psychiatric Association. (1994). *Diagnostic and statistical manual of mental disorders* (4th ed.), Washington, DC: Author.

Beahrs, J. O. (1982). *Unity and multiplicity.* New York: Brunner/Mazel.

Beale, E. W. (1978). The use of the extended family in the treatment of multiple personality. *American Journal of Psychiatry, 135,* 539-542.

Benjamin, L. R., & Benjamin, R. (1992). An overview of family treatment in dissociative disorders. *Dissociation, 5,* 236-241.

Bernstein, E. M., & Putnam, F. W. (1986). Development, reliability, and validity of a dissociation scale. *Journal of Nervous and Mental Disease, 174,* 727-735.

Bliss, E. L. (1980). Multiple personalities. *Archives of General Psychiatry, 37,* 1388-1397.

Bliss, E. L. (1984a). Auditory hallucinations and schizophrenia. *Journal of Nervous and Mental Disease, 171,* 30-33.

Bliss, E. L. (1984b). Spontaneous self-hypnosis in multiple personality disorder. *Psychiatric Clinics of North America, 14,* 135-148.

Boon, S., & Draijer, N. (1993). *Multiple personality disorder in the Netherlands: A study on reliability and validity of the diagnosis.* Amsterdam: Swets & Zeitlinger.

Boor, M., & Coons, P. M. (1983). A comprehensive bibliography of literature pertaining to multiple personality. *Psychological Reports, 53,* 295-310.

Bowers, M. K., et al. (1971). Therapy of multiple personality. *International Journal of Clinical and Experimental Hypnosis, 19,* 57-65.

Brandsma, J. M., & Ludwig, A. M. (1984). A case of multiple personality: Diagnosis and therapy. *International Journal of Clinical Hypnosis, 22,* 216-233.

Braun, B. G. (1980). Hypnosis for multiple personalities. In H. J. Wain (Ed.), *Clinical hypnosis in medicine.* Chicago: Year Book Publisher.

Braun, B. G. (Ed.). (1983a). *American Journal of Clinical Hypnosis, 26*(2).

Braun, B. G. (1983b). Psychophysiologic phenomena in multiple personality and hypnosis. *American Journal of Clinical Hypnosis, 26,* 124-137.

Braun, B. G. (1984a). Foreword. *Psychiatric Clinics of North America 7,* 1-2.

Braun, B. G. (1984b). Hypnosis creates multiple personality: Myth or reality? *International Journal of Clinical and Experimental Hypnosis, 32,* 191-197.

Braun, B. G. (1984c). *Multiplicity: Form and function.* Copyrighted paper.

Braun, B. G. (Ed.). (1984d). *Psychiatric Clinics of North America, 7*(1).

Braun, B. G. (1984e). Use of hypnosis with multiple personality. *Psychiatric Annals, 14,* 34-40.

Braun, B. G. (1986). Issues in the psychotherapy of multiple personality disorder. In B. G. Braun (Ed.), *The treatment of multiple personality disorder.* Washington, DC: American Psychiatric Press.

Braun, B. G. (1990). Unusual medication regimens in the treatment of dissociative disorder patients: Part I. Noradrenergic agents. *Dissociation, 3,* 144-150.

Brenner, I. (1994). The dissociative character. *Journal of the American Psychiatric Association, 42,* 819-846.

Buck, O. D. (1983). Multiple personality as a borderline state. *Journal of Nervous and Mental Disease, 171,* 62-65.

Caddy, G. R. (1985). Cognitive behavior therapy in the treatment of multiple personality. *Behavior Modification, 9,* 267-292.

Carlson, E. B., Putnam, F. W., Ross, C. A., Torem, M., Coons, P. M., Dill, D. L., Loewenstein, R. J., & Braun, B. G. (1993). Validity of the dissociative experiences scale in screening for multiple personality disorder: A multicenter study. *American Journal of Psychiatry, 150,* 1030-1036.

Caul, D. (1984). Group and videotape techniques for multiple personality disorder. *Psychiatric Annals, 14,* 43-50.

Caul, D., Sachs, R. G., & Braun, B. G. (1986). Group therapy for multiple personality disorder. In B. G. Braun (Ed.), *The treatment of multiple personality disorder.* Washington, DC: American Psychiatric Press.

Clary, W. F., Burstin, K. J., & Carpenter, J. S. (1984). Multiple personality and borderline personality disorder. *Psychiatric Clinics of North America, 7,* 89-100.

Coons, P. M. (1980). Multiple personality: Diagnostic considerations. *Journal of Clinical Psychiatry, 41,* 330-336.

Coons, P. M. (1984). The differential diagnosis of multiple personality. *Psychiatric Clinics of North America, 7,* 51-68.

Coons, P. M. (1985). Children of parents with multiple personality disorder. In R. P. Kluft (Ed.), *Childhood antecedents of multiple personality.* Washington, DC: American Psychiatric Press.

Coons, P. M. (1986). Treatment progress in twenty patients with multiple personality disorder. *Journal of Nervous and Mental Disease, 174,* 715-721.

Coons, P. M. (1994). Confirmation of childhood abuse in child and adolescent cases of multiple personality disorder and dissociative disorder not otherwise specified. *Journal of Nervous and Mental Disease, 182,* 461-464.

Coons, P. M., Bowman, E. S., Kluft, R. P., & Milstein, V. (1991). Cross-cultural occurrence of multiple personality disorder: Additional cases from a recent survey. *Dissociation, 4,* 124-128.

Coons, P. M., & Bradley, K. (1985). Group psychotherapy with multiple personality patients. *Journal of Nervous and Mental Disease, 173,* 515-521.

Coons, P. M., & Milstein, V. (1994). Factitious or malingered multiple personality disorder: Eleven cases. *Dissociation, 7,* 81-85.

Coryell, W. (1983). Multiple personality and primary affective disorder. *Journal of Nervous and Mental Disease, 171,* 388-390.

Damgaard, J. A., van Benschoten, S., & Fagan, J. (1985). An updated bibliography of literature pertaining to multiple personality. *Psychological Reports, 57,* 131-137.

Davis, D. H., & Osherson, A. (1977). The concurrent treatment of a multiple personality woman and her son. *American Journal of Psychotherapy, 31,* 504-515.

de Vito, R. (1993). The use of Amytal interviews in the treatment of an exceptionally complex case of multiple personality disorder. In R.P. Kluft, & C. G. Fines (Eds.), *Clinical perspectives on multiple personality disorder* (pp. 227-240). Washington DC: American Psychiatric Press.

Ellenberger, H. F. (1970). *The discovery of the unconscious.* New York: Basic Books.

Erickson, M. H., & Kubie, L. S. (1939). The permanent relief of an obsessional phobia by means of communications with an unsuspected dual personality. *Psychoanalytic Quarterly, 8,* 471-509.

Fagan, J., & McMahon, P. P. (1984). Incipient multiple personality in children: Four cases. *Journal of Nervous and Mental Disease, 172,* 26-36.

Fine, C. G. (1991). Treatment stabilization and crisis prevention: Pacing the therapy of the multiple personality disorder patient. *Psychiatric Clinics of North America, 14,* 661-675.

Fine, C. G. (1992). Multiple personality disorder. In A. Freeman & F. M. Dattilio (Eds.), *The comprehensive casebook of cognitive therapy* (pp. 347-360). New York: Plenum Press.

Fink, D. (1991). The comorbidity of multiple personality disorder and DSM-III-R axis II disorders. *Psychiatric Clinics of North America, 14,* 547-566.

Goettman, C., Greaves, G. B., & Coons, P. M. (1994). *Multiple personality and dissociation, 1791-1992: A complete bibliography.* (2nd ed.). Lutherville, MD: The Sidran Press.

Goodwin, J. (1982). *Sexual abuse: Incest victims and their families.* Boston: Wright/PSG.

Goodwin, J. (1985). Credibility problems in multiple personality patients. In R. P. Kluft (Ed.), *Childhood antecedents of multiple personality.* Washington, DC: American Psychiatric Press.

Greaves, G. B. (1980). Multiple personality: 165 years after Mary Reynolds. *Journal of Nervous and Mental Disease, 168,* 577-596.

Gruenewald, D. (1971). Hypnotic techniques without hypnosis in the treatment of dual personality: A case report. *Journal of Nervous and Mental Disease, 153,* 41-46.

Gruenewald, D. (1977). Multiple personality and splitting phenomena: A reconceptualization. *Journal of Nervous and Mental Disease, 164,* 385-393.

Gruenewald, D. (1984). On the nature of multiple personality: Comparisons with hypnosis. *International Journal of Clinical Hypnosis, 32,* 170-190.

Hall, R. C., Le Cann, A. F., & Schoolar, J. C. (1975). Amobarbital treatment of multiple personality. *Journal of Nervous and Mental Disease, 161,* 138-142.

Hall, P., & Steinberg, M. (1994). Systematic assessment of dissociative symptoms and disorders using the SCID-D in a clinical outpatient setting: Three cases. *Dissociation, 7,* 112-117.

Herman, J. L. (1992). *Trauma and recovery.* New York: Basic Books.

Hilgard, E. R. (1987). *Divided consciousness: Multiple controls in human thought and action.* (Expanded edition). New York: John Wiley & Sons.

Horevitz, R. P. (1983). Hypnosis for multiple personality disorder: A framework for beginning. *American Journal of Clinical Hypnosis, 26,* 138-145.

Horevitz, R. P., & Braun, B. G. (1984). Are multiple personalities borderline? *Psychiatric Clinics of North America, 7,* 69-88.

Hornstein, N., & Putnam, F. W. (1992). Clinical phenomenology of childhood and adolescent dissociative disorders. *Journal of the Academy of Child and Adolescent Psychiatry, 31,* 1077-1085.

Hornstein, N., & Tyson, S. (1991). Inpatient treatment of children with multiple personality/dissociative disorders and their families. *Psychiatric Clinics of North America, 14,* 631-648.

Howland, J. S. (1975). The use of hypnosis in the treatment of a case of multiple personality. *Journal of Nervous and Mental Disease, 161,* 138-142.

Kline, M. V. (1984). Multiple personality: Facts and artifacts in relation to hypnotherapy. *International Journal of Clinical and Experimental Hypnosis, 32,* 198-209.

Klonoff, E. A., & Janata, J. W. (1984, November). *Multiple personality.* Paper presented at the annual meeting of the Association for the Advancement of Behavior Therapy, Philadelphia, PA.

Kluft, R. P. (1982). Varieties of hypnotic interventions in the treatment of multiple personality. *American Journal of Clinical Hypnosis, 24,* 230-240.

Kluft, R. P. (1983). Hypnotherapeutic crisis intervention in multiple personality. *American Journal of Clinical Hypnosis, 26,* 73-83.

Kluft, R. P. (1984a). An introduction to multiple personality disorder. *Psychiatric Annals, 14,* 19-23.

Kluft, R. P. (1984b). Aspects of the treatment of multiple personality disorder. *Psychiatric Annals. 14,* 51-55.

Kluft, R. P. (1984c). Diagnosing multiple personality disorder. *Pennsylvania Medicine, 87,* 45-46.

Kluft, R. P. (1984d). Multiple personality in childhood. *Psychiatric Clinics of North America, 7,* 121-131.

Kluft, R. P. (Ed.). (1984e). *Psychiatric Annals, 14*(1).

Kluft, R. P. (1984f). The treatment of multiple personality disorder. *Psychiatric Clinics of North America, 7,* 9-30.

Kluft, R. P. (1984g, September). *The treatment of multiple personality: Approaches, goals, results.* Paper presented at the First International Conference on Multiple Personality/Dissociative States, Chicago.

Kluft, R. P. (Ed.). (1985a). *Childhood antecedents of multiple personality.* Washington, DC: American Psychiatric Press.

Kluft, R. P. (1985b). Introduction: Multiple personality disorder in the 1980s. In R. P. Kluft (Ed.), *Childhood antecedents of multiple personality.* Washington, DC: American Psychiatric Press.

Kluft, R. P. (1985c). The natural history of multiple personality disorder. In R. P. Kluft (Ed.), *Childhood antecedents of multiple personality.* Washington, DC: American Psychiatric Press.

Kluft, R. P. (1986). Personality unification in multiple personality disorder (MPD): A follow-up study. In B. G. Braun (Ed.), *The treatment of multiple personality disorder.* Washington, DC: American Psychiatric Press.

Kluft, R. P. (1987a). First-rank symptoms as a diagnostic clue to multiple personality disorder. *American Journal of Psychiatry, 144,* 293-298.

Kluft, R. P. (1987b). The simulation and dissimulation of multiple personality disorder. *American Journal of Clinical Hypnosis, 30,* 104-118.

Kluft, R. P. (1988a). The postunification treatment of multiple personality disorder: First findings. *American Journal of Psychotherapy, 42,* 212-228.

Kluft, R. P. (1988b). On treating the older patient with multiple personality disorder: "Race against time or make haste slowly." *American Journal of Clinical Hypnosis, 30,* 257-266.

Kluft, R. P. (Ed.). (1989a). *Dissociation,* 2(2).

Kluft, R. P. (1989b). On treating the older patient with multiple personality disorder: "Race against time or make haste slowly." *American Journal of Clinical Hypnosis, 32,* 90-98.

Kluft, R. P. (1991a). Clinical presentations of multiple personality disorder. *Psychiatric Clinics of North America, 14,* 605-630.

Kluft, R. P. (1991b). Multiple personality disorder. In A. Tasman, & S. M. Goldfinger (Eds.), *American Psychiatric Press review of psychiatry* (vol. 10). Washington, DC: American Psychiatric Press.

Kluft, R. P. (1992a). Hypnosis with multiple personality disorder. *American Journal of Preventative Psychiatry and Neurology, 3,* 19-27.

Kluft, R. P. (1992b). The use of hypnosis with dissociative disorders. *Psychiatric Medicine, 10,* 31-46.

Kluft, R. P. (1993a). The initial stages of psychotherapy in the treatment of multiple personality disorder patients. *Dissociation, 7,* 145-161.

Kluft, R. P. (1993b). The treatment of dissociative disorder patients: An overview of discoveries, successes, and failures. *Dissociation, 6,* 87-101.

Kluft, R. P. (1994a). Clinical observations on the use of the CSDS Dimensions of Therapeutic Movement Instrument (DTMI). *Dissociation, 7,* 272-283.

Kluft, R. P. (1994b). Countertransference in the treatment of multiple personality disorder. In J. P. Wilson & J. Lindy (Eds.), *Countertransference in the treatment of posttraumatic stress disorder* (pp. 122-150). New York: Guilford.

Kluft, R. P. (1994c). Metamorphoses. *Dissociation, 7,* 134-135.

Kluft, R. P. (1994d). Treatment trajectories in multiple personality disorder. *Dissociation, 7,* 63-76.

Kluft, R. P. (in press-a). The integration of an MPD patient in the course of a supervised classical psychoanalysis. In S. S. Marmer & R. P. Kluft (Eds.), *Psychoanalytic reflections on multiple personality disorder.*

Kluft, R. P. (in press-b). The psychodynamic psychotherapy of multiple personality disorder and allied forms of dissociative disorder not otherwise specified. In J. P. Barber & P. Crits-Cristoph (Eds.), *Handbook of dynamic therapy for Axis I disorders.* New York: Norton.

Kluft, R. P., Braun, B. G., & Sachs, R. G. (1985). Multiple personality, intrafamilial abuse, and family psychiatry. *International Journal of Family Psychiatry, 5,* 283-301.

Kohlenberg, R. J. (1973). Behavioristic approach to multiple personality: A case study. *Behavioral Therapy, 4,* 137-140.

Lampl-de Groot, J. (1981). Notes on multiple personality. *Psychoanalytic Quarterly, 50,* 614-624.

Lasky, R. (1978). The psychoanalytic treatment of a case of multiple personality. *Psychoanalytic Review, 65,* 355-380.

Levenson, J., & Berry, S. (1983). Family intervention in a case of multiple personality. *Journal of Marital and Family Therapy, 9,* 73-80.

Loewenstein, R. J. (1991a). An office mental status examination for complex chronic dissociative symptoms and multiple personality disorder. *Psychiatric Clinics of North America 14*, 567-604.

Loewenstein, R. J. (Ed.). (1991b). *Psychiatric Clinics of North America, 14*(3).

Loewenstein, R. J. (1991c). Rational psychopharmacology in the treatment of multiple personality disorder. *Psychiatric Clinics of North America, 14*, 721-740.

Loewenstein, R. J. (1993). Posttraumatic and dissociative aspects of transference and countertransference in the treatment of multiple personality disorder. In R. P. Kluft & C. G. Fine (Eds.), *Clinical perspectives on multiple personality disorder* (pp. 51-85). Washington DC: American Psychiatric Press.

Loewenstein, R. J., Hornstein, N., & Farber, B. (1988). Open trial of clonazepam in the treatment of posttraumatic stress symptoms in MPD. *Dissociation, 1*(3), 3-12.

Marmer, S. S. (1980a). Psychoanalysis of multiple personality. *International Journal of Psychoanalysis, 61*, 439-459.

Marmer, S. S. (1980b). The dream in dissociated states. In J.M. Natterson (Ed.), *The dream in clinical practice*. New York: Aronson.

Marmer, S. S. (1991). Multiple personality disorder: A psychoanalytic perspective. *Psychiatric Clinics of North America, 14*, 677-694.

McHugh, P. R. (1993). Multiple personality disorder. *The Harvard Mental Health Letter, 3*, 4-6.

Mersky, H. (1992). The manufacture of personalities: The production of multiple personality disorder. *British Journal of Psychiatry, 160*, 327-340.

Mesulam, M. (1981). Dissociative states with abnormal temporal lobe EEG. *Archives of Neurology, 38*, 176-181.

Nemiah, J. C. (1981). Dissociative disorders. In H. Kaplan, A. Freedman, & B. Sadock (Eds.), *Comprehensive textbook of psychiatry* (3rd ed.). Baltimore: Williams & Wilkins.

Orne, M. T. (1959). The nature of hypnosis: Artifact and essence. *Journal of Abnormal and Social Psychology, 58*, 277-299.

Orne, M. T. (1979). The use and misuse of hypnosis in court. *International Journal of Clinical and Experimental Hypnosis, 27,* 311-341.

Orne, M. T. (Ed.). (1984). *International Journal of Clinical Hypnosis, 32*(2).

Panos, P. T., Panos, A., & Allred, C. H. (1990). The need for marriage therapy in treatment of multiple personality disorder. *Dissociation, 3,* 10-14.

Price, J., & Hess, N. D. (1979). Behavior therapy as a precipitant and treatment in a case of dual personality. *Australian and New Zealand Journal of Psychiatry, 13,* 63-66.

Putnam, F. W. (1984). The psychophysiologic investigation of multiple personality disorder. *Psychiatric Clinics of North America, 7,* 31-40.

Putnam, F. W. (1989). *The diagnosis and treatment of multiple personality disorder.* New York: Guilford.

Putnam, F. W. (1991a). Dissociative phenomena. In A. Tasman, & S. M. Goldfinger (Eds.), *American Psychiatric Press review of psychiatry* (vol. 10). Washington, DC: American Psychiatric Press.

Putnam, F. W. (1991b). Recent research on multiple personality disorder. *Psychiatric Clinics of North America, 14,* 489-502.

Putnam, F. W. (1993). Diagnosis and clinical phenomenology of multiple personality disorder: A North American perspective. *Dissociation, 6,* 80-86.

Putnam, F. W., Guroff, J. J., Silberman, E. K., Balban, L., & Post, R. M. (1986). The clinical phenomenology of multiple personality disorder: A review of 100 recent cases. *Journal of Clinical Psychiatry, 47,* 285-293.

Putnam, F. W., Helmers, K, & Trickett, P. K. (1993). Development, reliability, and validity of a child dissociation scale. *Child Abuse and Neglect, 17,* 731-741.

Putnam, F. W., Loewenstein, R. J., Silberman, E. K. & Post, R. (1984). Multiple personality disorder in a hospital setting. *Journal of Clinical Psychiatry, 45,* 172-175.

Reis, H. (1958). Analysis of a patient with a split personality. *International Journal of Psychoanalysis, 39,* 397-407.

Rosenbaum, M. (1980). The role of the term schizophrenia in the decline of diagnosis of multiple personality. *Archives of General Psychiatry, 37,* 1383-1385.

Rosenbaum, M., & Weaver, G. M. (1980). Dissociated state: Status of a case after 38 years. *Journal of Nervous and Mental Disease, 168,* 597-603.

Ross, C. A. (1989). *Multiple personality disorder: Diagnosis, clinical features, and treatment.* New York: Wiley.

Ross, C. A. (1991). Epidemiology of multiple personality disorder and dissociation. *Psychiatric Clinics of North America, 14,* 503-518.

Ross, C. A., Anderson, G., Fleisher, W. P., & Norton, G. R. (1991). The frequency of multiple personality disorder among psychiatric inpatients. *American Journal of Psychiatry, 148,* 1717-1720.

Ross, C. A., Norton, G. R., & Wozney, K. (1989). Multiple personality disorder: An analysis of 236 cases. *Canadian Journal of Psychiatry 34,* 413-418.

Sachs, R. G., Frischholz, E. J., & Wood, J. I. (1991). Marital and family therapy in the treatment of multiple personality disorder. *Journal of Marital and Family Therapy, 14,* 249-259.

Saxe, G. N., van der Kolk, B. A., Berkowitz, R., Chinman, J., Hall, K., Lieberg, G., & Schwartz, J. (1993). Dissociative disorders in psychiatric inpatients. *American Journal of Psychiatry, 150,* 1037-1042.

Schenk, L., & Bear, D. (1981). Multiple personality and related dissociative phenomena in patients with temporal lobe epilepsy. *American Journal of Psychiatry, 138,* 1311-1316.

Schultz, R., Braun, B. G., & Kluft, R. P. (1989) Multiple personality disorder: Phenomenology of selected variables in comparison to major depression. *Dissociation, 2,* 45-51.

Spiegel, D. (1985). Multiple personality as a posttraumatic stress disorder. *Psychiatric Clinics of North America, 7,* 101-110.

Spiegel, D. (1991). Dissociation and trauma. In A. Tasman & S. M. Goldfinger (Eds.), *American Psychiatric Press annual review of psychiatry* (vol. 10). Washington, D.C.: American Psychiatric Press.

Steinberg, M. (1993). *Structured Clinical Interview for the Diagnosis of DSM-IV Dissociative Disorder (SCID-D)*. Washington DC: American Psychiatric Press.

Steinberg, M., Rounsavile, B., & Cicchette, D. V. (1990). The structured clinical interview for the diagnosis of DSM-III-R dissociative disorders: Preliminary report on a new diagnostic instrument. *American Journal of Psychiatry, 147,* 76-82.

Sutcliffe, J. P., & Jones, J. (1962). Personal identity, multiple personality, and hypnosis. *International Journal of Clinical and Experimental Hypnosis, 10,* 231-269.

Taylor, W. S., & Martin, M. F. (1944). Multiple personality. *Journal of Abnormal and Social Psychology, 39,* 281-300.

Thigpen, C. H., & Cleckley, H. M. (1984). On the incidence of multiple personality disorder: A brief communication. *International Journal of Clinical and Experimental Hypnosis, 32,* 63-66.

van der Hart, O. (1993). Multiple personality disorder in Europe: Impressions. *Dissociation, 6,* 103-118.

Victor, G. (1975). Sybil: Grand hysterie or folie a deux? *American Journal of Psychiatry, 132,* 202.

Watkins, J. G., & Watkins, H. H. (1988). The management of malevolent ego states in multiple personality disorder. *Dissociation, 1*(1), 67-72.

Wilbur, C. W. (1984). Multiple personality and child abuse. *Psychiatric Clinics of North America, 7,* 3-8.

Wilbur, C. W. (1985). The effect of child abuse on the psyche. In R. P. Kluft (Ed.), *Childhood antecedents of multiple personality*. Washington, DC: American Psychiatric Press.

Wilbur, C. B. (1986). Psychoanalysis and multiple personality disorder. In B. G. Braun (Ed.), *The treatment of multiple personality disorder*. Washington, DC: American Psychiatric Press.

Wilbur, C. B., & Kluft, R. P. (1989). Multiple personality disorder. In T. B. Karasu (Ed.), *Treatments of psychiatric disorders* (vol. 3). Washington, DC: American Psychiatric Press.

4

Therapeutic Approaches to Anxiety Disorders

Robert L. DuPont, MD

Dr. DuPont is President, Institute for Behavior and Health, Inc., Rockville, MD, and Clinical Professor of Psychiatry, Georgetown University School of Medicine, Washington, DC.

KEY POINTS

- The anxiety disorders are the most prevalent disorders in the United States, affecting 19.5% of women and 8% of men in the course of their lifetimes.
- The anxiety disorders are categorized into seven major syndromes: panic disorder and agoraphobia, specific phobia, social phobia, obsessive-compulsive disorder, posttraumatic stress disorder, generalized anxiety disorder, and anxiety disorder not otherwise specified.
- Normal anxiety can be useful in that it serves as a warning signal of serious internal or external threat; however, the clinically anxious client suffers from maladaptive anxiety, which leads to stress and disability.
- After decades in which people with anxiety disorders had no effective treatment at all, now a wide and growing range of psychological therapies and pharmacologic treatments are available. The techniques of some of the psychological therapies are presented: cognitive-behavioral therapy, psychotherapy, self-help, bibliotherapy, and adjunctive techniques.
- Psychological therapies of anxiety disorders are most effective when used in combination.

INTRODUCTION

The anxiety disorders have recently joined the affective disorders as another major focus of mental health research and practice. Even though much of the new interest centers on pharmacologic treatments, the psychological approach to anxiety disorders remains the foundation of clinical practice. This chapter deals with the psychological therapy of the anxiety disorders as well as with the epidemiology and diagnosis of these disorders.

THE CLINICALLY ANXIOUS CLIENT

Although anxiety can be a useful feeling in the sense that it serves as a warning signal of serious internal or external threat, the anxiety disorders are characterized by maladaptive anxiety, which leads to distress and disability. The hallmark of anxiety disorders is worry, which is understood by the client to be unrealistic and excessive (DuPont, 1983, 1986). The brain's normal alarm system is inappropriately triggered, leading primarily to unrealistic fear of danger, and often secondarily to loss of self-esteem and depression. Clinically anxious clients are often able to identify a tendency toward excessive worry that dated from childhood and to provide a history of family members who have suffered from similar anxiety disorders.

When talking with anxious clients, I use the metaphor that, based on my experience with other clients suffering from similar problems, they have a "worry machine" in their brain that churns out a never-ending stream of scary and upsetting "what if" scenarios. These are automatic, involuntary negative thoughts. Clients need to find ways to cope with the worry machine by separating "what is" problems from "what if" fears. I also explain that the anxiety disorder will not lead to psychosis or other mental or physical illness; their anxiety symptoms are distressing, but not dangerous (DuPont & DuPont, 1994).

Everyone experiences anxiety from time to time. Although many of the anxiety disorders have echoes in everyday life (such as mild fear of heights, flying, or public speaking), a diagnosis is made only when these anxieties persist and significantly reduce the quality of the client's life. The fourth edition of the *Diagnostic and Statistical Manual of Mental Disorders* (DSM-IV) (American Psychiatric Association, 1994) contains detailed descriptions of the anxiety disorders. Subsyndromal anxiety conditions may also respond to therapy. The boundaries between the individual anxiety disorders are not clear-cut: many clients suffer from more than one. The primary diagnosis is the one that dominates the clinical picture. The pattern of anxious symptoms typically remains reasonably stable even over many years.

RECOGNITION OF ANXIETY DISORDERS

The anxiety disorders are now categorized into seven major syndromes or clinical groupings, although future diagnostic classifications can be expected to lump and split these closely related syndromes in different ways. They are listed below with brief descriptions. See the DSM-IV (American Psychiatric Association, 1994) for the precise descriptions of each diagnostic category.

Panic Disorder and Agoraphobia (which may occur alone or in combination with each other):

Panic attacks are sudden, overwhelming feelings of terror, often associated with fear of going crazy, losing control, or dying. They are usually accompanied by physical symptoms including rapid heart rate, trembling, and difficult breathing. When panic attacks come unexpectedly, they are called "spontaneous," and when they come in predictable situations for a particular client (for example, in a shopping center or when driving on a freeway) they are called "situational." Early in the syndrome, spontaneous panic may predominate, but later in the evolution of the disorder, situational panic often is more frequent; spontaneous panic may even disappear.

Agoraphobia is "adult separation anxiety"; fears are commonly of separation from a safe person or a safe place. Panic attacks can occur without agoraphobia, and agoraphobia can occur without spontaneous panic attacks and sometimes without situational panic attacks.

The sudden flash of panic, with the catastrophic thoughts and sympathetic nervous system discharge, is called the "first fear." The anticipation of this fear, also known as anticipatory anxiety, is called the "second fear." The first fear commonly leads to the second fear, which usually predominates later in the course of the disorder. The second fear is usually followed by avoidance, the source of most of the disability in the disorder. Individuals who suffer from panic disorder and agoraphobia often seek to avoid experiences that will precipitate panic attacks, and, failing this, they seek to avoid situations in which panic attacks may cause danger or embarrassment. These three factors—panic, anticipatory anxiety, and avoidance—are locked together in a single vicious circle.

Specific Phobia:

Characterized by intense fear of particular situations or experiences, usually without spontaneous panic attacks and sometimes without prominent autonomic nervous system discharges associated with situational panic, specific phobia leads to avoidance of ordinary activities such as flying, heights, animals, and confining spaces. Specific phobias range in their effects on sufferers' lives from trivial to profoundly disabling, depending on the time spent thinking about the fears and the effects of avoidance in the clients' lives.

Social Phobia:

Social phobia is the morbid fear of embarrassment, which leads to avoidance of social experiences. Sometimes it is limited to public speaking, and at other times it is a pervasive shyness, which limits exposure to unfamiliar social situations and unfamiliar people. Public speaking phobics are often excellent speakers and are usually not shy in other social situations. The more pervasive social phobia syndrome can have profound negative effects on a person's life, commonly causing a premature departure from school and a failure to develop friends, as well as inhibiting dating and marriage.

Obsessive-Compulsive Disorder (OCD):

Obsessions are repeated unwanted, repugnant thoughts. Compulsions are ritualized actions taken to reduce the distressing feelings produced by the obsessions. Hand washing and checking are typical compulsions. Obsessive-Compulsive Disorder (OCD) thoughts and behaviors can consume many hours every day and leave the sufferers only when they sleep. (See Chapter 2.)

Posttraumatic Stress Disorder (PTSD):

Posttraumatic Stress Disorder (PTSD), sometimes not listed with the other anxiety disorders, is associated with depression, panic attacks, and anxiety. Avoidance and substance abuse may also become problems. PTSD follows an unusual and overwhelming stressor, such as a severe fire or assault. Nightmares and flashbacks that recall the trauma are common. Acute distress disorder is characterized by the same features as PTSD, but it *immediately* follows a severe emotional trauma. (See Chapter 1.)

Generalized Anxiety Disorder (GAD):

Generalized Anxiety Disorder (GAD) is characterized by excessive and unrealistic worries that persist for at least 6 months. Worries often focus on one or more life circumstances, usually health, finances, safety, or occupation. Like the other anxiety disorders, it tends to wax and wane over a lifetime and to range in severity among clients from minor to profoundly disabling.

Anxiety Disorder Not Otherwise Specified:

In addition to the six syndromes listed above, clinically significant anxiety can result from a general medical condition or from a substance-induced anxiety disorder. The category *anxiety disorder not otherwise specified* is used to code the disorders with prominent anxiety and/or phobia avoidance that do not meet full diagnostic criteria for the specific anxiety disorders but merit clinical attention.

As a group, the anxiety disorders are associated with excessive worry. As one of my anxious clients said, "I have had a terrible life, but most of it never happened." He did not mean that his suffering and the disabilities he endured because of his anxiety disorder did not happen. He meant that the events he feared, such as dreaded illnesses afflicting himself and his family members, accidents, and personal financial disasters, did not happen on the everyday basis as did his unrealistic but crippling worries. Anxious people tend to be perfectionistic and to have highly developed consciences. They often report that they are sensitive to medicines and are accordingly often reluctant to use them. I call the anxiety disorders "disorders of quality people," because so many anxious clients are good people with bad disorders.

EPIDEMIOLOGY

The Epidemiological Catchment Area (ECA) study of the National Institute of Mental Health, which is based on a sample of households (not a clinical sample of clients in therapy) and uses DSM-III diagnostic criteria, has rewritten the epidemiology of mental disorders (Regier et al., 1984). The anxiety disorders are the most prevalent mental disorders in the United States, affecting 19.5% of women and 8% of men in their lifetimes, and 9.7% of women and 4.7% of men in a 6-month period (see Figure 4.1). Figure 4.1 also shows the lifetime and 6-month prevalence of the other major groups of mental disorders, the affective disorders, and the substance use disorders.

Figure 4.1
One-Month Prevalence of Selected Mental Disorders (%)
U.S. Population Aged 18 and Older (ECA)

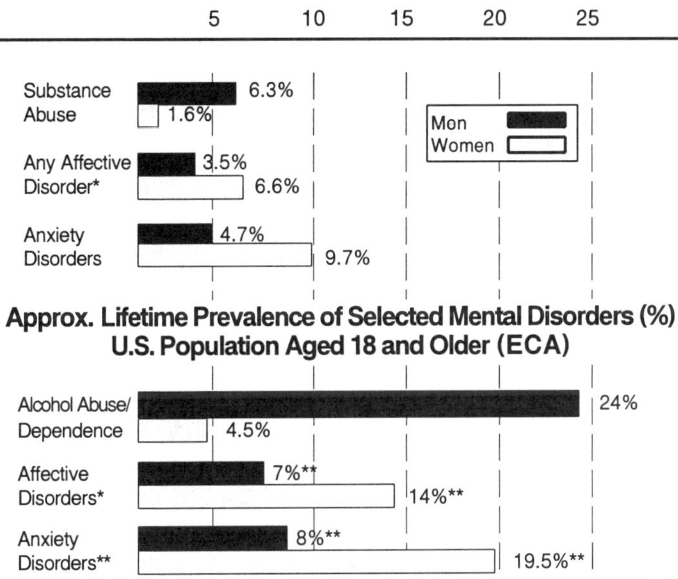

* Includes major depressive episode, dysthymia, manic episode

** Numbers are elevated slightly because persons with multiple diagnoses are counted more than once.

*** Includes panic disorder, agoraphobia, obsessive-compulsive disorder, simple phobia. Does not include social phobia, generalized anxiety disorder, posttraumatic stress disorder, or adjustment disorder with anxious mood.

Source: Robins L. N., Helzer, J. E., Weissman, M. M., Orvaschel, H., Burke, J. D., & Regier, D. A. (1989). Lifetime prevalence of specific psychiatric disorders in 3 sites. In T. J. McGlynn & H. L. Metcalf (Eds.), *Diagnosis and treatment of anxiety disorders: A physician's handbook.* Washington, DC: American Psychiatric Press, Inc. (Originally published in Archives in General Psychiatry, 41 [pp. 949-958]. Copyright 1984, American Medical Association.)

Among male clients with an anxiety disorder, about 24% have a lifetime substance abuse disorder. Conversely, about three out of four people with anxiety disorders have never had a substance use disorder or suffered from abuse of or dependence on alcohol or other drugs. People comorbid for anxiety and SUD are often seen in addiction treatment. They are less often seen in settings primarily treating anxiety disorders because of the primacy of the substance abuse disorder in the clinical picture for most dual diagnosis clients (U. S. Department of Health and Human Services, 1991).

Figure 4.2
LIFETIME PREVALENCE OF COMORBID MENTAL AND ADDICTIVE DISORDERS IN THE UNITED STATES

Noninstitutionalized household population
Ages 15-54, 1990
National Comorbidity Survey (NCS)

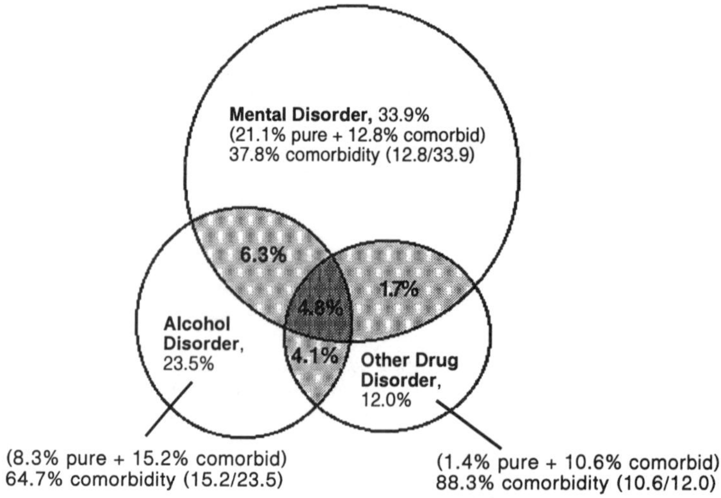

Source: Kessler, R. C., et al. (1995). *Comorbidity of DSM-III-R mental disorders and substance disorders in the National Comorbidity Survey*. Manuscript submitted for publication. Reprinted with permission of the authors.

More recently, the National Comorbidity Survey (NCS) from the University of Michigan focused on the problem of comorbidity using a national sample of Americans aged 15 to 54. It found that 24.9% met diagnostic criteria for anxiety disorders during their lifetimes (Kessler et al., 1994). In this sample, 35.6% of subjects with a substance use disorder suffered from an anxiety disorder during their lifetimes, whereas 15.2% of people with a diagnosis of an anxiety disorder suffered from a substance use disorder during their lifetimes (DuPont, 1995). See Figure 4.2 for a more detailed picture of the comorbidity of mental disorders with alcohol and other drug disorders.

The anxiety disorders created a total social cost of $46.5 billion in 1990, 31.5% of the burden of all mental disorders. This figure is larger than the costs generated by substance use disorders, affective disorders, or psychotic disorders, largely because the anxiety disorders are the most prevalent mental disorders. Lost productivity accounts for 73% of the costs of the anxiety disorders (DuPont et al., 1995).

DEFINING THE CLINICAL PROBLEM AND THE GOALS OF THERAPY

A cure for an anxiety disorder, as for all chronic illnesses, lies in knowing what is wrong and what to do about it. Health care professionals can educate clients about the anxiety disorders, helping them understand the available treatments and their likely results. Clients need to know that the anxiety disorder has biological roots—that it is not the result of poor coping skills or other failures of the client any more than are most other serious disorders. Like many other illnesses, the anxiety disorders also have important psychosocial dimensions. The anxiety disorders are associated with dreadful feelings. However, the anxious feelings will not lead to loss of consciousness, loss of control (other than avoidance), or physical illness (such as heart attacks). These facts are helpful to many anxious clients who suffer from guilt over their illness and from the fear that their panic and anxiety will lead to something even more dreadful.

Research has shown that clients with panic disorder suffer an excess of serious disorders such as heart attacks and suicide. After working with thousands of clinically anxious clients and finding them to be generally physically healthy despite their often extreme health fears (understandably fed by their experiences of panic), I have concluded that some panic disorder clients who do not know what is wrong with them, and who do not receive therapy, are indeed at added risk of many bad outcomes because of their own fears of the illness. However, once anxious clients understand their illness and get effective therapy, they appear not to have excessive rates of cardiac or other stress-related illnesses, including depression, suicide, and heart disease (DuPont, 1990).

Some clinically anxious people are involved in lawsuits, workers' compensation, or similar financial entanglements related to their anxiety disorders. It is especially common for PTSD clients. Although some of these anxious clients may be malingering, my experience is that malingering is uncommon. Rather, many of these compensation-related anxious clients are caught in a particularly cruel "what-if trap": if they get better, their claim is denied or is reduced in value. I have rarely seen one of these clients get better from their anxiety problem until the lawsuit is settled and they no longer have financial gain from being ill. If the clinically anxious client is to get well, it is essential that the anxiety problem be identified correctly as bad feelings that are inside the client. Only by accepting responsibility for these feelings and the behaviors to which the feelings give rise can anxious clients begin the process of recovering control of their lives.

In helping my clinically anxious clients to understand their illness, I personify the panic and other worry symptoms as a dragon who attacks the client in a terrifying fashion (DuPont, Spencer, & DuPont, 1994). The dragon can scare the client, but that is the limit of its power. The dragon's game is to use blackmail to get the client to stay in its dungeon. The dragon says, "If you don't do X, I will go easy on you!" The frightened sufferer from an anxiety disorder often agrees because of the nameless but overwhelming terror of the consequences of future dragon attacks. This is the basis of the avoidance that produces the disability commonly seen in anxious clients. Like all blackmailers, the dragon is never satisfied. Over time he wants more and more of the client's life. The dragon feeds on the client's fear. This is the only food the dragon can eat. The more the client fears the dragon, the larger the dragon grows. Once the client stops fearing the dragon, the dragon withers away and ultimately dies of starvation.

The most appropriate and achievable goal of therapy for anxiety disorders is a full, normal life without restrictions resulting from the anxiety disorder. The realistic goal of therapy is not to end the symptoms of anxiety. In fact, efforts to end the symptoms are part of the problem, because they set up expectations that cannot be fulfilled and lead to a sense of failure and demoralization for both the doctor and the client.

Cognitive therapies and other effective psychological therapies primarily affect the second fear—they reduce anticipatory anxiety. Behavioral therapies reduce avoidance. Because anticipatory anxiety and avoidance set the trigger for panic, these psychological approaches also reduce the panic, the first fear. The vicious cycle of panic, anticipatory anxiety, and avoidance is reduced at different points by different therapies. By reducing any component of the anxiety disorder, the cycle is slowed and the client's life is improved. Many clients benefit from concurrent combined treatments affecting all three components of the anxiety disorder cycle simultaneously.

Understanding anxiety and its treatment is the foundation for all successful approaches to the anxiety disorders, with or without pharmacotherapy. Therapy helps the client cope better with a seriously distressing disorder that is rooted in biology but has important psychosocial dimensions, even though the disorder cannot be banished. A cure is regaining control of one's life, not eliminating all the underlying feelings of anxiety arising from a hair-trigger alarm system. This approach is different from earlier psychological formulations of the anxiety disorders, which were based on the assumption that the client's anxious symptoms reflected poor coping skills (e.g., people who did not suffer from anxiety disorders were able to cope better with life's problems than were those who had anxiety disorder) or that the anxiety flowed from unique stresses that were not endured by those who did not have these painful chronic disorders.

This newer formulation of the anxiety disorders and their therapies is easily understandable by both therapists and clients. It respects the client's suffering, it offers important roles for both the mental health counselor and the client, and it fits with the understanding that these are biologically based, often lifelong disorders—and that the client is neither guilty nor weak. This formulation of the anxiety illness and its therapies is a basis for a solid therapeutic alliance between the client and the professional, one based on respect and a shared understanding of the disorder. It works equally well with psychological and pharmacologic therapies.

As with substance use disorders, clients suffering from anxiety disorders are not responsible for having the disorder, but they are fully responsible for what they do with it. Recovery is indeed possible, in the sense that clients can regain full control of their lives, but recovery from an anxiety disorder requires learning and hard work sustained over a long period of time, often with therapists and clients working together.

THE PSYCHOLOGICAL THERAPIES

Cognitive-Behavioral:

A wide variety of techniques are bundled in the descriptive phrase "cognitive-behavioral therapy." They have at their heart two characteristics (Barlow, 1988; Marks, 1982). The cognitive part of the new psychological prescription for anxiety disorders means helping clients develop a new understanding of the nature of the distress they experience and new ways to think about getting well. The key objectives of cognitive restructuring of clinically significant anxiety are to respect the suffering and to reduce the guilt and fear the clients often feel (Mavissakalian & Barlow, 1981).

Claire Weekes, an Australian general practitioner, was the guiding clinician in this new approach. Her short, easy-to-understand books—though by now quite old-fashioned—are still the most helpful to many clients (Weekes, 1969, 1972, 1987). Her four suggestions to clients for confronting panic in phobic situations were: facing, accepting, floating (not fighting), and letting time pass. More recently, Jerilyn Ross, Edna Foa, and Reid Wilson (Foa & Wilson, 1991; Ross, 1994; Wilson, 1987) have written books to help anxious patients.

When anxious clients do not manifest behaviors characteristic of their anxiety (for example, clients with GAD, panic disorder clients without avoidance, and OCD clients without compulsions), the psychological therapy is, paradoxically, often more difficult. It is not possible to conduct behavioral therapy because there is no pathological behavior to overcome. For these clients, effective therapy requires them to change their thoughts, making the cognitive aspects of therapy preeminent. Recovery often means helping clients learn to accept the symptoms and to put them into realistic perspective—as upsetting, but not scary. With such acceptance, the distressing thoughts usually diminish in both frequency of occurrence and severity over time, although they usually do not disappear completely. They become unimportant and thus no longer distressing.

The behavioral part of this new therapy is called *supported exposure*. It involves helping the client, as rapidly as possible but as slowly as necessary, to do precisely those things that produce the panic and other uncomfortable feelings of anxiety. Persuading anxious people to enter panic-generating situations is always difficult, and sometimes impossible. It is useful to work with anxious people in groups so they can meet fellow sufferers and see them confront their fears, thereby becoming free of disability. They are also pleased to find how normal other anxious people appear, because they fear that they themselves look and act bizarre.

The cure for anxiety disorders, and the understanding of the disorders, does not lie in the therapist's office but in the client's life outside the office. It can be helpful for the therapist or a person in recovery to accompany the client into the anxiety-generating experiences, especially at first. Psychologists can learn a great deal about the experience of anxiety and panic by accompanying their clients into phobic- or panic-generating situations. Dr. Weekes offers a succinct definition of a cure for anxiety disorders: "A cure is when the symptoms no longer matter."

It is essential in the behavioral approach to the anxiety disorders to have the client do the things that cause distress over and over again, every day. The client should stay in the anxiety-provoking situations for prolonged periods of time, learning that the panic subsides, over time, even without fleeing or avoiding panic-producing experiences. Only with repeated and prolonged exposure can desensitization to panic-generating experiences occur (Zane, 1989).

In talking with clients about the behavioral approach to a cure of an anxiety disorder, I use the analogy of an allergist desensitizing a client to bee venom: at first the dose of venom is small, but with repeated injections, the clients become easily able to endure exposures that would initially have been overwhelming. This analogy also explains why the panic-producing experiences are so difficult for the clinically anxious client: their nervous systems are sensitized to experiences to which other people are not sensitive, just as the person who has a bee sting allergy is unusually sensitive to bee venom. Both the problem (allergic sensitization) and the solution (desensitization) lie within the client who has the disorder, not in the bee. Also, like the allergic person, the anxious person's sensitization is not a sign of moral weakness or failure as a human being.

Why does desensitization in therapy work as well as it does? If all it took for a client to get well was to experience the distress of the panic, this should be a self-curing disorder, since clinically anxious clients, despite their often strenuous efforts to avoid panic-generating situations, are frequently confronted by panic in their everyday lives. These everyday exposures do not produce lowered sensitization, while exposures to panic in behavioral therapy do. The difference lies in the understanding of the anxiety disorder. White-knuckle exposure, which is how the anxious person outside of therapy experiences panic, worsens the disorder because it is rooted in fear.

In contrast, when clients understand their disorder and voluntarily and repeatedly submit themselves to panic-generating experiences, especially when they learn to do so without adding fearful thoughts to their painful feelings, when they can float through panic like a limp rag doll, then they move from sensitization to desensitization, from prison to freedom. In working with anxious clients, I find these phrases helpful: "Nothing is but thinking makes it so," and, "There is no heaven that thinking cannot make a hell, and no hell that thinking cannot make a heaven." In other words, "Your panic and anxiety are what you make them by your thoughts."

Psychotherapy:

In addition to cognitive-behavioral therapy, which is the mainstay of modern psychological treatments of anxiety disorders, clinically anxious clients often benefit from more traditional psychotherapy, including individual, family, and group therapy. It is important not to oversell such types of therapy to anxious clients. They are not likely to remove the anxiety or provide the quality of relief that cognitive-behavioral therapy can. Rather, these nonspecific psychological treatments can be effective in dealing with the real and important human problems the client has, which may or may not relate to the anxiety symptoms themselves.

Self-Help:

As part of the remarkable self-help movement that is sweeping the United States, especially during the last decade, increasing numbers of self-help groups have been created for anxious persons. Such groups offer a unique opportunity for support. They also help clients with anxiety disorders learn from other sufferers about the various therapists and therapies being used in their area, because mutual-aid meetings provide a consumers' eye view of the provider system. The one negative feature of self-help is that it can sometimes deteriorate into an environment in which anxious people complain about their illnesses and justify their failure to confront their fears—what Alcoholics Anonymous (AA) calls "the pity pot." Having leaders in mutual-aid groups, either professionals or people who are well along in their own recovery, can reduce this unhealthy tendency. Unlike AA and other established 12-step programs, self-help for the anxiety disorders lacks a clear program and a set of guidelines for recovery, although there have been attempts to use 12-step principles (Saylor, DuPont, & Brouillard, 1990).

Bibliotherapy:

Self-help books on anxiety have been popular for many decades. In fact, self-help books dealing with fear and anxiety were best sellers before the modern anxiety diagnoses were established. Today many such books are available, both for clients and for therapists using all therapy approaches.

Adjunctive Techniques:

In addition to specific cognitive-behavioral therapy and nonspecific psychotherapy, some anxious clients find a variety of adjunctive techniques useful, including exercise, diet, and the elimination of potentially anxiety-provoking substances, especially alcohol and caffeine. Aerobic exercise, which produces pounding heartbeats, can be frightening to clients suffering from panic and other anxiety problems, so they often quit exercising. Clients need to learn that this rapid heartbeat is not only normal, but beneficial. Aerobic exercise is also helpful in reducing depression and in building self-confidence. Some anxious clients find that by eliminating their use of caffeine and alcohol, they can reduce their panic and anxiety.

It is always desirable as part of therapy to have anxious clients stop drinking alcohol and beverages containing caffeine for a month. Caffeine is a stimulant that can precipitate panic attacks; alcohol reduces anxiety briefly after use, but when the effects of the alcohol wear off after a few hours, clients who are vulnerable to panic and other anxiety disorders often experience major and prolonged upsurges of symptoms. Many anxious clients have not made the connection between their distressing symptoms and their use of caffeine and alcohol because the increase in symptoms occurs some time after their use of the substances, whereas the acute effect, especially of alcohol, can be experienced as beneficial for the anxiety.

A variety of other nonspecific psychological therapies can also be useful in reducing anxiety symptoms and related disorders. They include assertiveness training, stress management, relaxation training, and therapy designed to assist individual clients with problems such as incest and rape as well as children of alcoholics and other life problems, which may be important factors in particular anxious clients' lives. These therapies, like traditional psychotherapy, are often useful for anxious clients, but they do not take the place of cognitive restructuring and active confrontation of the fear-generating experiences in real-life situations. People participating in these nonspecific therapies must also guard against excusing the disabilities resulting from their anxiety disorders and unwittingly perpetuating the disabilities. If the clients are to get well, they need to take personal responsibility for their own anxiety disorders and their own recoveries, no matter how the symptoms of anxiety got started.

INTEGRATION OF PSYCHOLOGICAL AND PHARMACOLOGIC THERAPIES

There is an unfortunate tendency to view psychological and

pharmacologic therapies as alternatives, as competitors, in the therapy marketplace. A more constructive and realistic view is that the goal of all therapy is intended to help anxious clients live full, normal lives without limitations because of their anxiety disorders. Both treatments can be useful in achieving this goal, often in combination. No therapy helps every anxious client who tries it, and no therapy fails to help anyone. Abundant clinical experience demonstrates that psychological and pharmacologic therapies do not detract from each other but often produce synergistic beneficial effects. After decades in which sufferers from anxiety disorders had no effective treatment at all, it is now a happy reality that a wide and growing range of effective therapies are available, all of which show promise. Anxious patients can often benefit from psychotherapy only after they have received medication to reduce their severe anxiety.

The heart of the psychological therapy of anxiety disorders is cognitive-behavioral therapy, which involves reeducating clients about the nature of their illnesses and the goals of therapy, as well as encouraging active and repeated entry into fear-generating experiences. These treatments view the anxious symptoms as distressing but not dangerous; the illnesses are held to be serious but curable, in the sense that the sufferer's life, which had been made unmanageable by the disorder, can be brought under control.

Therapy is unlikely to be successful without exposure to the anxiety-provoking situation on a routine basis. Thus, cognitive-behavioral therapy involves changing the way anxious people think about their symptoms—and changing their behaviors so that they move toward, rather than away from, the experiences that produce distressing feelings.

Many anxious clients benefit from traditional individual, family, and group psychotherapy. Self-help plays an increasing role in the therapy of anxiety disorders; for some clients, adjunctive therapy techniques, including aerobic exercises and the elimination of caffeine and alcohol intake, are also useful. A variety of other therapies are often helpful as well, including stress management, relaxation training, and assertiveness training. Clinically anxious patients are often intelligent and resourceful. Their suffering is intense. When they get better, their lives improve remarkably, and they are among the most grateful and gratifying of clients.

REFERENCES

American Psychiatric Association. (1994). *Diagnostic and statistical manual of mental disorders* (4th ed.). Washington, DC: Author.

Barlow, D. H. (1988). *Anxiety and its disorders: The nature and treatment of anxiety and panic.* New York: Guilford Press.

DuPont, R. L. (1983). Diagnosis and treatment of phobias. *Directions in Psychiatry, 3*(4).

DuPont, R. L. (1986). *Phobias and panic: A physician's guide to modern treatments.* Rockville, MD: Phobia Society of America.

DuPont, R. L. (1990). Anxiety: The burden of illness. *Journal of Clinical Psychiatry, 51*(suppl.), 11.

DuPont, R. L. (1995). Anxiety and addiction: A clinical perspective on comorbidity. *Bulletin of the Menninger Clinic, 59*(suppl. A), A53-A72.

DuPont, R. L. & DuPont, C. M. (1994). The treatment of anxiety: Realistic expectations and risks posed by controlled substances. *The Journal of Law, Medicine, and Ethics, 22,* 5-13.

DuPont, R. L., et al. (1995). *The economic costs of anxiety disorders.* Manuscript submitted for publication.

DuPont, R. L., Spencer, E. D., & DuPont, C. M. (1994). *The JumpStart Phobia Cure: Overcoming anxiety disorders and getting on with your life.* Rockville, MD: DuPont Associates, P.A.

Foa, E. B., & Wilson, R. R. (1991). *Stop obsessing! How to overcome your obsessions and compulsions.* New York: Bantam Books.

Kessler, R. C., et al. (1994). Lifetime and 12-month prevalence of *DSM-III-R* psychiatric disorders in the United States: Results from the National Comorbidity Survey. *Archives of General Psychiatry, 51,* 8-19.

Kessler, R. C., et al. (1995). *Comorbidity of DSM-III-R mental disorders and substance disorders in the National Comorbidity Survey.* Manuscript submitted for publication.

Marks, I. (1982). *Cure and care of neuroses: Theory and practice of behavioral psychotherapy.* New York: John Wiley & Sons.

Mavissakalian, M. & Barlow, D. H. (1981). *Phobia: Psychological and pharmacological treatment.* New York: Guilford Press.

Regier, D. A., et al. (1984). The NIMH Epidemiologic Catchment Area (ECA) program: Historical context, major objectives, and study population characteristics. *Archives of General Psychiatry, 41,* 934-941.

Ross, J. (1994). *Triumph over fear: A book of help and hope for people with anxiety, panic attacks, and phobias.* New York: Bantam Books.

Saylor, K. E., DuPont, R. L., & Brouillard, M. (1990). Self-help treatment of anxiety disorders. In R. Noyes, M. Roth, & G. D. Burrows (Eds.), *The treatment of anxiety* (4). Amsterdam: Elsevier, 483-495.

U. S. Department of Health and Human Services, National Institute on Alcohol Abuse and Alcoholism. (1991). Alcoholism and co-occurring disorders. *Alcohol Alert,* 14, 1-3.

Weekes, C. (1969). *Hope and help for your nerves.* New York: Hawthorne Books.

Weekes, C. (1972). *Peace from nervous suffering.* New York: Hawthorne Books.

Weekes, C. (1987). *More help for your nerves.* New York: Bantam Books.

Wilson, R. R. (1987). *Don't panic: Taking control of anxiety attacks.* New York: HarperPerennial.

Zane, M. D. (1989). A contextual approach to panic. In R. Baker (Ed.), *Panic disorder: Theory, research, and therapy* (pp. 117-140). Chichester, England: John Wiley & Sons, Ltd.

Further information about the nature and treatment of the anxiety disorders can be obtained from the following:

- Anxiety Disorders Association of America (ADAA)
  6000 Executive Boulevard, Suite 513
  Rockville, MD 20852
  (301) 231-9350

- National Anxiety Foundation
  3135 Custer Drive
  Lexington, KY 40501-4001
  (606) 272-7166

- Obsessive-Compulsive Disorder Foundation, Inc.
  P.O. Box 60
  Vernon, CT 06006

- National Institute of Mental Health
  Public Inquiries
  5600 Fishers Lane, Room 15C05
  Rockville, MD 20857
  (301) 443-4515

- Phobics Anonymous
  World Service Headquarters
  P. O. Box 1180
  Palm Springs, CA 92263
  (619) 322-COPE.

5

Psychotherapeutic Strategies for Borderline Personality Disorders

Glen O. Gabbard, MD

Dr. Gabbard is Bessie Walker Callaway Distinguished Professor at the Menninger Clinic; Training and Supervising Analyst, Topeka Institute for Psychoanalysis; and Clinical Professor of Psychiatry, University of Kansas School of Medicine, Topeka, KS.

KEY POINTS

- This chapter reviews the wide range of theories on the etiology of and treatment for borderline personality disorder (BPD).
- There is no single etiology of BPD; it seems to be a complex picture involving multiple pathways to the ultimate clinical syndrome.
- Many BPD patients have experienced some combination of loss, physical abuse, verbal abuse, and sexual abuse. However, 20–40% of borderline patients have experienced neither neglect nor abuse.
- All psychotherapeutic approaches to the treatment of BPD are linked implicitly or explicitly to etiologic hypotheses.
- The different types of BPD patients require different psychotherapeutic approaches. This chapter reviews some helpful approaches for the following types of patients: the neurologically compromised patient, the victim of childhood abuse, the patient suffering from annihilation panic, and the patient with no history of abuse or neglect.
- In treating BPD patients, shifting flexibly between expressive and supportive techniques is key. The therapist must tailor the psychotherapy to the relevant etiologic issues.

INTRODUCTION

A voluminous amount of literature has emerged in the last several decades on the subject of the psychotherapy of patients with borderline personality disorder. Virtually all clinicians agree that psychotherapy with this particular patient population is extraordinarily difficult. Indeed, some studies suggest that as many as 60% of patients discontinue therapy within the first 6 months (Frank, 1992).

Beyond the consensus on difficulty, however, little else about the treatment is viewed with any degree of unanimity. Much of the controversy in the literature involves the relative value of expressive versus supportive interventions. Some clinicians, such as Boyer (1977) and Kernberg (1975), believe that the intense negative transference that develops early in the process should be addressed through transference interpretations. Such interventions, they assert, help the patient form a more accurate picture of the therapist so that the establishment of a therapeutic alliance is possible.

Other clinicians, including Masterson (1976) and Modell (1976) have argued that interpretation must be delayed until the patient has developed sufficient trust in the therapist's intentions and reliability. Modell emphasizes that a "holding" environment must be established as a prerequisite to interpretive interventions. Adler (1985) offers a related perspective. He conceptualized the primary goal of psychotherapy with borderline patients as the establishment of a soothing-holding introject to sustain the patient in times of separation and loneliness.

Still other psychotherapists have advocated a strictly supportive approach. Zetzel (1971) was one of the strongest proponents of supportive psychotherapy, because she regarded interpretive comments as too disruptive of the therapeutic alliance. She also stressed that low frequency (once a week or less) was more successful than intensive psychotherapy several times a week. More recently, Rockland (1992) developed a systematic approach to the supportive psychotherapy of borderline patients based on specific ego strengthening interventions. He also emphasized that the majority of borderline patients require such treatment.

CAUSES OF BORDERLINE PERSONALITY DISORDER

Much of the controversy regarding appropriate treatment is undoubtedly related to the variability of patients who fall within the borderline spectrum. This variability, in turn, is related to the multiple pathways involved in the etiology and pathogenesis of the disorder. The optimal treatment approach is intimately related to the specific causative factors that come into play with any particular case. A review of the literature on the etiology of borderline personality disorder is crucial to the therapist who hopes to tailor psychotherapeutic work to the patient's needs.

Before the recent flurry of publications on childhood antecedents of borderline personality disorder, the primary etiologic theories were purely psychodynamic. Mahler and colleagues (1975) and Kernberg (1975) linked borderline personality disorder to a developmental crisis at the rapprochement subphase of separation-individuation. During this period of development, which occurs at approximately 16–30 months of age, the child fears that his or her mother may disappear. In Mahler's developmental studies of mother-infant pairs, she observed that children at this age often display a frantic sense of concern about the whereabouts of their mother. Both Kernberg and Mahler postulated that the adult borderline patient's anxiety about experiences of separation stem from disturbances in this particular developmental period. Kernberg hypothesized that either a disturbance of the mother's emotional availability during the rapprochement subphase or a constitutional excess of aggression in the child was responsible for the difficulties encountered at that point in childhood. Obviously, some combination of the two factors might also be involved.

Masterson and Rinsley (1975) also developed an etiologic model that was anchored to the rapprochement subphase of separation-individuation. However, their emphasis was more on the behavior of the mother rather than on innate factors in the child. They postulated that the mothers of borderline patients felt threatened about the prospect of their child growing up. Hence, they conveyed to the rapprochement toddler a sense that they would withdraw their love in response to the child's efforts to grow up and separate. Masterson and Rinsley suggested that this communication leads the child to feel an "abandonment depression."

To avoid feelings of abandonment, the child starts clinging to his or her mother to ensure a continued supply of emotional sustenance. The mother rewards such behavior, and the child develops a sense of self that is good only if obedient and passive. When the child attempts to separate, feelings of "badness" are pervasive. The borderline patient grows up feeling "stuck" at this developmental moment.

Whereas the foregoing models are essentially derived from conflict models of psychopathology, Adler's conceptualization of the etiology is based on a deficit model (Adler, 1985). Influenced by self-psychology, Adler suggested that inconsistent or unreliable mothering results in the patient's failure to develop a "holding-soothing" introject. Borderline patients thus go through life searching for idealized persons in the environment to provide external nurturing for them as a way of making up for the absence of internal sources of nurturing. Adler also stressed the lack of "evocative memory" in borderline patients. They are unable to summon an internal image of a soothing maternal figure because they regress to a developmental age between 8 and 18 months, before evocative memory has been achieved. Feelings of emptiness, separation anxiety, and clinging dependency are all related to this failure to internalize a nurturing parental figure.

EMPIRICAL STUDIES

The burgeoning literature on the causes of borderline personality disorder, as derived from empirical research, has challenged the assumptions inherent in the psychodynamic formulations. Gunderson (1984) stressed the heterogeneity of the family constellations, and he specifically pointed out that neglect is more common than overinvolvement in such families. Walsh (1977) reported a rather high incidence of frank abuse and parental hostility in the families of borderline patients.

In the last several years, numerous studies have confirmed that childhood physical, verbal, or sexual abuse occurs at higher rates among borderline patients than in other populations. Ogata and associates (1990) found that the incidence of childhood sexual abuse—as well as combined sexual and physical abuse—was significantly higher for borderline patients than for a control group of depressed patients. Herman and colleagues (1989) recorded a 71% prevalence of physical abuse and a 68% prevalence of sexual abuse in the childhood histories of borderline patients. Westen and associates (1990) found evidence of sexual and/or physical abuse in more than half of a sample of adolescent borderline inpatients.

Zanarini and colleagues (1989) performed a three-way outpatient comparison involving groups of patients with dysthymia, antisocial personality disorder, and borderline personality disorder. Although the borderline patients clearly had greater abuse histories than either of the other two groups, most striking was that 72% of borderline patients reported *verbal* abuse as compared with physical abuse in 46% and sexual abuse in 26% of the patients. Moreover, 76% reported significant neglect by parents or caretakers during childhood. When the researchers studied the prevalence of separation and loss in childhood, they found that 74% had experienced prolonged separation or loss involving a caretaker. Even though this finding was not vastly different from the figures for the patients with dysthymia and antisocial personality disorder, borderline patients had a significantly higher percentage than the other two groups when the prevalence of separations was narrowed to early childhood.

Given the rather extensive histories of trauma in the backgrounds of many borderline patients, Gunderson and Sabo (1993) studied the overlap between posttraumatic stress disorder (PTSD) and borderline personality disorder (BPD). They noted that some degree of overlap exists between the two that often can be disentangled through a careful history that distinguishes rapid, adult-onset symptomatic pictures (PTSD) from enduring patterns or personality traits (BPD). Swartz and colleagues (1990) cautioned, however, that fully one third of borderline patients also fulfilled criteria for PTSD.

Several major studies (Frank & Paris, 1981; Goldberg et al., 1985; Paris & Frank, 1989; Paris & Zweig-Frank, 1992; Soloff & Millward, 1983; Zweig-Frank & Paris, 1991) have demonstrated that patients with borderline personality disorder tend to experience their parents as emotionally neglectful. In contrast to the emphasis on the mother's role in many of the psychodynamic formulations, this research has suggested that *both* parents create difficulties for the child. The children, who felt their parents prevented them from separating but did not provide much emotional support even when the child would attempt to cling, perceived a pattern of "affectionless control."

A MULTIFACTORIAL PICTURE

If we attempt to sift through this plethora of empirical data, one clear conclusion emerges—there is no single etiology of borderline personality disorder. A mixed, complex picture surfaces that involves multiple pathways to the ultimate clinical syndrome. Although a great many patients have experienced some combination of loss, physical abuse, verbal abuse, and sexual abuse, in each study, between 20% and 40% of borderline patients have experienced neither neglect nor abuse.

Moreover, the presence of childhood sexual abuse does not necessarily imply that it is of paramount importance as a pathogenic factor. As Paris and Zweig-Frank (1992) emphasized, almost one third of all women in North America have experienced some form of childhood sexual abuse, but only an estimated 2% suffer from borderline personality disorder. Most of the studies do not differentiate between incest and extrafamilial childhood sexual abuse. Research literature on childhood sexual abuse has established that incest is far more pathogenic than other forms of childhood molestation (Browne & Finkelhor, 1986).

The diversity of findings in the research on early childhood experiences of borderline patients supports the view that the different psychodynamic approaches to psychotherapy may reflect the clinical reality that mental health professionals see different kinds of borderline patients. Even though the empirical research may lead to "parent-blaming" models of etiology, the fact that 20%–40% experience neither abuse nor neglect suggests important constitutional factors may be at work as well. Silverman and colleagues (1991) found some evidence of familial transmission of the affective and impulsive personality traits in families of borderline patients. Coccaro and associates (1989) reported a significantly decreased level of serotonergic activity in a male population of borderline patients. In addition, some research (Andrulonis, 1991; Andrulonis et al., 1981) suggests that borderline patients have soft signs of neurologic deficit, including a history of poor impulse control, learning problems, attention deficit disorder, and conduct disorder.

To complicate matters further, none of these etiologies is mutually exclusive. In the real world of clinical work, the psychotherapist often encounters different etiologic factors in the same patient. For example, one borderline patient in the Menninger Treatment Interventions Project (Horwitz et al., in press) clearly demonstrated a combination of constitutional factors and childhood trauma. She was born with a constitutional temperament that made it difficult for her to be soothed. Indeed, her parents found that they were unable to get her to sleep at night, despite a great deal of holding, rocking, and comforting. Each time they set her in her crib, she would scream at the top of her lungs and keep both her parents awake for hours. Finally, they took her to a pediatrician, who told them that they were not being firm enough. He instructed them to let her cry in the crib until she went to sleep. When she was old enough to crawl out of the crib and open the door to her room by herself, he suggested they put a door stop underneath the door to keep her from leaving the room.

In this clinical example, we clearly have a hyperirritable temperament acted on by environmental trauma. The child was undoubtedly terrified to the point of panic as she cried all night, wondering why her parents would not rescue her as they had in the past. Moreover, it would be difficult to portray the parents as "monsters": they were simply following the pediatrician's orders as conscientiously as they could. To be sure, etiology is not an "either/or" proposition.

PSYCHOTHERAPEUTIC CONSIDERATIONS

All psychotherapeutic approaches are linked implicitly or explicitly to etiologic hypotheses. By providing this overview of the literature on the causative factors involved in borderline personality disorder, I am encouraging an *explicit linkage* between the presumed etiology and the psychotherapeutic technique. Obviously, the psychotherapist may have incomplete information about the relevant etiologic issues in a particular patient. Much can be inferred, however, from a careful history and a detailed neuropsychiatric evaluation.

The Neurologically Compromised Patient:

Patients who have fundamental neurophysiologic impairment will reveal themselves to the clinician through subtle or not-so-subtle soft signs, such as an inability to discriminate left from right, difficulties in processing verbal information, a history of poor impulse control, various forms of learning disability or dyslexia, and a childhood history of attention deficit disorder. Neuropsychological testing may be the most accurate way of identifying these signs.

Neurologically compromised patients respond to a predominantly supportive approach. Part of the difficulty they face as a result of their cognitive limitations is an inability to think abstractly. If the therapist offers interpretations of unconscious meaning and expects the patient to think symbolically, the patient is likely to feel like a failure. Psychotherapy will be one more situation in which the patient is failing to live up to the expectations of others. Borderline patients may mask their shame and humiliation over their inability to work expressively through outbursts of anger and contempt directed toward the therapist or through impulsive acting-out behavior.

On the other hand, these patients may respond much better to a psychotherapeutic approach in which the therapist takes an active role as an auxiliary ego figure. The therapist addresses defective areas of ego functioning by providing some of those functions for the patient. For example, with an impulsive patient who uses poor judgment, the therapist might help him or her think through the consequences of impulsive behavior. A sample intervention follows:

> I know you feel like overdosing to get back at your boyfriend, but let's think through what will probably happen if you do that. First, you'll probably end up in the emergency room or even the intensive care unit, and you know how you hate hospitals. Also, it may backfire in the sense that your boyfriend will then want nothing to do with you because he sees you as a suicide risk.

The Victim of Childhood Abuse:

Patients who have experienced severe childhood physical or sexual abuse also require an individually tailored approach. The psychotherapy of such patients can be understood best as the unfolding of a drama involving three principal characters: a victim, an abuser, and an omnipotent rescuer (Davies & Frawley, 1991; Gabbard, 1991, 1994; Gabbard & Wilkinson, 1994). In the process of growing up, abused children have internalized an abusive parent or parental figure and a view of themselves as a victim. They have also internalized either the fantasy of someone who would rescue them from their victimization or, in some cases, an actual person who did intervene to extricate them from the abuse they were suffering. These three internal self- and object-representations oscillate between patient and therapist through projective and introjective processes.

Most psychotherapeutic processes with victims of childhood abuse begin with the patient in the role of victim and the therapist in the role of omnipotent rescuer who sets out to provide a better parenting experience than the patient's traumatic childhood offered. However, such patients soon begin to demonstrate feelings of entitlement to compensation for their mistreatment by having the therapist go to extraordinary means to show caring. They may demand extra sessions, phone calls in the middle of the night, extended sessions, hugs during the session, reassurances that they are loved, exception from paying a fee, and so forth. The demands soon escalate to the point that the therapist begins to feel tormented by the patient. The roles have now shifted so that the patient is the abuser and the therapist is the victim.

Therapists may begin to show resentment when they begin to feel "fed up" and angry about the patient's unrelenting demands. When patients detect growing resentment in their therapist, they reexperience the situation as one of traumatic abuse. The patient may say to the therapist, "You don't really care about me. You're just doing this for money. You hate me." Therapists in the midst of such attacks may begin to make sarcastic comments to the patient or use interpretations as counterattacks.

A psychotherapist who treats a borderline patient suffering from severe childhood trauma must keep in mind that he or she may be needed to play the role of abuser or "bad object" for lengthy periods in psychotherapy. The therapist may be tempted to offer transference interpretations at such moments. For example: "I know you think I'm being abusive to you, but actually you're the one who's being abusive to me." These transference interpretations *merely confirm* to the patient that the therapist is indeed an abusive bad object. The therapist must be able to contain the projections of the patient's internal abuser and not respond defensively in a way that lends some credence to the patient's transference distortions. This containment often involves holding the feeling and riding it out until the patient calms down. After the patient has overcome the anger or rage, the therapist may then be able to process what happened with the patient and provide some insight about the interaction. In other words, a considerable amount of support and empathic validation may need to precede interpretive comments.

Some of the difficulties encountered in the psychotherapy of patients who have been victims of childhood abuse can be managed by establishing firm boundaries at the outset of treatment. A contractual agreement that clearly outlines what therapy is and what therapy is not should be established during the first few meetings with the patient (Gabbard & Wilkinson, 1994; Kernberg et al., 1989). Matters such as length and frequency of sessions, payment for the psychotherapy, willingness to enter a hospital in a suicidal crisis, and arrangements for missed sessions should be discussed openly so that the patient has reasonable expectations of the psychotherapist. In doing so, therapists establish that they have rights just as patients do, and these ground rules also help the patient understand that the psychotherapist is not a parent. Needless to say, these boundaries must be maintained as the therapy proceeds. When the patient wants to be hugged, the therapist may need to say, "I know this is disappointing and upsetting to you, but psychotherapy is a verbal treatment, and we need to use words here rather than touch." To do otherwise raises false hopes in the patient.

Annihilation Panic:

Patients who have experienced early object loss may have failed to internalize a soothing-holding introject, as described by Adler (1985). They lack the evocative memory to remember the therapist's looks, the sound of the therapist's voice, and a sense of the therapist as an internal presence to sustain them between sessions. Such patients may feel panic over weekends and during vacations because they feel as if the therapist has died or disappeared.

One patient became convinced, every time her therapist took a vacation, that she had been abandoned and that the therapist would never return. Such feelings also occurred over weekends, and the patient would call the therapist at home in a frenzied state. When the therapist answered the phone, the patient would explain that she could no longer picture him and feared he had died or would never come back. The therapist reassured her that he was fine and would see her at the next appointment. The patient's panic immediately ceased; she apologized for calling him and hung up. Allowing panicky patients brief phone calls may head off hospitalizations or suicide attempts. Adler has also suggested that sending such patients postcards during long vacations may help them get through the therapist's absence with the postcard as a kind of transitional object. Ultimately, the therapist will be internalized over a long-term psychotherapy process so that separations become more tolerable for the patient.

The Patient With No History of Abuse or Neglect:

A subgroup of borderline patients has not experienced profound abuse, neglect, or early object loss. Many can use a highly expressive psychotherapeutic approach, provided they have several key characteristics. They must demonstrate a capacity for abstract thinking, a specific type of psychological mindedness in which they view their problems as having an internal origin, and a motivation to understand the repetitive patterns in their lives. Also, some patients with masochistic tendencies may receive partial transference gratification from the therapist's interpretations and confrontations, which are experienced as attenuated attacks.

Even with these psychologically sophisticated, higher-level

borderline patients, however, transference interpretations are always high-risk, high-gain interventions (Horwitz et al., in press). If they are well-timed and delivered with empathic attunement, they may result in increased collaboration between therapist and patient in the pursuit of insight. However, if poorly timed or laden with countertransference contaminants, the transference interpretations may backfire and cause the patient to explode in anger at the therapist.

In general, most psychotherapists tend to be biased toward a highly expressive or interpretive technique. Patients, on the other hand, often are less interested in insight. A frequent pattern in the psychotherapy of borderline patients is for the therapist to try to force the patient to be more reflective than he or she is capable of being. Borderline patients often show steady improvement in functioning, even though they may not demonstrate a great deal of insight; the therapist is well advised to monitor the actual improvements in the patient's external life rather than the acquisition of insight.

CONCLUDING COMMENTS

Waldinger and Gunderson (1987) studied five successfully terminated cases of long-term psychotherapy with borderline patients. They concluded that no particular technique or theoretical orientation was appropriate for all patients: different approaches seemed to be effective in different cases. A recurrent theme in all the cases, however, was the patient's perception that the therapist was durable and would continue in the treatment—no matter how difficult.

Lack of rigidity is probably one of the most important attributes of the therapist who hopes to treat borderline patients successfully. Shifting flexibly between expressive and supportive techniques is necessary in many of the treatments; to a large extent, it is artificial to speak of technical strategies that are either exclusively expressive or exclusively supportive. Interpretations may be heard and understood much better when they are delivered in the context of a supportive holding environment. In all cases, the therapist must tailor the psychotherapy to the relevant etiologic issues so that it has a rational basis in addressing the problems that were central to the pathogenesis of the disorder.

REFERENCES

Adler, G. (1985). *Borderline psychopathology and its treatment.* New York: Jason Aronson.

Andrulonis, P. A. (1991). Disruptive behavior disorders in boys and the borderline personality disorder in men. *Annals of Clinical Psychiatry, 3*, 23–26.

Andrulonis, P. A., et al. (1981). Organic brain dysfunction and the borderline syndrome. *Psychiatric Clinics of North America, 4*, 47–66.

Boyer, L. B. (1977). Working with borderline patients. *Psychoanalytic Quarterly, 46*, 386–424.

Browne, A., & Finkelhor, D. (1986). Impact of child sexual abuse: A review of the research. *Psychological Bulletin, 99*, 66–77.

Coccaro, E. F., et al. (1989). Serotonergic studies in patients with affective and personality disorders: Correlates with suicidal and impulsive aggressive behavior. *Archives of General Psychiatry, 46*, 587–599.

Davies, J. M., & Frawley, M. G. (1991). Dissociative processes and transference-countertransference paradigms in the psychoanalytically oriented treatment of adult survivors of childhood sexual abuse. *Psychoanalytic Dialogues, 2*, 5–36.

Frank, A. F. (1992). The therapeutic alliances of borderline patients. In J. F. Clarkin, B. Marziali, & H. Munroe-Blum (Eds.), *Borderline personality disorder: Clinical and empirical perspectives* (pp. 220–247). New York: Guilford Press.

Frank, H., & Paris, J. (1981). Recollections of family experience in borderline patients. *Archives of General Psychiatry, 38*, 1031–1034.

Gabbard, G. O. (1991). Commentary on: 'Dissociative processes and transference-countertransference paradigms. . . .' by Jody Messler Davies and Mary Gail Frawley. *Psychoanalytic Dialogues, 2*, 37–47.

Gabbard, G. O. (1994). *Psychodynamic psychiatry in clinical practice: The DSM-IV edition*. Washington, DC: American Psychiatric Press.

Gabbard, G. O., & Wilkinson, S. M. (1994). *Management of countertransference with borderline patients*. Washington, DC: American Psychiatric Press.

Goldberg, R. L., et al. (1985). Parental qualities as perceived by borderline personality disorders. *Hillside Journal of Clinical Psychiatry, 7*, 134–140.

Gunderson, J. G. (1984). *Borderline personality disorder*. Washington, DC: American Psychiatric Press.

Gunderson, J. G., & Sabo, A. N. (1993). The phenomenological and conceptual interface between borderline personality disorder and PTSD. *American Journal of Psychiatry, 150*, 19–27.

Herman, J. L., Perry, J. C., & van der Kolk, B. A. (1989). Childhood trauma in borderline personality disorder. *American Journal of Psychiatry, 146*, 490–495.

Horwitz, L., et al. (in press). *Borderline personality disorder: Tailoring the psychotherapy to the patient*. Washington, DC: American Psychiatric Press.

Kernberg, O. F. (1975). *Borderline conditions and pathological narcissism*. New York: Jason Aronson.

Kernberg, O. F., Selzer, M. A., Koenigsberg, H. W., et al. (1989). *Psychodynamic psychotherapy of borderline patients*. Washington, DC: American Psychiatric Press.

Mahler, M. S., Pine, F., & Bergman, A. (1975). *The psychological birth of the human infant: Symbiosis and individuation*. New York: Basic Books.

Masterson, J. (1976). *Psychotherapy of the borderline adult: A developmental approach*. New York: Brunner/Mazel.

Masterson, J. F., & Rinsley, D. B. (1975). The borderline syndrome: The role of the mother in the genesis and psychic structure of the borderline personality. *International Journal of Psychoanalysis, 56,* 163–177.

Modell, A. H. (1976). 'The holding environment' and the therapeutic action of psychoanalysis. *Journal of the American Psychoanalytic Association, 24,* 285–307.

Ogata, S. N., Silk, K. R., Goodrich, S., et al. (1990). Childhood sexual and physical abuse in adult patients with borderline personality disorder. *American Journal of Psychiatry, 147,* 1008–1013.

Paris, J., & Frank, H. (1989). Perceptions of parental bonding in borderline patients. *American Journal of Psychiatry, 146,* 1498–1499.

Paris, J., & Zweig-Frank, H. (1992). A critical review of the role of childhood sexual abuse in the etiology of borderline personality disorder. *Canadian Journal of Psychiatry, 37,* 125–128.

Rockland, L. H. (1992). *Supportive therapy for borderline patients.* New York: Guilford Press.

Silverman, J. M., Pinkham, L., Horvath, T. B., et al. (1991). Affective and impulsive personality disorder traits in the relatives of patients with borderline personality disorder. *American Journal of Psychiatry, 148,* 1378–1385.

Soloff, P. H., & Millward, J. W. (1983). Developmental histories of borderline patients. *Comprehensive Psychiatry, 24,* 574–588.

Swartz, M., Blazer, D., George, L., et al. (1990). Estimating the prevalence of borderline personality disorder in the community. *Journal of Personality Disorders, 4,* 257–272.

Waldinger, R. J., & Gunderson, J. G. (1987). *Effective psychotherapy with borderline patients: Case studies.* New York: Macmillan.

Walsh, F. (1977). Family study 1976: 14 new borderline cases. In R. R. Grinker & B. Werble (Eds.), *The borderline patient* (pp. 158–177). New York: Jason Aronson.

Westen, D. et al. (1990). Physical and sexual abuse in adolescent girls with borderline personality disorder. *American Journal of Orthopsychiatry, 60,* 55–66.

Zanarini, M. C., Gunderson, J. G., Marino, M. F., et al. (1989). Childhood experiences of borderline patients. *Comprehensive Psychiatry, 30,* 18–25.

Zetzel, E. R. (1971). A developmental approach to the borderline patient. *American Journal of Psychiatry, 127,* 867–871.

Zweig-Frank, H., & Paris, J. (1991). Parents' emotional neglect and overprotection according to the recollections of patients with borderline personality disorder. *American Journal of Psychiatry, 148,* 648–651.

6

The Criminal Personality

Stanton E. Samenow, PhD

Dr. Samenow is Clinical Psychologist and Consultant in Alexandria, VA.

KEY POINTS

- Contrary to broadly accepted ideas of the origins of criminality, it is neither a product of environmental adversity nor of mental illness.
- The cause of criminality, which cannot be fully understood within the context of current psychological theory, lies in criminal thought patterns.
- Criminal thought patterns include: dissatisfaction with responsible life, a pattern of defaulting on responsibilities that are not to the criminal's liking or interest, calculated lying, the lack of a concept of personhood and of interdependence, concrete thinking, extreme changeability, fearfulness, and unrealistic expectations of the world.
- The key to changing criminal behavior is not to rehabilitate criminals, but to *habilitate* them, or to change the way that they *think*.
- Essential to the process of change are three factors: full disclosure, receptivity, and constructive self-criticism.
- It is the change agent's task to point out errors in thinking, define them, and to help criminals to see the role such errors have played in their lives.
- Since 1977, community and institutional programs have adapted contemporary research on the criminal personality to their own settings.

INTRODUCTION

For decades, criminality has been perceived as a product of forces external to the individual or as resulting from a mental illness. Moreover, it is argued that the definition of criminality changes, depending upon the laws and mores of society. A person might be regarded as a "criminal" today but not tomorrow, according to the law. In other words, criminality is a relative concept. Those who hold these views reject the idea that there is such a thing as a "criminal personality." They regard such a concept as a throwback to outmoded 19th century theories or as a dubious argument that there is a "bad seed." The concept of a "criminal personality" has surfaced again based largely upon the findings of a 17-year research-treatment program by Yochelson and Samenow (Samenow, 1984; Yochelson & Samenow, 1976, 1977, 1986). Before discussing their concept, let us first examine why other long-standing explanations of criminal behavior are unsatisfactory.

SOCIOLOGICAL EXPLANATIONS

Nearly every environmental adversity has been cited as causative of crime. The conventional wisdom has been that poverty, racism, trouble-filled schools, and lack of employment opportunities have driven youngsters and adults into crime. Such thinking, however, has been based on sociological theories or on what criminals have told others when they are held accountable for their offenses. Crime knows no social or economic boundaries. If a person lives in a slum and does not know what or when he or she will next eat, this certainly constitutes a severe hardship. Most poor people are not criminals, however, and many prosperous individuals are.

Members of poor families perceive and react to adversities in different ways. They may or may not turn to crime. People will argue that it is safer to walk in an affluent suburb than in most inner-city neighborhoods; however, this may be explained by the fact that criminals often gravitate to areas of instability in the urban core. The locations in which they congregate are inhabited by many responsible citizens who are afraid to leave their homes.

The same sort of argument holds for other alleged environmental causes of crime. As mentioned above, schools have their problems, and unemployment is considerably high in parts of the United States. Again, different people deal with social problems in different ways. They choose how to respond.

The conventional wisdom is that people become criminals because they are shut out of the mainstream—that they have a hard time in school and fail, or that they are unable to find work. The reality is that some people reject the mainstream before the mainstream rejects them. They despise doing things on others' terms and find requirements of school or the workplace insufferably boring. The person who becomes a criminal may attend school or hold a job only because he or she hopes to provide to others a convincing facade of responsibility. Having satisfied others, the person is then free to do as he or she pleases. Some criminals use a classroom or job site as an arena for committing crimes.

This is not meant to ignore the impact of serious social problems, but society does not cause crime. It may, however, provide opportunities for crime to occur by offering greater or lesser deterrence, but the role of individual choice has been understated or entirely overlooked. After all, it is the individual who chooses to commit a crime. Only later, when the offender is held accountable, does he or she contend that unfavorable environmental conditions are responsible for his or her having broken the law.

The above discussion has not addressed the matter of peer pressure, which has long been regarded as critical to the etiology of criminal behavior. Anyone who raises a child or observes adolescents knows that peer pressure is a powerful force nearly from womb to tomb. What is ignored is that peers are chosen. Youths are not forced into crime at knifepoint.

Every high school has groups with a variety of names (depending on location and the particular terms in use), such as "preppies," "nerds," "jocks," or "freaks."

To be a member of a group of illegal drug users who are committing crimes not only requires a series of choices, but also a determination to show that one can be trusted, will not "snitch" (or inform), and that one will go along with the group. Even in neighborhoods and schools where a significant criminal element exists, many youths reject participating in such activities.

Sociological explanations of criminal behavior fail to provide an answer as to why people turn to crime. Indeed, such explanations only provide rationalizations that render the criminal a victim of adverse forces that he or she cannot control.

PSYCHOLOGICAL FACTORS

A second major category of explanation for criminal behavior is psychological. It has long been taken for granted that a great deal of what people do results from their upbringing. If the child turns out to have problems, it is invariably believed that the parents must be at fault. The thinking, in turn, has been that if the child is engaging in criminal behavior, his or her home life must have contributed. Inadequate parenting, poor role models, and child abuse are among the factors regarded as causative of criminal behavior. However, no findings confirm this belief. It is how the child perceives and reacts to adversity that is of critical importance.

Child abuse is a case in point. In the first place, criminals may often lie and allege that they have been abused when, in reality, abuse has never occurred. Second, if one asks these individuals how their siblings were treated, they may candidly acknowledge that their brothers and sisters were not harshly treated because their behavior conformed to acceptable standards. Third, by no means do all children who are abused become criminals. They suffer and have problems, but they do not necessarily turn to crime.

Yet another dimension should be considered. Unless one has an antisocial youngster of his or her own, it is almost impossible to grasp what life is like in such a family. Future criminals may turn home life into a never-ending nightmare. They steal from parents and siblings. From an early age, they resist authority. The simplest request may result in a battle. They sneak around or blatantly defy their parents at every turn. Such youngsters ferret out and exploit any weakness or vulnerability in other family members. They exacerbate whatever friction naturally exists among family members. Their parents are constantly anxious, for whenever the phone or doorbell rings, they wonder if it is a complaining neighbor, a frustrated school official, the police, or even a hospital official telling them that their child is dead. Living in such fear and turmoil destroys family life. It is not unlikely that a besieged parent will react with physical punishment only to have the child threaten to report child abuse. Thus, those who blame parents for their offspring's criminality totally ignore the child's role in creating the problems. They see the child as a victim rather than a cause of family problems.

Some crimes are thought to have been committed by individuals suffering from mental illness and, therefore, these individuals are not responsible for the results. Yochelson and Samenow (1976) hypothesize that the insanity defense is often a charade participated in by criminals wanting to avoid long prison terms, by well-meaning mental health professionals, and by the courts. Criminals are often adept at "feeding" psychiatrists and others what they believe these professionals want to hear. Recognizing that insanity is a passport out of prison, their malingering is limited only by their imaginations. Unsophisticated "street" criminals have been successful at convincing others that they were insane at the time the particular crime was committed. Regarded as mentally ill and admitted to a psychiatric hospital, all they need do is continue to play the game and convince others that they have been rehabilitated so they can eventually be discharged.

Yochelson and Samenow (1976) found that a small number of criminals go through alternating phases of psychosis and crime. They may be psychotic following a crime, but interviewers erroneously conclude they were psychotic before committing the crime. When psychotic, these individuals are too confused to commit an organized crime. Furthermore, the thought content of the psychosis is often anticrime, even religious in nature. A person can, however, be both psychotic and a criminal, but one condition does not cause the other. By analogy, one can have cancer and heart disease, but these are separate disease entities. It is necessary to ask the proper questions in order to determine that, even though psychotic, the person who committed the crime was still free to make a choice. When the criminal is in legal jeopardy, however, he or she is not likely to acknowledge this unless approached by a very skilled interviewer. Although cases in which a crime is committed by a person who is not responsible may exist, neither Samenow nor Yochelson have so far found this to be true.

CAUSATION: STILL AN ENIGMA

If people do not become criminals due to external circumstances; if their criminality is not a product of their upbringing; if their crime is not a product of mental illness — what then is the etiology of criminal behavior? Genetics may help explain the cause for some individuals. Although some findings support such an explanation, researchers regard them as merely preliminary, and, in some cases, find them questionable. Yochelson and Samenow, (1976) who also conducted physical studies (e.g., blood, EEG, XYY chromosome), remained unable to explain why people become criminals. They abandoned the search for causes for two reasons: no factor or set of factors that they explored turned out to be necessary or sufficient to explain why a person becomes a criminal. Furthermore, they discovered that criminals used the search for "reasons why" to further explain and justify their criminality. One criminal said in a moment of candor, "If I didn't have excuses for crime before psychiatry, I certainly have enough now." Instead of focusing on why these people were criminals, Yochelson and Samenow generally studied their thinking processes.

THE CONCEPT OF THE CRIMINAL PERSONALITY

Yochelson and Samenow (1976) conducted a phenomenological study in which they found it necessary to see the world from the criminal's point of view. Behavior is largely a product of thinking; thus, it was the criminal's thought patterns that became their focus. Some thinking patterns are common to all criminals, whatever their background or their particular criminal pattern.

Critics of Yochelson and Samenow have pointed out that there is no such entity as a criminal personality. They correctly observe that what constitutes a criminal act changes with the times. However, some people, regardless of their society, will run afoul of the laws and mores. In other words, for life to be personally exciting is to do the forbidden, whatever the forbidden happens to be. This view is expressed by one man who declared, "If rape were legalized today, I wouldn't rape, but I'd do something else."

Like other issues, criminality lies along a continuum. If one were to speak of criminal acts, the continuum might range from a minor traffic offense to mass murder. But Yochelson and Samenow did not speak in terms of criminal acts, whose definitions may be different from jurisdiction to jurisdiction or from one era to another. Rather, they spoke in terms of thinking patterns, which also lie along a continuum. Their approach was not unlike that of Alfred Adler (1930/1977), who stated that he was not looking into crimes but rather into individual lives. In their study, Yochelson and Samenow found that the thinking patterns of criminals also lie along a continuum.

They also questioned whether larceny exists in every soul. Certainly, they reasoned, each person has been irresponsible at some point in his or her life. Thus, the thinking patterns of the criminal are shared, to an extent, by people who are not criminals. In the career criminal, all the patterns are present to an extreme. The whole, then, is more than the sum of its parts. The career criminal *thinks differently* from the responsible person.

HOW CRIMINALS VIEW THEMSELVES AND THE WORLD

From an early age, criminals are dissatisfied with the way that their responsible peers are living their lives. They view the world as a chessboard with people and objects for them to use in serving their own ends. Human relationships serve as avenues for conquests and triumphs. They pursue power and control for their own sake. For them, becoming a success is to become important overnight. It is not the step-by-step process of working toward, and then achieving, a goal. Being entrusted with power and legitimate control over others is not enough. They do the forbidden in order to *be* someone; they take risks that others would never take.

Because they lie so often to get what they want, others think they have become "compulsive" liars who are unable to tell the truth. Herein lies another myth. In order to understand criminals, one must recognize that lying serves a purpose for them—beyond that of covering their tracks and avoiding punishment. By lying, criminals preserve a view of themselves and the world. There is power in lying, in believing that they have "pulled the wool" over the eyes of others.

Responsible people tell an occasional white lie. They do so to avoid embarrassment, to protect others from bad news, or to cover up wrongdoing; however, lying does not become a way of life—as it does for criminals.

Although they may be of average intellectual potential, criminals think concretely. On an intelligence test, they may be able to abstract. They might appear highly conceptual, as they philosophize about matters remote from them. However, they never acquired the concepts of responsible living that most of us learned early in grade school, for they are antithetical to their way of life. Ask a religiously observant criminal what he or she means by "religious" and, almost invariably, he or she will respond in terms of the act of going to church, reading the Bible, or celebrating a holy day. For such criminals, religion is not an operational guide to life, to dealing with fellow human beings.

Criminals never develop a concept of personhood. To them, human beings are mere instruments to use as they please. Even criminals' mothers—the women who stand by them, who bail them out of difficulty, and who provide for them—are never seen as people in their own right. They are simply here to serve.

That criminals are concrete in their thinking also means they do not develop a concept of injury to others. They do not think of themselves as victimizing others. Rather, *they* are the victims when others interfere with their objectives. The criminal's idea of injury is as literal as leaving a person in a pool of blood.

Criminals are extremely changeable. People who are perplexed by this quality tend to regard it as a sign of mental illness. Criminals may be charming, helpful, and considerate in the morning and transform into complete tyrants in the afternoon. With great sincerity, they may tell others that they want to change and be more responsible—yet, within 24 hours, they commit a terrible crime. Although changeable, they are able to choose what they want. They are not simply at the mercy of uncontrollable inner forces.

Criminals are fearful people, but they do not want to show

fear. They have a remarkable capacity to shut off fears of getting caught—just long enough to do as they please. To put it more graphically, they can change from tearfulness to brutality within minutes.

A great deal of what the criminal does seems impulsive and senseless to observers, yet there is nothing impulsive about their behavior. Criminals know what they want and do whatever they think necessary to get it. If they spot an opportunity for excitement and personal gain, they will strike in an instant. They become so proficient at committing crimes that they often do so without prior planning. Invariably, however, they know exactly what they are doing. A crime that appears to have no motive simply has a hidden motive—the criminal's attempt to build himself or herself up at the expense of others.

Some crimes are so bizarre and morbid that experts conclude they could only be the product of a sick mind. Criminals know right from wrong, and they know the occupational hazards of crime—getting caught, convicted, confined, injured, or even killed—yet they can shut this awareness off long enough to do as they please. To kill and mutilate the body of a stranger is not "normal." However, to say it is a "sick" act reveals more about the reaction of the observer than about the mind of the criminal. The killer gets a "high" from reducing a person to a quivering, pleading speck of humanity, and then destroying him or her. The act itself is the product of a deliberate, calculating mind.

No matter how many crimes they have committed, no matter how brutal and diverse the crimes are, criminals regard themselves as decent human beings. Criminals maintain the view that they are, at heart, good people in several ways. First, they know they have done kind deeds and others think well of them. (Some people hold individual criminals in high esteem because they know nothing of their criminality.) Second, they have talents and skills for which they have been recognized. (Much artistic and musical talent exists behind bars.) Third, their aspirations for a good life fortify their view of their personal goodness. Perhaps, most important, they know they have broken the law but, in their view, they have only done what they needed to do to fulfill their own objectives. Their intentions remained good. As one man said, "If I thought of myself as evil, I couldn't live."

Many other thinking patterns are characteristic of people who have made crime a way of life. One is that they have no concept of interdependence. Put nine criminals on a baseball team, and each will consider himself or herself to be the captain.

Another prominent criminal thinking pattern is that of deferring or eventually defaulting on responsibilities that are not to the criminal's liking or interest. Criminals generally consider a responsible life to be intolerably boring. Thus, they simply do not bother. They break promises, they do not pay their bills, and they fail to recognize their obligations.

A third characteristic of criminal thinking is unrealistic expectations of the world. While thinking of something, they are positive it will happen. Without finding facts, they make assumptions about the world that they then expect to operate on their terms.

There are numerous other criminal thinking patterns. One that pervades criminals' daily existence is the fear of being put down. Criminals have a "thin skin." They can "dish out" anything; however, they will not take even the slightest criticism. If one expected the world always to operate on their terms, the number of threats to that world view would near infinity. Because they think in extremes, it takes little to threaten their artificially inflated self-concept. When even a tiny detail of life does not go according to plan, it is as though their entire self-worth is on the line. Criminals are constantly warding off the most trifling of inconveniences. Thus, they are angry most of the time, even if they do not show it. When they feel threatened, they perceive the threat to be global.

Perhaps readers of this account of criminal thinking patterns will argue that some people show aspects of these patterns who are not criminals. This is not the issue. When one understands criminals' mental processes, one finds that these and other thinking patterns are integral parts of the criminal personality. Criminals are extreme in these features. In the case of criminals, such thinking patterns are errors in that they inevitably lead to criminal behavior and injury to others. If criminals are to change, the errors of their thinking must be addressed.

HELPING THE CRIMINAL CHANGE: MOTIVATION

Many professionals in correctional facilities, mental health, social services, and other segments of the criminal justice system and in society at large believe criminals do not change and cannot change. Billions of dollars have been channeled into rehabilitation programs with few positive results. Yet the concept of "rehabilitation" as applied to the criminal personality is a misconception and a misnomer. To "rehabilitate" means to restore to an earlier constructive state or condition. Offender-rehabilitative measures have included providing educational opportunities, job skills, social skills, counseling, and therapy. This has resulted in criminals who have education, job skills, social skills, and occasional personal insights. However, many—if not most—of them remain criminals.

The rehabilitative measures were well-conceived and somewhat useful, but they did not touch the core of criminals—the way they understand their place in the world. Thus, the scope of the task is broader than rehabilitation. Rather, it is to *habilitate* criminals, or help them change the way they *think*. Psychotherapeutic and counseling approaches that have been successful with a variety of client populations have not been successful with criminals, since they constitute a very different group. Only when the individual criminal's mind is understood does it become possible to develop an approach for helping him or her become a responsible human being.

Criminals, like anyone else, have only two effective sources of motivation to change long-standing patterns: external and internal. For a criminal to make significant and enduring change, leverage must come from the outside. This does not imply that change can or should be coerced. Rather, life provides consequences for ongoing, irresponsible, or illegal behavior.

The process of change can begin in a variety of settings. Professionals can work with criminals in the community who are on probation or parole. If criminals are already in an institution, the work can begin there. The most important part of the process of change, however, is to help criminals see themselves as they are and to reject their criminal behaviors. None of us changes anything about ourselves unless we become disgusted with certain behaviors. How then is this accomplished with criminals who see themselves as above others and who are reluctant to give up an exciting way of life for one that they have renounced?

OVERVIEW OF THE HABILITATIVE PROCESS

Essential to the process of change is a wide-open channel with three components: full disclosure, receptivity, and constructive self-criticism. Criminals, however, open and close the channel to suit their own purposes. The method by which an increasingly open channel is created is one of phenomenological reporting. It requires criminals to report whatever they are thinking. This method is similar to obtaining a computer printout of the mind, without explanation, addition, subtraction, or tailoring the report.

Even though criminals are unlikely fully to disclose their thoughts at the outset, almost every time they open their mouths, an error in thinking becomes evident. It is the change agent's task to point out errors of thinking, define them, and help criminals to see the role such errors have played in their lives. Especially important is the injury criminals have inflicted on others, even those about whom they say they care. A thought or afterthought can provide a theme for a discussion about a life pattern. The objective is to proceed from the concrete to the conceptual. It is the incipient thought of today that leads to the crime of tomorrow.

This approach goes beyond other rational/cognitive treatment approaches. It requires more than rational problem solving. Most rehabilitation counselors and therapists have probably had the frustrating experience of believing their client had gained insight into a problem, only to have the client fail to apply the insight to a similar event later. Yochelson and Samenow recognize that this concrete thinker will remain incapable of actualizing their insight unless they develop an error in thinking as a concept and then relate it to life—past, present, and future.

Such an approach has virtually no emphasis on feelings. Rather, the focus is on thought: when thinking changes, feelings also change. The stance that Yochelson and Samenow take toward anger is vastly different from that in traditional psychotherapy. They suggest that criminals be encouraged to control their anger first, not express it. In turn, they find that as their thinking about themselves and the world becomes more realistic and responsible, they feel less anger. The objective is to get as close to eliminating anger as possible. Criminals should avoid anger in the same way that alcoholics should avoid the first sip of a martini.

Initially, the motivation for change is all negative—fear of external consequences and the client's increasing loathing for the kind of person that he or she is. As criminals practice the correctives of thinking errors, however, they find that positive things occur. They do not have to continually look over their shoulders for the police and others who want to hold them accountable. They have a sense of "being clean." People they have admired and those who have wanted to trust them start to regard them in a new way. And, finally, they have accomplished things they do not want to jeopardize by returning to old patterns.

The process is not quick, simple, or infallible. Many cycles comprise the change process. Numerous offenders drop out or try to play "both sides of the street," inevitably returning to crime. However, it is possible to work with some people—either in the community or in the institution—who are fed up with the kind of life they have been leading. It is mandatory that if this habilitative work is started with an inmate while he or she is confined that there be a follow-up when he or she returns to the community.

THE CRIMINAL PERSONALITY IN PERSPECTIVE

Contemporary work on the criminal personality has been available to professionals since 1977. Throughout the country, community and institutional programs have adapted this work to their own settings. The controversy as to whether a "criminal personality" exists has largely abated as people have endeavored to determine how the concept can be most helpful to them in their work with offenders.

REFERENCES

Adler, A. (1977). Individual psychology and crime. *Quarterly Journal of Corrections,* 7-13 (Original work published 1930).

Samenow, S. E. (1984). *Inside the criminal mind.* New York: Times Books.

Yochelson, S. & Samenow, S. E. (1976). *The criminal personality: A profile for change.* New York: Jason Aronson.

Yochelson, S. & Samenow, S. E. (1977) *The criminal personality: The change process.* New York: Jason Aronson.

Yochelson, S. & Samenow, S. E. (1986). *The criminal personality: The drug user.* New York: Jason Aronson.

FOR FURTHER READING

Samenow, S. E. (1989). *Before it's too late: Why some kids get into trouble and what parents can do about it.* New York: Times Books.

7

Pathological Gambling

Richard A. McCormick, PhD

Dr. McCormick is Chief, Psychology Service at the Cleveland V.A. Medical Center, and Assistant Clinical Professor of Psychology, Case Western Reserve University, Cleveland, OH.

KEY POINTS

- The therapist or counselor who treats pathological gambling must target not only the gambling behavior, but also the multiple needs and complex dynamics of the client.
- *Depressive* gamblers exhibit a cognitive style that feeds the depression and tends to exaggerate their responsibility for negative life events. *Narcissistic* gamblers feel entitled to special consideration and treatment, making unreasonable demands for attention and displaying exhibitionistic tendencies.
- It is valuable to understand the nature of the addictive cycle for each particular gambler, as it can reveal a complex interaction of biological and environmental factors that puts the gambler at risk for the disorder.
- Clinical treatment can be aided by an evaluation of the client's personality type; assessment should also include the tracking of significant life events and the gambler's development of personal relationships with others.
- Information on treatment effectiveness for pathological gambling is limited. Integrated approaches utilizing inpatient treatment (often modeled after programs for substance abusers), peer counseling, group therapy, and cognitive therapy have demonstrated various degrees of effectiveness.

INTRODUCTION

With the expansion of opportunities for us to gamble—from the stock market to government lotteries, from Atlantic City to the Caribbean islands—the prevalence of pathological gambling has undoubtedly increased. This increase has been accompanied by a serious rise in the personal and familial catastrophes it leaves in its wake.

In some ways, pathological gambling resembles substance abuse, and the two often go together; however, the problem is much more complex than that. Some pathological gamblers are extremely narcissistic; they feel entitled to special privileges, even to the point of defying the rules of chance. Others are covering up loneliness or anxiety. Still others are expressing rage at some major figure in the past—a demanding and perhaps abusing parent for instance—and, at the same time, their guilt for such feelings. Many enjoy the excitement of flirting with danger. Most manifest the dynamics of habituation and addiction.

There appear to be two major subgroups of pathological gamblers. The first is the depressive gambler, who has a negative cognitive style: assuming responsibility for all that has gone wrong in life, being pessimistic about the future, communicating poorly about emotional needs, feeling anxious, guilty, and beset with high expectations of performance that are seldom achieved. The second type is the narcissistic gambler: sociable, verbal, projecting the image of handling life well, but using and manipulating others, displaying little insight into the reasons for failure, desperately in need of stimulation, grandiose, with poorly developed internal value systems.

In treatment, focusing on the gambling behavior alone appears to be insufficient. A broader approach that targets intervention to the multiple needs and complex dynamics of clients is necessary. This integration may include individual and group therapy, support groups, and even, at times, inpatient care.

DEFINITION

In the fourth edition of the *Diagnostic and Statistical Manual of Mental Disorders* (DSM-IV) (American Psychiatric Association, 1994), pathological gambling is defined as "persistent and recurrent maladaptive gambling behavior that disrupts personal, family, or vocational pursuits." Pathological gambling may also be seen as an addictive behavior, and therapists treating pathological gamblers have long noted its addictive quality (Adler & Goleman, 1969; Moran, 1975; Tyndel, 1963; Zimmerman, Meeland, & Krug, 1985). Pathological gambling and substance abuse often occur together, both in identified clients and in their biological families (Ramirez et al., 1983). Gamblers have personality profiles similar to substance abusers (Graham & Lowenfeld, 1986; McCormick, 1987).

A phenomenon comparable to tolerance develops as the pathological gambler increases the amount and intensity of gambling. By the same token, the gambler reports a short-term "withdrawal syndrome" following the cessation of gambling that is similar in symptomatology to that of the substance abuser (Custer, 1984; Wray & Dickerson, 1981). Further underscoring the similarity of pathological gambling to other addictive behavior, the DSM-IV sets criteria for pathological gambling that are very similar to those for substance dependence, except for the physiological effects of the exogenous substance.

PREVALENCE OF PATHOLOGICAL GAMBLING

A study by the U.S. Government's Commission on the Review of the National Policy Toward Gambling estimated that in 1976 there were over 1.1 million pathological gamblers in the United States. It is likely that the number has continued to climb as more people are exposed to increased opportunities for gambling. Recent studies of prevalence rates in three states have found that between 2.4% and 2.8% of adults were classified as problem gamblers, and another 1.4% were classified as probable pathological gamblers (Volberg & Steadman, 1989). Among substance abusers, the incidence of significant gambling problems exceeds 13% (McCormick, 1993).

The number of places where casino gambling is legal increased significantly during the past 20 years. Sports betting, which alone is estimated to exceed $70 billion annually, has expanded to include legalized off-track betting. Publicly administered lotteries in the United States are now offered in almost every state in the union, with wagering exceeding $25 billion annually.

All these increases are accompanied by tremendous media exposure, promoting gambling as a recreational option or financial salvation. Lotteries invest large sums in paid advertising, and the most recent super-lottery winner becomes front-page news on a recurring basis. More subtle forms of gambling are also increasing. The volatile commodities and futures markets, as well as speculative investing in the stock market, are options for the upper- and middle-class gambler.

PERSONALITY DYNAMICS OF THE PATHOLOGICAL GAMBLER

The earliest writings on the personality of the pathological gambler are to be found in the psychoanalytic literature. Freud (1975) analyzed the personality of the novelist Dostoevsky, a heavy gambler in the casinos during the nineteenth century, and found similarities between pathological gambling and the compulsive neuroses. It seemed that gambling was used to cope with recurrent anxiety states related to his preoccupation with the sudden death of his father when the novelist was 18 years old. Freud suggested that a parent figure who was perceived as demanding and punishing in the gambler's early life was hypothesized to produce guilt and depression.

Fenichel (1945) stressed the narcissistic qualities of the pathological gambler: he or she feels entitled to special privileges, expecting to be exempted even from the rules of chance, and has unrealistic faith in his or her ability to overcome the odds. Fenichel also noted the parallel between the mood swings of the gambler and the win-lose cycle of gambling.

Bergler (1958) synthesized his observations of the more than 60 pathological gamblers he treated and provided the basis for modern concepts on the disorder. He noted that gamblers seem to search for a "pleasurable-painful" tension level that is more important than winning itself, and he focused on the gamblers' anger and aggressive impulses. This anger generates guilt, since the anger is unconsciously directed at the parent who previously had been the socializing influence on the child's development. Bergler felt that gambling, with its inevitable losses, satisfies a masochistic need for self-punishment.

Greenberg (1980) noted the overconfidence, impatience, and even grandiosity of some gamblers, but considered this to be a cover for loneliness or anxiety generated by the threat of intimacy. Gamblers are preoccupied with the present. They have come to value competition and material success highly but are driven by needs that cause them to demand too much too soon. They narcissistically ignore the reality factors necessary for enduring success.

In a similar vein, Rosenthal (1986) hypothesized that gamblers build an illusion of omnipotence in order to defend against a deep sense of helplessness. They flirt constantly with danger to test their self-worth and power. In addition, Rosenthal suggests that the gamblers use the primitive defenses of denial, projection, and splitting. Bettors (i.e., those who bet) dichotomize themselves and others, uncertain of their own boundaries and identities. They are forced to rely on the value system of others, and consequently seek continual approval. Intimacy is difficult, so arousal and physical gratification are used as substitutes.

In a sociological study of gamblers, Lesieur (1977) offers insight into their personality dynamics. Observing that gamblers are preoccupied with wagering to the exclusion of other activities, he argues that as the behavior progresses, gamblers become increasingly unable to see that rational alternatives to gambling may be available. Gamblers enter a spiral of decreasing options and come to see gambling as the solution for their problems rather than as the source of them.

SUBTYPES OF PATHOLOGICAL GAMBLERS

The diagnostic classification of pathologic gambling varies significantly. Consequently, establishing subtypes has some clinical utility. Two major subtypes emerge—the depressive gambler and the narcissistic gambler.

The Depressed Gambler:

Depression has been established in a substantial portion of pathological gamblers entering treatment (McCormick et al., 1984). Whereas for some the depression seems to be primarily situational, for a significant number it is a lifetime pattern that precedes their gambling. Many have a life history of significant trauma (Taber, McCormick, & Ramirez, 1987). A history of child abuse, often at the hands of an alcoholic parent, is remarkably common. Seriously depressed gamblers exhibit a cognitive style that feeds the depression, and tend to exaggerate their responsibility for negative life events. When things go poorly, they generalize the results of a setback in one portion of their lives, believing that they are total failures. They are pessimistic about future events and interpret the past in a most negative light.

Depressed gamblers often display an avoidant personality style. They tend to communicate very little about their emotional needs and will minimize the intensity of their affect. Symptoms of anxiety disorders may be present, including intrusive thoughts and nightmares, but they are seldom volunteered. Guilt and remorse are intense, but they do little to change the repetitive gambling behavior. Seriously depressed gamblers tend to minimize their accomplishments and perceive themselves as underachievers.

They will often go through periods during which they display responsibility and control. They may have stable work or family histories and, even in the midst of an impulsive gambling spree, may display some capacity for control. Depressive gamblers generally have strong—in fact, overly rigid—value systems, and their histories often reveal a strong, hard-driving parent whom the client was never able to satisfy.

The Narcissistic Gambler:

Narcissistic gamblers are outwardly sociable and verbal. They project an image of being able to manage things; however—despite fleeting successes—their accomplishments seldom match their claims. They focus primarily on their own needs, and although they can be charming, people who attempt to form relationships with them tend to feel used and manipulated. Narcissistic gamblers feel entitled to special consideration and treatment, making unreasonable demands for attention and displaying exhibitionistic tendencies. They display little insight into the reasons for their failures and tend to project blame for their losses onto others or factors outside their control (e.g., the market was in a period of unpredictable adjustment).

Narcissistic gamblers are more likely to engage in forms of risk-taking that have high visibility and stimulation, such as stocks, commodities, and high-stakes casino gambling. Although their behavior may, in fact, be an attempt to compensate for deep-seated feelings of emptiness and inadequacy, they have little awareness of any such feelings or of dysphoria. Probing will often reveal some awareness of the negative feeling that a lack of stimulation produces for them, and they will acknowledge being easily bored and having a "need" for excitement.

Narcissistic gamblers may have a poorly developed internal value system. They attempt to read the expectations of others and attempt to project values that they believe will be accepted and thus attain their goals. The lack of clear internal values and beliefs may contribute to their feelings of emptiness.

THE ADDICTIVE CYCLE

The addictive cycle for the pathological gambler reveals a complex interaction of biological and environmental factors that puts the gambler at risk for the disorder. The biological/hereditary factors might include an unusually large need for stimulation, an endocrine disorder, or a catecholamine imbalance that aggravates dysphoria. The environmental factors could include inadequate early socialization experiences and traumatic experiences. Then the person is exposed to gambling as a recreational option. The high-arousal gambling experience provides excitement and, in the case of the depressive gambler, relief from the ongoing dysphoria. Pathological gamblers report that while they are gambling they experience euphoria and a marked change in mood. They are able to focus all their attention on the gambling experience and are thus relieved of all awareness of their life problems.

Once exposed to gambling as an option, the return of a need state reactivates the addictive cycle. In the case of narcissistic gamblers, the need state may be the boredom that the bettor experiences or the emptiness and fears of loneliness hypothesized by personality theorists. While in the need state, they perceive the options available for relief, but as the addiction progresses and intensifies, their perception of the available options diminishes. In choosing gambling, the pathological gambler finds temporary relief and—in some cases—euphoria. Such relief may have its biological underpinnings in the activation of the hypothalamic pituitary adrenal axis by the high-arousal gambling behavior. That activation may, in turn, stimulate a modulating endorphin system that is intended to control the activation (Gold & Rea, 1983). In the depressed gambler, catecholamine and endocrine changes involved in the activation of these systems may have an antidepressant effect.

However, for psychological and perhaps physiological reasons, the relief is temporary. Losses are inevitable and they compound gamblers' difficulties. They increasingly lie, steal, or embezzle in order to provide the money necessary to support their gambling behavior. They further alienate their family and friends. Gamblers are left feeling that they are more of a failure and, in the case of depressive gamblers, more guilty and dysphoric. At the physiological level, the constant arousal and activation lead to compensatory adjustments in biological systems, which gamblers may experience as "withdrawal." These adjustments may also raise the threshold of arousal necessary to experience mood changes, an effect comparable to tolerance.

The rebound need-state may then be more intense than the state that originally precipitated the gambling. The addiction escalates, and the gambler becomes increasingly desperate in his or her search for the "action" and the psychological relief it provides.

THE CLINICAL MANAGEMENT OF THE PATHOLOGICAL GAMBLER

Case management must be based on a thorough assessment of a variety of psychological, environmental, and biophysical variables. When interviewing gamblers, the therapist or counselor must bear in mind that, as with other addictions, denial, minimization, and rationalization are likely. Gamblers may relabel some of their gambling behavior, referring to it as "investing" or their "profession." Gamblers' stories may be so rich as to be seductive. They will tend to concentrate on finances and see money as both the problem and the solution (American Psychiatric Association, 1994). A thorough history of the nature, frequency, and intensity of the client's gambling experience must be obtained. It is also important to assess the degree to which the gambling behavior affects major elements of the client's life, including family and vocation. Equally important, but often more difficult, is the assessment of the gambler's subjective experience during the anticipation phase of gambling and his or her progression to actual gambling behavior. It is often helpful to encourage the use of analogies or metaphors to describe these subjective experiences.

Pathological gambling is a stressful lifestyle, and consequently gamblers tend to have a high incidence of cardiovascular and stress-related physical disorders. The assessment of psychosomatic conditions also provides supportive data for the assessment of personality style. Hyperactivity is common in gamblers (McCormick et al., 1984), and it is therefore important to consider the possibility of endocrine dysfunction. Undiagnosed hypothyroidism can contribute to the gambling cycle in a small but clinically significant subset of cases.

A thorough history should track significant life events, particularly those of a traumatic nature, as well as the development of interpersonal relationships. Having the gambler complete a written autobiography can be especially helpful in this regard (Adkins, Taber, & Russo, 1985). The client's history of mood shifts and the development of internalized values should also be probed, with special emphasis on the development of a competitive outlook towards life. Other addictive behavior may contribute to gambling or recur with it over the course of the client's life. Again, the gambler will tend to underestimate the severity of those addictive behaviors such as substance abuse and sexual promiscuity.

Personality testing can be useful in understanding the dynamics of the client and in subtyping the disorder. Work to date has primarily focused on the Minnesota Multiphasic Personality Inventory (MMPI) (Bolen, Caldwell, & Boyd, 1975; Graham & Lowenfeld, 1986). The depressive gambler shows high elevations on scales measuring depression and anxiety. Although elevations on scales measuring impulsivity and hyperactivity may be high compared to a normal sample, they are moderate when compared with other types of pathological bettors. The depressive gambler may also show elevations on scales measuring social introversion, contradicting the stereotype that all gamblers are gregarious. The California Personality Inventory (CPI), which measures personality dimensions of a nonpathological nature, can also be of unique value. The CPI provides measures on personality dimensions which are directly relevant to treatment, such as responsibility, ego control, and self-control (McCormick et al., 1987).

In the assessment process, it is also valuable for one to understand the nature of the addictive cycle for each particular gambler. Cues that seem to trigger the cycle can include internal phenomena, such as vague feelings of uneasiness, boredom, or anxiety, and external cues such as sights, sounds, or angry interchanges with family or friends. Potentially competing responses to gambling behavior should also be noted. They may include functional behaviors that also tend to take on an addictive quality—for instance, many pathological gamblers are workaholics when not gambling.

Information on the treatment of pathological gambling is limited. Bergler (1958) claimed a 75% success rate with the gamblers he treated, but he provided no clear data on the criteria used to define success or the severity of the clients' problems. A variety of behavioral approaches has been attempted, including one by Barker and Miller (1968) that reported favorable results for three patients treated with electric-shock aversion therapy.

In a subsequent report that compared the results of aversion therapy with 10 patients against the results of imaginal desensitization for 10 other patients (McConaghy et al., 1983), the aversion therapy was shown to be unsuccessful as measured by a 1-year follow-up. Some modest improvements were seen among the desensitization subjects, however. Greenberg and Rankin (1982) reported on 26 male compulsive gamblers at an outpatient clinic who were treated with a variety of behavioral methods, but results were again modest. The less-than-dramatic results achieved with behavioral methods may indicate that focusing on the gambling behavior itself is insufficient. A broader approach that targets therapeutic interventions to the multiple needs of the client is likely to be necessary.

Inpatient programs for severe pathological gamblers have become more common in recent years, and many are modeled after the rehabilitation programs available for substance abusers. One of the oldest and best-studied is the program at the Brecksville Veterans Administration Medical Center in Ohio (Russo et al., 1984). This program provides a highly structured treatment approach and uses the inevitable conflicts that the participants have with the rules and expectations of the therapeutic environment as "grist" for the therapeutic mill. A variety of modalities are available, but the primary thrust of the program is group therapy and peer counseling.

In peer counseling, a recovering pathological gambler provides support, role modeling, and—when necessary—confrontation. The peer counselor can model assertive action, provide advice and encouragement, and be effective in confronting the gambler's denial and in breaking through the gambler's deflection of responsibility and blame to others.

Gambler's Anonymous (GA) has a long history of successful intervention with many pathological gamblers. The GA step-work system for spiritual or psychological growth concretely focuses the client away from gambling behavior and toward the psychological steps necessary for effective recovery.

The concept of "serenity," which the self-help groups encourage, has a number of positive aspects for the gambler. Gamblers tend to overvalue material goods and accomplishments, concentrate on external stimulation and confirmation, and have difficulty accepting and rewarding themselves for moderate, less-than-spectacular accomplishments. The concept of serenity urges self-acceptance and highlights the value of everyday personal accomplishments; it is a useful method for the gambler to conceptualize the changes that need to be made in all these areas.

The therapist should bear in mind, however, that GA meetings vary considerably. They may not have the degree of structure and discipline characteristic of Alcoholics Anonymous (AA) meetings, so it may be important to prepare some clients for the particular GA group they will encounter. On balance, the GA experience is almost always a positive one. Preparing clients for the aspects that may be less tolerable for their particular personality can help ensure that they will not use the aspects of the experience they find unpleasant as an excuse to abandon the whole experience. Family members are also strongly encouraged to join a Gam-Anon group. It focuses on their feelings and provides them with the guidance and support necessary to cope with living with a pathological gambler and often to change their pattern of enabling the gambler's behavior.

Group therapy is the other cornerstone of the program. Therapy is conducted by mental health professionals familiar with gamblers and addictions in general. Pathological gamblers generally tend to be highly verbal, so the therapist must keep the process in focus. While the peer group sessions may begin working through gamblers' denial, it is in group therapy that the process of supporting and working through the pain of change can occur (Taber & McCormick, 1987). In therapy, gamblers may reveal their irrational beliefs, such as the delusion that continuing to bet will inevitably result in a recouping of all losses; the therapist may also discover that the client has irrational beliefs about the self that are similar to those of depressed or narcissistic individuals in general. One such belief common among gamblers is that you can only be cared for if you are bestowing large monetary presents on those around you. The narcissistic gambler may have irrational beliefs that border on grandiosity about his or her gambling "skills" or "system."

An integrated inpatient approach has been shown to provide good results for many gamblers entering treatment (Graham & Lowenfeld, 1986). In one outcome study, 56% of persons followed in the community 6 months after treatment were totally abstinent (Taber et al., 1987). Subjects in this study had been given a battery of psychological measures on entry into treatment, and those with a depressogenic cognitive style were significantly less likely to be abstinent at follow-up. These individuals, who tended to attribute the cause for negative events to internal reasons and to generalize the negative event to other areas of their lives, were apparently less able to cope effectively with the inevitable setbacks that occurred during the recovery process. In general, psychopathologic symptoms subsided with abstinence, but in some cases depression and anxiety continued at high levels despite such abstinence. This further underscores the therapeutic utility of evaluating the independence of the dysphoria and the gambling and adjusting treatment accordingly.

Clearly, not all clients require a highly structured inpatient approach. Many do very well in GA alone. Individual therapy can also be effective. The therapist or counselor, however, must strive to provide structure for gamblers. Education about the realities of pathological gambling—including helping the client to be clear on what gambling is—and confrontation of denial and other defenses early in the process is critical. GA can be used to provide additional assistance in these areas. The therapist can also effectively intervene with the irrational beliefs of the gambler. Cognitive therapy, with homework assignments that extend the therapy outside of the treatment sessions, is a potentially effective approach. Once abstinence is obtained, longer-term therapy can focus on underlying depression and identity conflicts.

Reports on the use of pharmacotherapy to treat pathological gamblers are sparse. Moskowitz (1980) cited four cases in which lithium provided improvement. This is likely to occur primarily when case assessment indicates significant hypomania. Antidepressant medication can be of use in cases where the depression is documented to be recurring and long-standing. The strong tendency for gamblers to establish other addictive behaviors must be considered when psychoactive medication is prescribed. Depressive gamblers are also frequently suicidal (McCormick et al., 1984); if they demonstrate suicidal behavior, it should be addressed in the prescribing process.

REFERENCES

Adkins, B. J., Taber, & J. I., & Russo, A. M. (1985). The spoken autobiography: A powerful tool in group psychotherapy. *Social Work, 30,* 435–439.

Adler, N., & Goleman, D. (1969). Gambling and alcoholism: Symptom substitution and function equivalents. *Quarterly Journal of the Study of Alcoholism, 30,* 733–736.

American Psychiatric Association (1994). *Diagnostic and statistical manual of mental disorders* (4th ed). Washington, DC: Author.

Barker, J. C., & Miller, M. (1968). Aversion therapy for compulsive gambling. *Journal of Nervous and Mental Disorders, 146,* 285–302.

Bergler, E. (1958). *The psychology of gambling.* New York: International Universities Press.

Bolen, D. W., Caldwell, A. B., & Boyd, W. H. (1975). Personality traits of pathological gamblers. In W. R. Eadington (Ed.), *The gambling papers: Proceedings of the 1975 Conference on Gambling.* Reno: University of Nevada.

Commission on the Review of the National Policy Toward Gambling. (1976). *Gambling in America.* Washington, DC: Government Printing Office.

Custer, R. L. (1984). Profile of the pathological gambler. *Journal of Clinical Psychiatry, 45,* 35–38.

Fenichel, O. (1945). *The psychoanalytic theory of neurosis.* New York: W. W. Norton.

Freud, S. (1975). Dostoevsky and parricide. In J. Halliday & P. Fuller (Eds.), *The psychology of gambling.* New York: Harper and Row.

Gold, M. S., & Rea, W. S. (1983). The role of endorphins in opiate addiction, opiate withdrawal, and recovery. *Psychiatric Clinics of North America, 6*(3), 489–520.

Graham, J. R., & Lowenfeld, B. H. (1986). Personality dimensions of the pathological gambler. *Journal of Gambling Behavior, 2*(1), 58–66.

Greenberg, A., & Rankin, H. (1982). Compulsive gamblers in treatment. *British Journal of Psychiatry, 140,* 364–366.

Greenberg, H. (1980). Psychology of gambling. In H. I. Kaplan, A. H. Freedman & B. J. Sadock (Eds.), *Comprehensive textbook of psychiatry* (Vol. 3, 3rd ed.). Baltimore: Williams & Wilkins.

Lesieur, H. R. (1977). *The chase.* New York: Doubleday.

McConaghy, N., et al. (1983). Controlled comparison of aversive therapy and imaginal desensitization in compulsive gambling. *British Journal of Psychiatry, 142,* 366–372.

McCormick, R. A. (1993). Disinhibition and negative affectivity in substance abusers with and without a gambling problem. *Addictive Behaviors, 18,* 331-336.

McCormick, R. A., et al. (1984). Affective disorders among pathological gamblers seeking treatment. *American Journal of Psychiatry, 141,* 215–218.

McCormick, R. A., et al. (1987). Personality profiles of pathological gamblers: The California Personality Inventory. *Journal of Clinical Psychology, 43,* 521–527.

Moran, E. (1975). Pathological gambling. *British Journal of Psychiatry, 9,* 416–428.

Moskowitz, J. A. (1980). Lithium and lady luck. *New York State Journal of Medicine, 5,* 785-788.

Ramirez, L. F. G., et al. (1983). Patterns of substance abuse in pathological gamblers undergoing treatment. *Addiction and Behavior, 8,* 425–428.

Rosenthal, R. J. (1986). The psychodynamics of pathological gambling. *Journal of Gambling Behavior, 2*(2), 108-120.

Russo, A. M., et al. (1984). An outcome study of an inpatient treatment program for pathological gamblers. *Hospital and Community Psychiatry, 36,* 823-827.

Taber, J. I., et al. (1987). Pathological gamblers following treatment: An outcome study. *American Journal of Psychiatry, 144,* 757-761.

Taber, J. I., & McCormick, R. A. (1987). The pathological gambler in treatment. In T. Galski (Ed.), *The clinical handbook of pathological gambling.* New York: Thomas.

Taber, J. I., McCormick, R. A., & Ramirez, L. F. (1987). The prevalence and impact of major life stressors among pathological gamblers. *International Journal of Addiction, 22,* 71-79.

Tyndel, M. (1963). Gambling—an addiction. *Addictions, 10,* 40-48.

Volberg, R. A., & Steadman, H. J. (1989). Prevalence estimates of pathological gambling in New Jersey and Maryland. *American Journal of Psychiatry, 146,* 1618-1619.

Wray, I., & Dickerson, M. G. (1981). Cessation of high frequency gambling and withdrawal symptoms. *British Journal of Addiction, 76,* 401-405.

Zimmerman, M. A., Meeland, T. G., & Krug, S. E. (1985). Measurement and structure of gambling behavior. *Journal of Personal Assessment, 49,* 76-81.

FOR FURTHER READING

Eadington, W. R. (Ed.). (1985). *The gambling papers: Proceedings of the 1985 Conference on Gambling.* Reno: University of Nevada.

McCormick, R. A., & Ramirez, L. F. (1988). Pathological gambling. In J. G. Howells (Ed.), *Modern perspectives in psychosocial pathology.* New York: Brunner/Mazel.

McCormick, R. A., & Taber, J. I. (1987). The pathological gambler: Salient personality variables. In T. Galski (Ed.), *The clinical handbook of pathological gambling.* New York: Thomas.

McCormick, R. A., et al. (1989). The relationship between attributional style and PTSD in addicted patients. *Journal of Traumatic Stress, 2,* 477-487.

Taber, J. I., & McCormick, R. A. (1987). Treatment of the pathological gambler. In T. Galski (Ed.), *The clinical handbook of pathological gambling.* New York: Thomas.

8

Pervasive Developmental Disorders

Sam Goldstein, PhD

Dr. Goldstein is a clinical instructor and psychologist at the Developmental Disabilities and Mental Retardation Clinic, Department of Psychiatry, University of Utah School of Medicine, Salt Lake City, UT.

KEY POINTS

- The term *pervasive developmental disorder* (PDD) refers to a group of disorders that appear to exert a significant negative impact on children's general development, communication, behavior, and interpersonal relations.
- Included in this group are: autistic disorder, Rett's disorder, childhood disintegrative disorder, Asperger's disorder, and atypical patterns of pervasive developmental disorders. All of these are referred to colloquially as *autism*.
- Symptoms of PDD frequently include: perceptual disorders, language deficits, cognitive difficulties, memory weaknesses, and social impairment.
- To date, PDD has no cure. Although medication might help certain symptomatic problems, it does not lead to major changes for most children with autistic disorder or Asperger's disorder.
- A combination of school- and home-based behavioral interventions involving behavior modification and the reinforcing of small changes has proved effective in many cases. A treatment program should emphasize the development of language skills and provide psychological support for the child's family.

INTRODUCTION

The term *pervasive developmental disorder* refers to a group of disorders that appear to exert a significant negative impact on children's general development, communication, behavior, and interpersonal relations. Included in this group are autism, Rett's disorder, childhood disintegrative disorder, Asperger's disorder, and atypical patterns of pervasive developmental disorder. Despite recent research and clinical advances in distinguishing these different types of pervasive developmental disorders, all of them continue to be referred to colloquially as *autism,* the term affixed to them in the literature prior to 1980.

EARLY DESCRIPTIONS

Kanner (1943) first described autism as an innate condition in which children experienced a profound disturbance of social functioning. According to Kanner's description, autistic children experienced:

- An inability to relate normally to people
- Excellent rote memory skills
- Language difficulties ranging from mutism to spoken language characterized by lack of communicative intent, echolalia (involuntary repetition of a word or words just spoken by someone else), personal pronoun reversal and literalness
- Fear of loud noises and moving objects
- Repetitious behaviors and an obsessive desire for the maintenance of a static environment and routines
- Lack of spontaneous activity

- (Occasionally) good cognitive potential

Until the 1970s, autism was considered a form of schizophrenia. However, it was clear that the behavior of young autistic children was very different from the psychotic problems of later childhood or teenage years. It has also been clear that young autistic children suffer in many other areas of their development (Kolvin, 1971).

COMMON CHARACTERISTICS

Autism is a spectrum disorder in which patients may present with a range of problems—from those that are almost totally impairing to others that allow some, although not optimal, functioning. The population of autistic and pervasively impaired children experiences a wide range of developmental difficulties involving communication, socialization, thinking, cognitive skills, interests, activities, and motor abilities.

There is a consensus that autism and pervasive developmental disorder consist of three major areas of problems: social relations, communication, and behavior. It is likely that cognitive deficits form a fourth component. Although the age of onset was originally specified in the revised third edition of the *Diagnostic and Statistical Manual of Mental Disorders* (DSM-III) as before 30–36 months, it is no longer included among the essential diagnostic criteria (Wing, 1990). Gillberg (1986) reports that autism may have its onset long after 3 years of age.

Although critics suggest that the use of the diagnosis "pervasive developmental disorder" is inconsistent and not well-defined because it does not refer to *all* pervasive developmental disorders (e.g., retardation), this term appears to define this group of children best. There is no doubt, however, that some children experience specific or partial pervasive impairment (Gillberg, 1990). Symptomatic problems frequently include perceptual disorders (Ornitz & Ritvo, 1968), language deficits (McCann, 1989), cognitive difficulties (Rutter, 1983), memory weaknesses (Boucher, 1981), and impairment in social relations (Fein, Pennington, Markowitz, Braverman, & Waterhouse, 1986; Fein, Pennington, & Waterhouse, 1987).

Due to the unusual combination of weaknesses in behavior and the lack of a physiologic model to understand this disorder, autism appears to be a most perplexing condition (Schopler & Meisobov, 1987). Autism is best conceptualized as a biologically determined set of behaviors that occur with varying presentation and severity as the result of varying cause.

Autistic children often demonstrate a variable and mixed combination of impairments. Many do not meet all the criteria for autism; some of these children may experience what has been referred to as a "schizoid disorder of childhood" (Wolff & Barlow, 1979). The higher intellectually functioning group of autistic children may represent a mild case of the disorder or a variant called Asperger's Disorder (Wing, 1981), which appears to involve impairment in social interaction, self-absorbed behavior, odd interests and routines, speech and language problems (despite superficially competent expressive language skills), nonverbal communication problems, and motor clumsiness (Gillberg & Gillberg, 1989). These six criteria appear to define this variant of the disorder most precisely.

Rutter (1979) finds that the pattern of cognitive disabilities in autistic children, especially those with Asperger's Disorder, is distinctive and different from that found in children with general intellectual handicaps. Most commonly, language and language-related skills involving problems with semantics and pragmatics are present (Rutter, 1983). Hobson (1989) found that higher functioning autistic children are unable to make social or emotional discriminations or read social or emotional cues well. These deficits appear to impact social relations and likely stem from cognitive weaknesses. The inability to read social and emotional cues and understand others' points of view leads to marked interpersonal difficulties (Baron-Cohen, 1989; MacDonald, Rutter, & Howlin, 1989).

The DSM first used the term *pervasive developmental disorder* in 1980. This helped set more firmly the opinion that autism is developmental in nature and distinct from mental illness occurring later in life. It is now recognized as an organically-based neurodevelopmental disorder (Rutter, 1970). It appears to occur significantly more often in males (Smalley, Asarnow, & Spence, 1988) and presents across all social classes (Gillberg & Schaumann, 1982). It is estimated that one in four autistic children experience physical problems, including epilepsy (Rutter, 1970). Up to 80% are generally found to experience intellectual deficiencies. Lotter (1974) suggests that the level of intellectual functioning and the amount of useful language by 5 years of age are the best predictors of outcome for autistic children. This finding is supported by the work of Gillberg & Steffenburg (1987).

DSM-IV CRITERIA

The DSM-IV (American Psychiatric Association, 1994) includes diagnostic criteria for a group of several pervasive developmental disorders.

Autistic Disorder:

Autistic disorder has remained fairly consistent in the last three versions of the DSM. Its diagnosis includes three parts, the first of which involves three sets of behavioral descriptions.

The first set of behaviors includes qualitative impairment in social interaction, as manifested by at least two of the following: marked impairment in the use of multiple nonverbal behaviors (e.g., eye-to-eye gaze, facial expression, body postures, and gestures to regulate social interaction); failure to develop peer relationships appropriate to the child's developmental level; a lack of spontaneous seeking to share enjoyment, interests, or achievements with other people; and lack of social or emotional reciprocity.

The second set of behaviors involves qualitative impairments in communication as manifested by one of the following: delay in, or total lack of, the development of spoken language without efforts to compensate through alternative modes of communication such as gestures or mime; marked impairment in the ability to initiate or sustain conversation with others; use of stereotyped and repetitive language or idiosyncratic language; and lack of varied, spontaneous, make-believe, or social imitative play appropriate to the child's developmental level.

The third set of behaviors involves repetitive and stereotyped patterns of behavior, interest and activities, as manifested by at least one of the following: encompassing preoccupation with one or more stereotyped and restricted patterns of interest that is abnormal in either intensity or focus; apparently inflexible adherence to specific, nonfunctional routines or rituals; stereotyped and repetitive motor mannerisms (e.g., hand or finger flapping or twisting, or complex whole-body movements); and persistent preoccupation with parts of objects.

A delay in social interaction, language as used in social communication, and/or symbolic or imaginative play prior to age 3 is a universal characteristic of the autistic population. Finally, the child's clinical description should not be better accounted for by Rett's disorder or childhood disintegrative disorder.

Rett's Disorder:

DSM-IV criteria describe Rett's disorder as being manifested by: (a) apparently normal prenatal and perinatal development, (b) apparently normal psychomotor development through the first 5 months after birth, and (c) normal head circumference at birth. Between 5 and 48 months, head growth decelerates. The child loses previously acquired purposeful hand skills between ages 5 and 30 months and begins to develop characteristic stereotyped hand movements that resemble hand wringing or hand washing. Interest in social environment diminishes, problems develop in the coordination of gait or trunk movements, and expressive and receptive language become impaired, with severe psychomotor retardation.

Childhood Disintegrative Disorder:

Another new disorder in DSM-IV is *childhood disintegrative disorder*. Children with this problem develop normally for the first 2 years and then lose skills in at least two of the following areas: expressive or receptive language, social skills or adaptive behavior, bowel or bladder control, and play or motor skills. In addition, they begin to manifest qualitative impairment of social interaction (e.g., the impairment of nonverbal behaviors, failure to develop peer relationships, lack of social or emotional reciprocity), and qualitative impairments in communication (e.g., delay or lack of spoken language, inability to initiate or sustain a conversation, use of stereotyped and repetitive language, lack of varied make-believe play). The behavior of a child with childhood disintegrative disorder should not be accounted for by another specific pervasive developmental disorder or schizophrenia.

Asperger's Disorder:

The DSM-IV includes Asperger's disorder under the pervasive developmental disorders. The diagnostic description includes: (a) qualitative impairment in social interaction involving difficulty with nonverbal behavior; (b) failure to develop peer relationships; (c) impaired expression of pleasure; (d) lack of social or emotional reciprocity; (e) restricted, repetitive, and stereotypic patterns of behavior; (f) lack of any significant delay in language; and (g) lack of significant delay in cognitive development. Furthermore, the child should not meet the criteria for another specific pervasive developmental disorder. These criteria clearly represent a productive start in acknowledging this group of higher functioning children with pervasive developmental disorder. However, in my opinion, these criteria do not extend far enough—nor are they operationalized well enough, based on the data reviewed earlier in this chapter.

EPIDEMIOLOGY

Wing and Gould (1979) refer to the triad of social, language-oriented, and behavioral impairments with autistic-like conditions. This triad has been reported in approximately 21 out of 10,000 children (Gillberg, 1986; Wing & Gould, 1979). Full-syndrome autism likely occurs in 6 or 7 out of 10,000 children (Steffenburg & Gillberg, 1986). Other authors suggest an incidence as high as 21 out of 10,000 children, with a male-to-female ratio of approximately 4:1 (Cialdella & Mamelle, 1989). Asperger's disorder appears to be at least 3–5 times more common than full-syndrome autism, occurring in approximately 2 or 3 children per 1,000 (Gillberg & Gillberg, 1989; Wing, 1990).

ETIOLOGY

Fotheringham (1991, p. 689) concludes that the core behavioral disorder in autism is "a disturbance of reciprocal social relations which [*sic*] is due to an information processing defect in assigning social-emotional value to stimuli. The constancy of the core behavioral signs of autism suggests a defined neurologic mechanism within the brain that is disrupted." Brain-related causative theories for autistic populations include deficits in the frontal or temporal lobes, amygdala, septal nuclei, corpus striatum, thalamus, and vestibular regions or gray matter (Reichler & Lee, 1987). Courchesene (1989) and Courchesene, Yeung-Courchesene, and Press (1988) suggest that cerebellar dysfunction is responsible for autism. Kinsbourne (1987) points to a disorder of the cerebral brain stem. Finally, Fein and colleagues (1987) maintain that the limbic system is most likely involved in this group of disorders. It may be that autism does not represent a single disorder but results from a variety of causes and represents a series of disorders with overlapping symptoms (Reichler & Lee, 1987).

In rare cases, environmental factors, such as infection (Chess,

Fernandez, & Korn, 1978), genetics (Rutter, 1970), or perinatal trauma (Deykin & McMahon, 1980) have been implicated. Although at one time it was suspected that this group of disorders was caused by cold and unemotional parents, research over the past 25 years has not confirmed this hypothesis (Cantwell, Baker, & Rutter, 1978; Gillberg & Coleman, 1993).

It is likely that genetic factors play a major role in autism with regard to risk and extent of problems (Ritvo et al., 1989). The prevalence of autism in siblings of autistic persons has been reported as just under 3% (MacDonald, Rutter, Rios, & Bolton, 1989; Smalley, Asarnow, & Spence, 1988); this is significantly higher than its occurrence in the general population. The rates of language delay and intellectual problems in first-degree relatives of autistic persons are also much higher than in controls (Bartak, Rutter, & Cox, 1975). In addition, MacDonald and colleagues (1989) found that 15% of siblings of autistic persons demonstrated learning disabilities and 12% experienced social problems.

Also significant is the incidence of identifiable medical conditions that may coexist with autism (Gillberg, 1988). Common conditions include fragile X syndrome (Hagerman, 1990), tuberous sclerosis (Gillberg & Steffenburg, 1987), neurofibromatosis (Gaffney, Kuperman, Tsai, & Minchin, 1988), rubella embryopathy (Wing, 1990), and Rett's disorder in females. Fragile X chromosome studies suggest there may be a linkage to autism, with approximately 5% of autistic persons carrying the fragile X chromosome (Bloomquist et al., 1985; Ho & Kalousek, 1989). Gillberg and Forsell (1984) found a relationship between neurofibromatosis and autism. A total of 3 in 51 autistic children experienced neurofibromatosis, a rate significantly higher than expected in the population.

Neurologic and central nervous system problems are reported in at least one third of all autistic persons (Cialdella & Mamelle, 1989); epilepsy is reported in 5% (Bryson, Clark, & Smith, 1988) to 33% (Gillberg & Steffenburg, 1987). Abnormal brain functioning as measured by electroencephalogram, visual and auditory evoked potentials, neuroimaging, and neuropsychological testing consistently has been found in a significant percentage of children and adults with autism (Hooper, Boyd, Hynd, & Rubin, 1993). At a neurostructural level, abnormalities in autistic persons have been found in the left hemisphere as well as the frontal and temporal regions of the brain (Gillberg & Svendsen, 1983).

Nonetheless, other researchers have not found clear localizable patterns of neurologic abnormality in this population. Autism, therefore, is best conceptualized as a behaviorally defined disorder with a wide array of underlying medical conditions. These problems do not occur randomly in autism, and thus are likely to be either the cause or consequence of the disorder.

Despite these associations, Rutter (1983) suggests that better assessment with regard to systematic and standardized observations and data collection will lead to lower association rates as clinicians become more proficient in accurately diagnosing autism and pervasive developmental disorders. This certainly speaks to the significant importance of providing a full and detailed neurodevelopmental assessment when autism or pervasive developmental disorders are suspected. Gillberg and Steffenburg (1987) also report that at least one in five persons with autism or pervasive developmental disorders appears to deteriorate in functioning at the time of puberty.

EVALUATION

Gillberg (1990) suggests that diagnosis of autism should include observations of severity, cognitive level, specific clinical traits, and associated medical conditions. However, with the exception of aberrations in language development and communication skills, there continues to be little agreement as to what neurobiologic, neurophysiologic, and neuropsychological features are consistently or differentially characteristic of the spectrum of autistic disorders (Hooper, Boyd, Hynd, & Rubin, 1993). Although some children with autism demonstrate evidence of lateralized dysfunction involving the left cerebral hemisphere, this is not an exclusive characteristic of the syndrome. For the time being, assessment of autism and pervasive developmental disorders must rely heavily on history and observed behavior. Given that children with Asperger's disorder usually do not demonstrate early symptomatic problems of sufficient severity to place them in clinical settings or to receive diagnoses, they are likely the most common autistic group to confront the practicing therapist.

The case presentation of a 12-year-old boy with a history of Asperger's Disorder provides a number of critical issues for therapists to consider when faced with a pattern of somewhat atypical, but previously unidentified or untreated, problems.

> John was referred by his classroom teacher due to a history of difficulty with socialization, problems with written work, and inattention. His family history was unremarkable for similar problems in any of John's six siblings. In fact, two older siblings were participating in gifted educational programming. His family history was also unremarkable for similar behavior in nieces, nephews, uncles, or aunts.
>
> John experienced separation anxiety at 2–3 years of age. His medical history was noted by difficulty in sleeping consistently through the night and poor appetite. Developmental milestones appeared to be reached within normal limits, but his parents indicated he reached them later than did his siblings. His motor skills were awkward.
>
> John's parents recalled that he was rather shy when he entered school. He eventually adjusted to school but continued to be on the periphery of social interaction. Academically, his basic rote skills seemed adequate in kindergarten and first grade. By fourth grade, however, he was experiencing difficulty with concept development and comprehension.
>
> Within the home and school settings, John was described as

exhibiting problems sustaining attention and responding appropriately to rewards, with restless and somewhat impulsive behavior. He had a number of odd interests. Teacher reports reflected a child who was perceived as having low self-esteem, being cooperative, and not demonstrating significant behavioral problems in the classroom. Socially, he was rarely accepted or in demand for activities. He was described as "quite sweet" but insecure and isolated. Cognitive assessment reflected lower average skills with good rote verbal ability (general information) but much weaker complex language skills (verbal reasoning). His fine motor skills (i.e., eye-hand coordination) were weak.

During assessment, John was mildly echolalic and would repeat his own statements at a low volume. Language skills were atypical and somewhat tangential. A mild degree of performance anxiety was observed. Habitual mannerisms included tapping on the desk, rubbing his hands, placing his fingers in his mouth, and contorting his body into somewhat odd positions.

Further neuropsychological assessment revealed John's excellent rote memory skills but markedly weaker ability to integrate, comprehend, and recall more complex verbal and visual information. Computerized tasks of sustained attention and ability to modulate impulsive responding reflected marked problems. John's simple reading and spelling skills appeared to be below average, and his mathematics ability was significantly weaker. Although he read with good awareness, phrasing, intonation, and language skill, he often did not appear to understand what he was reading. His mathematics scores reflected a lack of conceptual knowledge.

John appeared to possess a history of early separation anxiety, continued social problems, a temperamental quality reflecting difficulty warming up to others, a somewhat odd verbal and interpersonal style, a pattern of tic-like behaviors, intermittent echolalia, and some degree of passive-aggressive behavior. John appeared to worry and was more unhappy than others.

Diagnostically, these symptomatic problems appeared to reflect attention deficit disorder (ADD), oppositional defiance, avoidance, depression, anxiety, language, and learning problems. In combination, however, these factors appeared to fit the proposed diagnostic criteria for Asperger's disorder. (The Childhood Autism Rating Scale [CARS] [Schopler, Reichler, & Renner, 1988] and the Autism Behavior Checklist [Krug, Arrick, & Almond, 1978] may be the most useful observation scales to identify children who appear at risk for a diagnosis of autism or Asperger's disorder.)

TREATMENT

Although Rimland (1987) suggested that large doses of vitamin B_6 and magnesium might be helpful for autism, his data is inconclusive and unreplicated. The stimulant fenfluramine (Pondimin) was initially considered beneficial for this population (Campbell, 1988). Campbell, Perry, Small, and Green (1987) suggested that a variety of drugs may be helpful for symptomatic treatment of autistic problems, including disruptive behavior, overactivity, emotional outbursts, and anxiety. Based on my observation, many children with Asperger's Disorder also appear to experience concomitant symptoms of ADD that in many cases respond to stimulants. Overall, however, it has been demonstrated that although medication may help certain symptomatic problems, it does not lead to major changes for most children with autism or Asperger's disorder (Campbell, 1988).

Although intensive behavioral methods using operant conditioning (Lovaas, 1987) have been reported to be curative for many autistic children, they have never become popular. This method of treatment is likely to be unpopular because of its labor- and time-intensive nature. Critics of the Lovaas method contend young children entering these studies may have constituted a biased sample, identifying only a group with good prognosis for this type of treatment (Schopler & Meisobov,

1987). It appears that most autistic children are best helped through a specialized education program, focusing on both the development of cognitive skills and behavioral self-control (Rutter & Bartak, 1973).

As a result of special-education impetus and laws requiring the education of all children, school districts have developed specialized programs for autistic children. According to Le Couteur (1990), such programs focus on accurate assessment of the child's skills, involvement of parents to facilitate the generalization and learning process that occurs at school, and the use of successive behavioral approximations to make small changes that eventually lead to significant improvement.

To date, pervasive developmental disorders have no cure; we do not truly understand how persons afflicted with them, especially those who function at a higher level, progress as adults. Howlin and Rutter (1987) provide convincing evidence that a combination of school- and home-based behavioral interventions that involve behavior modification, reinforcement of small changes, emphasis on the development of language skills, and psychological support for the child's family all make a positive difference in the overall functioning of this population. However, a note of caution provided by Gillberg (1990) reminds us that although these programs yield encouraging data, they are not curative.

REFERENCES

American Psychiatric Association (1994). *Diagnostic and statistical manual of mental disorders* (4th ed.). Washington, DC: Author.

Baron-Cohen, S. (1989). The autistic child's theory of mind: A case of specific developmental delay. *Journal of Child Psychology and Psychiatry, 30,* 285–297.

Bartak, L., Rutter, M., & Cox, A. (1975). A comparative study of infantile autism and specific developmental receptive language disorder, I: The children. *British Journal of Psychiatry, 126,* 127–145.

Bloomquist, H. K., Bohman, M., Edvinsson, S. O., Gillberg, C., Gustavson, K. H., Holmgren, G., & Wahlstrom, J. (1985). Frequency of the fragile X syndrome in infantile autism: A Swedish multicentre study. *Clinical Genetics, 27,* 113–117.

Boucher, J. (1981). Memory for recent events in autistic children. *Journal of Autism and Developmental Disorders, 11,* 293–302.

Bryson, S. E., Clark, B. S., & Smith, I. M. (1988). First report of a Canadian epidemiologic study of autistic syndromes. *Journal of Child Psychology and Psychiatry, 29,* 443–445.

Campbell, M. (1988). Fenfluramine treatment in autism (annotation). *Journal of Child Psychology and Psychiatry, 29,* 1–10.

Campbell, M., Perry, R., Small, A. M., & Green, W.H. (1987). Overview of drug treatment in autism. In E. Schopler & G. B. Mesibov, (Eds.), *Neurobiological issues in autism.* New York: Plenum Press.

Cantwell, D., Baker, L., & Rutter, M. (1978). Family factor. In M. Rutter & E. Schopler (Eds.), *Autism: A reappraisal of concepts and treatment.* New York: Plenum Press.

Chess, S., Fernandez, P., & Korn, S. (1978). Behavioral consequences of congenital rubella. *Journal of Pediatrics, 92,* 662–703.

Cialdella, P., & Mamelle, N. (1989). An epidemiologic study of infantile autism in a French department (Rhone): A research note. *Journal of Child Psychology and Psychiatry and Allied Disciplines, 30,* 165–175.

Courchesne, E. (1989). Neuroanatomical systems involved in infantile autism: The implications of cerebellar abnormalities. In G. Dawson (Ed.), *Autism: Nature, diagnosis, and treatment.* New York: Guilford Press.

Courchesne, E., Yeung-Courchesne, B.A., & Press, G.A. (1988). Hypoplasia of cerebellar vermal lobules VI and VII in autism. *New England Journal of Medicine, 318,* 1349–1354.

Deykin, E. Y., & McMahon, B. (1980). Pregnancy, delivery and neonatal complications among autistic children. *American Journal of Diseases of Children, 134,* 860–864.

Fein, D., Pennington, B., Markowitz, P., Braverman, M., & Waterhouse, L. (1986). Toward a neuropsychological model of infantile autism: Are the social deficits primary? *Journal of the American Academy of Child Psychiatry, 25,* 198–212.

Fein, D., Pennington, B., & Waterhouse, L. (1987). Implications of social deficits in autism for neurological dysfunction. In E. Schopler & G. B. Mesibov (Eds.), *Neurobiological issues in autism.* New York: Plenum Press.

Fotheringham, J. B. (1991). Autism: Its primary psychological and neurological deficit. *Canadian Journal of Psychiatry, 36,* 686–692.

Gaffney, G. R., Kuperman, S., Tsai, L. Y., & Minchin, S. (1988). Morphological evidence for brainstem involvement in infantile autism. *Biological Psychiatry, 24,* 578–586.

Gillberg, C. (1986). Onset at age 14 of a typical autistic syndrome: A case report of a girl with herpes encephalitis. *Journal of Autism and Developmental Disorders, 16,* 569–575.

Gillberg, C. (1988). The neurobiology of infantile autism. *Journal of Child Psychology and Psychiatry, 29,* 257–266.

Gillberg, C. (1990). Autism and pervasive developmental disorders. *Journal of Child Psychology and Psychiatry, 31,* 99–119.

Gillberg, C., & Coleman, N. (1993). *Biology of the autistic syndromes* (2nd ed.). London: Cambridge University Press.

Gillberg, C., & Forsell, C. (1984). Childhood psychosis and neurofibromatosis—more than a coincidence. *Journal of Autism and Developmental Disorders, 14,* 1–9.

Gillberg, I. C., & Gillberg, C. (1989). Asperger syndrome—some epidemiologic considerations: A research note. *Journal of Child Psychology and Psychiatry, 30,* 630–638.

Gillberg, C., & Schaumann, H. (1982). Social class and infantile autism. *Journal of Autism and Developmental Disorders, 12,* 223–228.

Gillberg, C., & Steffenburg, S. (1987). Outcome and prognostic factors in infantile autism and similar conditions: A population-based study of 46 cases followed through puberty. *Journal of Autism and Developmental Disorders, 17,* 271–285.

Gillberg, C., & Svendsen, P. (1983). Childhood psychosis and computer tomography brain scan findings. *Journal of Autism and Developmental Disorders, 13,* 19–32.

Hagerman, R. (1990). Genes, chromosomes, and autism. In C. Gillberg (Ed.), *Autism: Diagnosis and treatment.* New York: Plenum Press.

Ho, H. H., & Kalousek, D. K. (1989). Brief report: Fragile X syndrome in autistic boys. *Journal of Autism and Developmental Disorders, 19,* 343–347.

Hobson, R. P. (1989). Beyond cognition: A theory of autism. In Dawson, G. (Ed.). *Autism: Nature, diagnosis, and treatment.* New York: Guilford Press.

Hooper, S. R., Boyd, T. A., Hynd, G. W., & Rubin, J. (1993). Definitional issues and neurobiological foundations of selected severe neurodevelopmental disorders. *Archives of Clinical Neuropsychology, 8,* 279–307.

Howlin, P., & Rutter, M. (1987). *Treatment of autistic children.* New York: John Wiley & Sons.

Kanner, L. (1943). Autistic disturbance of affective contact. *Nervous Child, 2,* 217–250.

Kinsbourne, M. (1987). *Cerebral-brainstem relations in infantile autism.* In E. Schopler & G. B. Mesibov (Eds.), *Neurobiological issues in autism.* New York: Plenum Press.

Kolvin, I. (1971). Psychoses in childhood—a comparative study. In M. Rutter (Ed.). *Infantile autism: Concepts, characteristics and treatment.* London: Churchill Livingstone.

Krug, D. A., Arrick, J. R., & Almond, P. J. (1978). *Autism behavior checklist.* Portland, OR: ASIEP.

Le Couteur, A. (1990). Autism: Current understanding and management. *British Journal of Hospital Medicine, 43,* 448–452.

Lotter, V. (1974). Factors related to outcome in autistic children. *Journal of Autism and Developmental Disorders, 4,* 263–277.

Lovaas, O. I. (1987). Behavioral treatment and normal educational and intellectual functioning in young autistic children. *Journal of Consulting and Clinical Psychology, 55*, 3–9.

MacDonald, H., Rutter, M., & Howlin, P. (1989). Recognition and expression of emotional cues by autistic and normal adults. *Journal of Child Psychology and Psychiatry, 30*, 865–878.

MacDonald, H., Rutter, M., Rios, P., & Bolton, P. (1989). *Cognitive and social abnormalities in first-degree relatives of autistic and Down's syndrome probands.* Paper presented at the First World Congress of Psychiatric Genetics, Churchill College, Cambridge, UK.

McCann, B. S. (1989). Hemispheric asymmetries and early infantile autism. *Journal of Autism and Developmental Disorders, 11*, 401–411.

Ornitz, E. M., & Ritvo, E. R. (1968). Perceptual inconsistency in early infantile autism. *Archives of General Psychiatry, 18*, 76–98.

Reichler, R. J., & Lee, E. M. C. (1987). Overview of biomedical issues in autism. In E. Schopler & G. B. Mesibov (Eds.), *Neurobiological issues in autism.* New York: Plenum Press.

Rimland, B. (1987). Megavitamin, B_6 and magnesium in the treatment of autistic children. In E. Schopler & G. B. Mesibov (Eds.), *Neurobiological issues in autism.* New York: Plenum Press.

Ritvo, E. R., Freeman, B. J., Pingree, C., Mason-Brothers, A., Jorde, L., Jenson, W. R., McMahon, W. M., Petersen, P. B., Mo, A., & Ritvo, A. (1989). The UCLA-University of Utah epidemiologic survey of autism: Prevalence. *American Journal of Psychiatry, 146*, 194–199.

Rutter, M. (1970). Autistic children: Infancy to adulthood. *Seminars in Psychiatry, 2*, 435–450.

Rutter, M. (1979). Language, cognition, and autism. In R. Katzman (Ed.), *Congenital and acquired cognitive disorders.* New York: Raven Press.

Rutter, M. (1983). Cognitive deficits in pathogenesis of autism. *Journal of Child Psychology and Psychiatry, 24*, 513–531.

Rutter, M., & Bartak, L. (1973). Special educational treatment of autistic children: A comparative study, II: Follow-up findings and implications for services. *Journal of Child Psychology and Psychiatry, 14*, 241–270.

Schopler, E., & Meisobov, G. B. (1987). *Neurobiological issues in autism.* New York: Plenum Press.

Schopler, E., Reichler, R. J., & Renner, B. R. (1988). *A childhood autism rating scale.* Los Angeles, CA: Western Psychological Services.

Smalley, S. L., Asarnow, R. F., & Spence, M. A. (1988). Autism and genetics: A decade of research. *Archives of General Psychiatry, 45,* 953-961.

Steffenburg, S., & Gillberg, C. (1986). Autism and autistic-like conditions in Swedish rural and urban areas: A population study. *British Journal of Psychiatry, 149,* 81-87.

Wing, L. (1981). Asperger's syndrome: A clinical account. *Psychological Medicine, 11,* 115-129.

Wing, L. (1990). Diagnosis of autism. In C. Gillberg (Ed.), *Autism: Diagnosis and treatment.* New York: Plenum Press.

Wing, L., & Gould, J. (1979). Severe impairments of social interaction and associated abnormalities in children: Epidemiology and classification. *Journal of Autism and Developmental Disorders, 9,* 129-137.

Wolff, S., & Barlow, A. (1979). Schizoid personality in childhood: A comparative study of schizoid, autistic, and normal children. *Journal of Child Psychology and Psychiatry, 20,* 19-46.

9

Parent Training for Children with Attention-Deficit/ Hyperactivity Disorder

Robert F. Newby, PhD, ABPP

Dr. Newby, a child neuropsychologist, is Associate Professor of Neurology, Medical College of Wisconsin, Milwaukee, WI.

KEY POINTS

- Symptoms of attention-deficit/ hyperactivity disorder (ADHD) include: inattention, impulsivity, and motor restlessness. The two most effective treatment approaches are behavior management and medication.
- Parent training serves the need for specific guided practice in behavior management.
- Most parent training concentrates on behavior management of childrens' problems with noncompliance and poor rule-governed behavior.
- Treatment goals include: increasing parents' knowledge of causes of children's behavior problems; improving parents' ability to manage these problems; and increasing children's compliance.
- Format of treatment is flexible, and it can be delivered in both the individual and group settings.
- Two crucial areas of parent training are building parent-child rapport and enhancing parents' attending skills.
- Behavior modification systems such as token economies are useful for supporting positive behaviors. Used consistently, time-outs are effective punitive measures for negative behaviors.

INTRODUCTION

Attention-deficit/hyperactivity disorder (ADHD), one of the most common problems facing mental health professionals who work with children today, affects approximately 5% of the school-age population (Barkley, 1990). Because the major symptoms—inattention, impulsivity, and motor restlessness—usually persist to some degree throughout childhood and adolescence despite treatment (Fischer, Barkley, Edelbrock, & Smallish, 1990), effective treatment for this disorder attempts to manage or ameliorate symptoms rather than to cure the core problems.

Behavior management and medication are the two treatment approaches that appear to have the most reliable impact on ADHD symptoms. Behavior management involves a broad set of methods such as structuring the physical environment, delivering commands, and planning behavioral consequences, with the goal of attaining what Barkley (1990) terms a "prosthetic social environment" in which to contain and direct ADHD symptoms. In order to have a significant impact in a given setting (such as home or school), behavior management methods must be applied directly and continuously in each environment. Stimulant medication can provide varying degrees of benefit for approximately three fourths of children with ADHD, and other classes of medication (e.g., antidepressants) sometimes help when stimulants are not effective. Other approaches such as cognitive-behavioral therapy have produced mixed results in research studies (Abikoff, 1991), but they may provide supplementary benefit in some cases.

Parent Training:

Parents of children with ADHD require information about the disorder itself, training in behavior management skills, and emotional support in dealing with the stress engendered by their children's behavioral problems. The need for specific guided practice in behavior management can be well-served through the format of parent training. The primary aim of this chapter is to familiarize professionals with the core elements of several prominent models for parent training that are applicable for ADHD children in the preschool through elementary school years. The parent-training approaches incorporated here are drawn from the programs of Barkley (1987, 1990), Patterson (1976, 1982), and Forehand and McMahon (1981). Although designed for noncompliant children in general rather than children with ADHD in particular, these programs are highly relevant for the problems with rule-governed behavior (Barkley, 1990) in the ADHD population. The references cited previously provide clear, detailed instructions for therapists who work with parents of children with ADHD, and they should be read by professionals who are serious about engaging in this work. These three programs have been outlined and reviewed concisely in a special issue of the *School Psychology Review* on ADHD (Newby, Fischer, & Roman, 1991). This chapter is organized around several core issues in parent training with ADHD, and is not an outline of the separate programs themselves.

DEFINITION AND DIAGNOSIS

The definition of ADHD has evolved gradually over the last several decades. The previous term, *minimal brain dysfunction*, was based on the inference that subtle neurological problems were the main cause of the disorder. In the 1960s and 1970s, child psychology and psychiatry reoriented toward diagnostic terms that provided essential descriptions of behavioral syndromes, rather than terms with etiological implications; as a consequence, the labels *hyperactivity* and *hyperkinetic syndrome* became prominent. Research in the 1970s suggested that attention problems were more ubiquitous and central in the syndrome than motor overactivity itself; therefore, the third edition of the *Diagnostic and Statistical Manual of Mental Disorders* (DSM-III) (American Psychiatric Association [APA], 1980) changed the label to *attention deficit disorder with hyperactivity*. A partial syndrome of attention deficit disorder *without* hyperactivity was also recognized at that time and was presumed to consist of inattention and impulsivity without prominent overactivity. More recently, attention deficit disorder without hyperactivity has been suspected to represent a different class of child psychopathology from ADHD. The diagnostic term was modified slightly to *attention-deficit hyperactivity disorder* in the revisions of DSM-III in the late 1980s (DSM-III-R) (APA, 1987) and mid-1990s (DSM-IV) (APA, 1994).

Clinicians who conduct parent training for ADHD should be familiar with three definitions of the disorder. It is appropriate to use all three definitions in some combination, both in selecting children who are appropriate for a certain treatment approach and in directly applying specific treatment methods.

Definition I:

Barkley (1990, p. 47) presented a conceptualization of ADHD that reflects current accepted clinical theory and research:

> Attention-deficit/ hyperactivity disorder is a developmental disorder characterized by developmentally inappropriate degrees of inattention, overactivity, and impulsivity. These often arise in early childhood; are relatively chronic in nature; and are not readily accounted for on the basis of gross neurological, sensory, language, or motor impairment, mental retardation, or severe emotional disturbance. These difficulties are typically associated with deficits in rule-governed behavior and in maintaining a consistent pattern of work performance over time.

Definition II:

Operational diagnostic criteria for ADHD are necessary in clinical practice. The most commonly accepted diagnostic criteria at present are drawn from DSM-IV, which are presented in Table 9.1.

Table 9.1
DIAGNOSTIC CRITERIA FOR ATTENTION-DEFICIT/HYPERACTIVITY DISORDER (ADHD) (DSM-IV)

A. Either (1) or (2):

1. six (or more) of the following symptoms of inattention have persisted for at least 6 months to a degree that is maladaptive and inconsistent with developmental level:

   Inattention

   (a) often fails to give close attention to details or makes careless mistakes in schoolwork, work, or other activities

   (b) often has difficulty sustaining attention in tasks or play activities

   (c) often does not seem to listen when spoken to directly

   (d) often does not follow through on instructions and fails to finish schoolwork, chores, or duties in the workplace (not due to oppositional behavior or failure to understand instructions)

   (e) often has difficulty organizing tasks and activities

   (f) often avoids, dislikes, or is reluctant to engage in tasks that require sustained mental effort (such as schoolwork or homework)

   (g) often loses things necessary for tasks or activities (e.g., toys, school assignments, pencils, books, or tools)

   (h) is often easily distracted by extraneous stimuli

   (i) is often forgetful in daily activities

Table 9.1
DIAGNOSTIC CRITERIA FOR ATTENTION-DEFICIT/HYPERACTIVITY DISORDER (ADHD) (DSM-IV)
CONTINUED

2. six (or more) of the following symptoms of hyperactivity-impulsivity have persisted for at least 6 months to a degree that is maladaptive and inconsistent with developmental level:

   Hyperactivity

   (a) often fidgets with hands or feet and squirms in seat

   (b) often leaves seat in classroom or in other situations in which remaining seated is expected

   (c) often runs about or climbs excessively in situations in which it is inappropriate (in adolescents or adults, may be limited to subjective feelings of restlessness)

   (d) often has difficulty playing or engaging in leisure activities quietly

   (e) often is "on the go" or often acts as if "driven by a motor"

   (f) often talks excessively

   Impulsivity

   (g) often blurts out answers before questions have been completed

   (h) often has difficulty awaiting turn

   (i) often interrupts or intrudes on others (e.g., butts into conversations or games)

B. Some hyperactive-impulsive or inattentive symptoms that caused impairment were present before age 7 years.

C. Some impairment from the symptoms is present in two or more settings (e.g., at school [or work] and at home).

D. There must be clear evidence of clinically significant impairment in social, academic, or occupational functioning.

E. The symptoms do not occur exclusively during the course of a Pervasive Developmental Disorder, Schizophrenia, or other Psychotic Disorder and are not better accounted for by another mental disorder (e.g., Mood Disorder, Anxiety Disorder, Dissociative Disorder, or a Personality Disorder).

Source: American Psychiatric Association. (1994). *Diagnostic and statistical manual of mental disorders* (4th ed.). Washington DC: Author. Copyright 1994 American Psychiatric Association. Reprinted with permission.

In clinical practice, the DSM-IV criteria are often supplemented with standardized behavior rating questionnaires by parents and teachers. In order to confirm a diagnosis of ADHD, inattention, impulsivity, and/or hyperactivity scales should show elevations greater than 1.5–2 standard deviations above normal population means. Commonly used questionnaires include the Conners Questionnaire (Conners, 1985) and the Child Behavior Checklist (Achenbach & Edelbrock, 1983, 1986).

Definition III:

Barkley (1990) presented another cutting-edge definition of ADHD, which is highly relevant to parent training models and is likely to influence future operational diagnostic schemes for the disorder:

> ADHD consists of developmental deficiencies in the regulation and maintenance of behavior by rules and consequences. These deficiencies give rise to problems with inhibiting, initiating, or sustaining responses to tasks or stimuli, and adhering to rules or instructions, particularly in situations where consequences for such behavior are delayed, weak, or nonexistent. The deficiencies are evident in early childhood and are probably chronic in nature. Although they may improve with

> neurological maturation, the deficits persist in comparison to same-age normal children, whose performance in these areas also improves with development.

Most parent training programs for ADHD focus on behavior management of children's problems with noncompliance and poor rule-governed behavior. This focus is consistent with the high prevalence of comorbid oppositional-defiant disorder or conduct disorder in the ADHD population. Clinicians should be aware that children with ADHD who also have prominent comorbid internalizing problems, such as anxiety or depressive disorders, may not respond ideally to a behavior management emphasis in parent training. The multiple problems of these children may be better addressed through individual or family psychotherapy, sometimes supplemented with the type of parent training outlined here.

Similarly, children with ADHD who have reached adolescence usually present complex developmental issues of emerging independence and may not respond favorably to the "top down" management style that is implicit in the behaviorally oriented parent-training approaches described herein. The needs of families with adolescents with ADHD are probably better addressed through pragmatically-oriented family methods that develop both parents' and adolescents' skills in negotiation and conflict resolution, such as the program of Robin and Foster (1989).

OUTLINE OF A TYPICAL PARENT-TRAINING SEQUENCE

As noted above, the ideas outlined here are integrated from other original sources. The general recommended treatment sequence and most of the specific content generally follow Barkley (1987), whose written handouts for parents represent excellent supplements to direct verbal instruction and demonstration of methods by the therapist.

Diagnostic Assessment:

Any parent-training intervention should be preceded by a careful assessment of the child, family, and environment. Most assessment procedures for ADHD involve some combination of parent interviews, child interviews, clinical observations, observations in naturalistic environments, parent- and teacher-completed behavior rating questionnaires, and/or direct psychological testing.

Treatment Goals:

The primary goals of parent training are: (a) increasing parents' knowledge of the causes of children's difficult behavior patterns, particularly in terms of relevant research on ADHD and social learning theory; (b) improving parents' skills in managing children's behavior problems; and thereby (c) increasing children's compliance with commands and rules.

Several core principles underlie the methods in parent training for ADHD. Among the most prominent of these principles is the importance of delivering immediate, specific, and consistent consequences to children's positive and negative behaviors. In addition, a strong emphasis is placed on interrupting what Patterson (1982) terms *coercive interaction* and *coercive escalation*. In coercive interaction, parents and children vie for control by, for instance, presenting aversive stimuli (e.g., the parent issuing a command, or the child arguing) then withdrawing the aversive stimuli (e.g., the parent not enforcing the command, or the child desisting the protest). In coercive escalation, more aversive stimuli are presented (e.g., the parent yelling and threatening), which lead to negative reinforcement of both noncompliance and aversive interactions.

Treatment Format:

There is considerable flexibility in choosing a treatment format for parent training. Forehand and McMahon (1981) worked with mother-child dyads in the clinic, with repeated demonstrations and guided practice in behavior management methods, often using two cotherapists. This approach represents an intensive, direct intervention into family interactions, which facilitates detailed feedback to parents and close monitoring of treatment compliance and progress. The program of Patterson (1982) typically involves six to eight sessions with parents from one family at a time, in a tutorial format with instruction, demonstration of techniques, and action homework assignments. The program of Barkley (1987, 1990) is often, but not necessarily, conducted in a group parent-training format, with approximately eight sessions with a group of parents from five to eight different families. The group format can provide extremely valuable social support among participants, many of whom feel socially isolated or even ostracized in their struggles with their children's ADHD behaviors. The group also enhances the program by eliciting spontaneous ideas on child management that are shared among parents and by encouraging treatment compliance as parents are asked to review their homework in the presence of other group members.

Building Parents' Knowledge Base:

Up to two sessions at the beginning of the parent training sequence can be devoted to increasing parents' understanding of ADHD, behavioral principles that influence parent-child interactions, and general child development. Details on the first two areas are available in Barkley (1990).

The therapist should present the following information on several aspects of ADHD: definition and diagnosis; commonly associated problems; prevalence; theories about etiology; prognosis; and commonly recommended treatment approaches. It is often useful to supplement direct discussion of ADHD in treatment sessions with handbooks written in understandable language (Gordon, 1991).

Parent-child interactions are presented as being determined by many different influences: child and parent factors, environmental factors, and situational consequences. The powerful influence of consequences on children's behavior patterns is emphasized, with particular attention paid to issues such as the importance of immediacy and consistency in behavior management consequences for children with ADHD. Several exercises that may be useful in eliciting parental contributions to this discussion include: asking the parents to list reasons why children misbehave; asking them to describe the characteristics of favorable and unfavorable employers for whom they have worked; and eliciting examples of typical sequences of behaviors surrounding commands between parents and children, in order to demonstrate the principles of coercive interactions and coercive escalations.

Many parents of ADHD children lack knowledge about typical child behavior patterns at different stages of development. This can lead to frustrating, unrealistic expectations regarding behavior control. Both at the beginning of the parent training sequence and at various relevant points throughout the training, it can be very helpful to educate parents about the degree and type of behavior control that they can expect from normal children in the age range with which they are working at home.

Building Parent-Child Rapport and Enhancing Parents' Attending Skills:

Barkley (1987) begins interactive training with parents by teaching them to practice paying attention to their children's positive behaviors in nondirective one-to-one special play times for 15–20 minutes daily. Parents are instructed to avoid questions and commands during these times, and to increase the variety and frequency of their attention toward their children's positive behaviors. For instance, they can practice joining in play activities chosen by the children, directly watching their children play without distracting thoughts about other matters, narrating the play activities out loud, and avoiding questions and commands.

Although the explicit purpose of this exercise is to increase parent attending skills, several other benefits often accrue at this critical junction early in the therapy. First, parents often rediscover a sense of rapport with their behaviorally-difficult children, because of the frequent positive interactions that they almost invariably experience during the special play times. Second, children often rediscover a personal sense of pleasure and value in their parents' attention toward them, which in many families of children with ADHD has become a largely negative, coercive interaction pattern. Third, parents learn to "turn on" and "turn off" their directive guidance roles, which increases their discretion and flexibility later in the program when they need to focus their own attention on carefully selected commands; this way, they avoid bombarding their children with an unrealistically high flood of commands. It is often helpful to emphasize to parents that this exercise is more for *them* than for their children, and to predict no particular behavioral benefits from this early step in the parent training process; when faced with such a prediction, they are often pleasantly surprised by changes in the rapport that evolves through the activity.

Delivering Commands:

Forehand and McMahon (1981) provided a particularly cogent analysis of the form of relatively successful parental commands (termed *alpha commands*). Alpha commands are more specific and direct, involve only one request at a time, and allow the child adequate time to enact the command before presenting other verbalizations. Behavioral parent-training methods emphasize that *consequences* for children's behavior can be powerful influences on behavior; therefore, work on command presentation helps with a secondary—but still very important—influence on behavior (i.e., its antecedents).

Barkley (1987) provides a pragmatic list of specific guidelines for command presentation: (a) select only those commands that are truly important or that the parent "really means," (b) phrase the command as a statement rather than a question or favor, (c) obtain the child's attention before delivering the command, and (d) give only one command at a time. Clinical training and practice in command presentation and/ or assignments to practice these methods at home represent an important step in parent training. Parents can benefit from this experience, as they learn that many behavioral methods *improve* compliance even if they do not *guarantee* it.

Developing Informal Social Reinforcement:

The parent-training programs discussed here vary widely—from emphasizing informal social reinforcement on the one hand, to formal token economy systems on the other. Because most parents of ADHD children do not take full advantage of their capacity to influence their children's behavior through informal praise and compliments, explicit training in this approach usually makes a significant impact on their success in gaining compliance regardless of the extent and type of formal systems that are employed. In addition, direct training in social reinforcement increases generalization and maintenance of desired behaviors when formal behavior modification systems are faded, or when the management systems are used inconsistently and/or are discontinued covertly by today's busy families. Working concertedly on informal social reinforcement before formal systems often helps parents become more willing to exert the vigilant effort that it takes to evolve their everyday interactions with their children toward more adaptive patterns, rather than believing that only contrived, formal methods can have a significant impact.

In this aspect of the training, parents must learn how to give praise frequently and immediately (with specific information about what is being praised) for partial or small behavioral successes as well as major behavioral goals. Parents should be taught not to include implicit or explicit criticisms in their compliments (e.g., "I'm glad to see that you did better cleaning up your room today than yesterday"). The positive feedback that parents begin to develop during special play times can be expanded by giving them lists of methods for increasing the variety as well as the frequency of their verbal and nonverbal praise. The use of praise can be diversified and expanded by having parents practice chains of commands interspersed with praise after each compliance, or by using shaping (gradually spacing out the timing of attention and praise) to reinforce children for independent play while the parent is occupied in some other activity such as talking on the phone.

Teaching Formal Behavior Modification Systems:

Virtually all parents of ADHD children can obtain modest to dramatic improvement in their children's behavior with token economy systems. The main advantages of formal systems involve their use of individually meaningful rewards (e.g., privileges) that can be delayed while the child accumulates concrete symbols of the rewards (e.g., tokens), as well as the attractive element of choice on the child's part (e.g., a menu of privileges on which to spend the tokens). The variety of techniques available are numerous; pragmatic, detailed outlines are available in Barkley (1987) and Patterson (1982).

Although their exact specifications are beyond the scope of this chapter, five general guidelines are worth emphasizing here. First, many parents can be convinced that the time and energy necessary to consistently apply a formal behavior modification system is worthwhile if the method is presented as a tool rather than a way of life. Explicit instruction about starting (with cooperative family meetings) and stopping (through deliberate fading rather than covert progressive disuse) these systems is essential. Second, some families respond best to an overarching system that includes many target behaviors, chores, and routines, whereas others cope better with more limited, partial systems (e.g., morning routine or mealtime behavior). Third, it is usually recommended that parents "sell" the system to their children by emphasizing that the system will give them credit for all the helpful things that they do at home, and by starting the system for at least the first week with credits for positive behaviors, then adding debits for negative behaviors later. Fourth, developmental cognitive considerations would suggest concrete tokens in small numbers for preschool and early elementary school children, versus point charts with larger, richer-appearing numbers for older children. Finally, many families are able to extend the influence of token economy systems to the school setting by working out a reliable, carefully targeted daily-behavior report card with the child's teacher; the incentives for obtaining positive ratings on the card are applied on the same day as soon as the child comes home from school.

Using Time-Out:

All three of the parent training programs detailed here use time-out from social reinforcement as the primary punishment method, but the specifics of the time-out procedures vary. Patterson (1982) advocates a physical barrier to contain the noncompliant child for a brief period of time (e.g., placing the child in a closed bathroom for several minutes), whereas Barkley (1987) uses a time-out chair where the parent remains in close enough physical proximity to the child to enforce a backup if the child violates the expectation that he or she stay in time-out (e.g., spanking or physically restraining the child if he or she gets out of the chair).

The main advantage of the physical barrier is that it precludes continued interactions between the parent and child during time-out, thereby minimizing coercive escalation. The time-out chair has the advantage of being the most popular punishment method in many schools and day care settings, so children are often familiar with this method.

As with token economy procedures, the specifics of an effective time-out procedure are beyond the scope of this lesson, and the reader is referred to Barkley (1987). However, several central principles can be highlighted briefly. First, the positive methods outlined above must be taught and used extensively before introducing punishment methods such as time-out. Parents can use their usual, familiar punishment procedures in the meantime, unless they are too severe or abusive. Second, because children with ADHD often present such a high frequency of problematic behaviors, parents should be instructed to pick only one or two target behaviors with which to punish with a time-out at first. Third, the complex time-out procedure must be broken into several steps for parents. Barkley (1987), for instance, separately considers the issues of how the child gets to the chair, where the chair should be placed, what needs to happen before the child is allowed to leave the chair, and how parents should reinforce the time-out procedure if the child leaves the chair without permission. Finally, parents need particularly strong support and encouragement from the therapist when first instituting this always-confrontational and often-dramatic procedure.

Unfortunately, most parents of children with ADHD have tried some version of time-out before entering treatment, usually in ways that undermine its effectiveness. Mistakes often include: talking to the child on the chair, not having effective backups if the child gets out of the chair, using a bedroom full of attractive toys, or using time-out inconsistently. Many parents confuse the central use of time-out as punishment (i.e., an aversive consequence designed to reduce the frequency or intensity of an undesirable behavior) with other important behavior management methods, such as containment of disruptive behavior or a cooling-off period when the child is upset. These alternative uses might allow the child to choose when to leave time-out, whereas a compliance-oriented time-out procedure would let the parent decide when time-out ends and would require the child to agree to fulfill the target command as soon as he or she leaves time-out. The common parental protest, "I've tried that before, and it doesn't work," must be met by emphasizing that the method must be used exactly to work successfully; there is no presumed magic in the mere use of the chair.

Managing Behavior in Public Places:

Barkley (1987) makes the pragmatic recommendation that

parents apply new behavior management methods in the home setting first, then expand to community settings. This approach takes advantage of the relative ease of establishing routines at home, and it helps make some of the more basic management skills automatic for parents before venturing into more complex environments in which a high degree of vigilance and anticipation of contingencies is required. Many parents find this step particularly compelling, because their children's behavior becomes especially problematic in public places, often constraining and limiting family activities.

Three basic steps are helpful for parents in managing their children's behavior in public places (Barkley, 1987). First, parents should establish, teach, and verbally review with their children a small number of key rules for each particular public place. For instance, the rules for a preschool child with ADHD in a grocery store might consist of "stay by me, don't touch, and walk." Second, an incentive system needs to be implemented to reward children for following the key rules. (In the grocery store, the child could receive a token at the end of each aisle for successful performance.) Third, parents should carefully plan a modified time-out procedure to be used in the public place when the child fails to follow the key rules to a major extent. Many parents are reluctant or embarrassed about the prospect of placing a disruptive, noisy child in time-out in a public place; however, they are often encouraged by the marked effectiveness of the method, and by the frequent finding that time-out can have the same impact with a shorter punishment period than at home.

HANDLING FUTURE BEHAVIORAL PROBLEMS

Children with ADHD will continue to present new types of behavioral problems as they develop and as situational demands change. It is helpful to teach parents a general model for troubleshooting future problems. An adaptive four-step process involves: (a) observing and specifying the problem behavior in detail, (b) formulating positive alternative behavior(s) that will represent the target of the behavioral intervention, (c) informally and/or formally reinforcing the positive alternative behavior as effectively as possible, and (d) introducing a punishment if the reinforcement approach yields weak or inconsistent results.

CONCLUSION

This chapter is intended to provide a general orientation on parent training for children with ADHD, and to offer pragmatic directions for the individual clinician to formulate a program that suits the needs of the client.

The wide variety of principles and methods in parent training for children with ADHD leaves many choices for the individual clinician. The effectiveness of these types of programs has been demonstrated in extensive research with noncompliant children in general, with positive but more limited research in ADHD populations in particular (Pisterman et al., 1989). The complex nature of many aspects of these behavior management programs, particularly the formal behavior modification procedures and the nuances of time-out, require study of the original references cited in this chapter.

REFERENCES

Abikoff, H. (1991). Cognitive training in ADHD children: Less to it than meets the eye. *Journal of Learning Disabilities, 24*, 205–209.

Achenbach, T. M., & Edelbrock, C. S. (1983). *Manual for the teacher report form and the child behavior profile.* Burlington, VT: University of Vermont, Department of Psychiatry.

Achenbach, T. M., & Edelbrock, C. S. (1986). *Manual for the child behavior checklist and revised child behavior profile.* Burlington, VT: University of Vermont, Department of Psychiatry.

American Psychiatric Association (1980). *Diagnostic and statistical manual of mental disorders* (2nd ed.). Washington, DC: Author.

American Psychiatric Association (1987). *Diagnostic and statistical manual of mental disorders* (3rd ed. rev.). Washington, DC: Author.

American Psychiatric Association. (1994). *Diagnostic and statistical manual of mental disorders* (4th ed.). Washington, DC: Author.

Barkley, R. A. (1987). *Defiant children: A clinician's manual for parent training.* New York: Guilford Press.

Barkley, R. A. (1990). *Attention-deficit/ hyperactivity disorder: A handbook for diagnosis and treatment.* New York: Guilford Press.

Conners, C. K. (1985). *The Conners rating scales: Instruments for the assessment of childhood psychopathology.* Unpublished manuscript, Children's Hospital National Medical Center, Washington, DC.

Fischer, M., Barkley, R. A., Edelbrock, C., & Smallish, L. (1990). The adolescent outcome of hyperactive children diagnosed by research criteria, II: Academic, attentional and neuropsychological status. *Journal of Consulting and Clinical Psychology, 58,* 580–588.

Forehand, R. L., & McMahon, R. J. (1981). *Helping the noncompliant child: A clinician's guide to parent training.* New York: Guilford Press.

Gordon, M. (1991). *ADHD/hyperactivity: A consumer's guide for parents and teachers.* DeWitt, NY: GSI Publications.

Newby, R. F., Fischer, M., & Roman, M.A. (1991). Parent training for families of children with ADHD. *School Psychology Review, 20,* 252–265.

Patterson, G. R. (1976). *Living with children: New methods for parents and teachers.* Champaign, IL: Research Press.

Patterson, G. R. (1982). *A social learning approach to family intervention: Vol. 3. Coercive family process.* Eugene, OR: Castalia.

Pisterman, S., McGrath, P., Firestone, P., Goodman, J. T., Webster, I., & Mallory, R. (1989). Outcome of parent-mediated treatment of preschoolers with attention deficit disorder with hyperactivity. *Journal of Consulting and Clinical Psychology, 57,* 628–635.

Robin, A. L., & Foster, S. (1989). *Negotiating parent-adolescent conflict.* New York: Guilford Press.

10

Teaching Self-Help Strategies to Manic Clients

Mary Ellen Copeland, MS, MA

Ms. Copeland is a mental health counselor and educator based in Brattleboro, VT.

KEY POINTS

- This chapter offers safe, noninvasive, inexpensive strategies for counselors to use in helping their manic clients (many of whom may be receiving mood-stabilizing medications) alleviate or eliminate manic episodes. Such strategies include: relaxation and stress reduction techniques, peer counseling, focusing, and journal writing.
- The counselor plays a key role in helping manic clients achieve long-term stability by: providing a safe space to discuss issues, helping them recognize that long-term stability is *their* responsibility, encouraging them to educate themselves about the disorder, offering strategies to reduce or prevent episodes, assisting them in developing a strong support system, and providing advice about medical treatment and healthy living habits.
- Issues that arise when working with manic clients are discussed, including: problematic behavior; alternating episodes of depression with episodes of mania; the normalcy, acceptability, and desirability of the early warning signs of mania; medication issues; seasonal patterns; increased clarity; embarrassment and guilt; and issues that present during and between manic episodes.

BACKGROUND INFORMATION

Although a substantial amount of information is available on the medical and clinical management of mania, it is difficult to find information about working with people who are manic, what a counselor can do to assist in relieving related problems, and self-help strategies to reduce the impact of a manic episode or help avoid one altogether. This chapter describes safe, noninvasive, inexpensive strategies that manic clients have found to be helpful in alleviating or eliminating manic episodes; it will not address medical treatment options.

Periods of mania and depression are experienced in what is commonly known as bipolar disorder or manic-depressive disorder. A client with this disorder experiences recurring, alternating—but not usually regular—cycles of severe mania and depression.

The following is a description of mania from a person who has experienced it:

> I couldn't stop—moving, talking, doing, thinking. I wanted to rest, but my body wouldn't let me. Firecrackers were going off in my brain. My bizarre actions—I didn't know they were bizarre—embarrassed my family and got me in serious trouble. I thought I could do anything. I spent money recklessly—money I didn't have. Everyone else seemed boring. I thought I knew everything. I felt so strong and creative. It seemed like fun then, but now it seems like a horror story. I'm so ashamed I can't face anyone.

The fourth edition of the *Diagnostic and Statistical Manual of Mental Disorders* (DSM-IV) (American Psychiatric Association, 1994, p. 332) describes a manic episode as:

> . . .a distinct period of abnormally and persistently elevated, expansive, or irritable mood, lasting at least 1 week (or any duration if hospitalization is necessary) . . . . during [which] three (or more) of the following symptoms have persisted (four if the mood is only irritable) and have been present to a significant degree:

(1) inflated self-esteem or grandiosity

(2) decreased need for sleep (e.g., feels rested after only 3 hours of sleep)

(3) more talkative than usual or feels pressure to keep talking

(4) flight of ideas or subjective experience that thoughts are racing

(5) distractibility (i.e., attention too easily drawn to unimportant or irrelevant external stimuli)

(6) increase in goal-directed activity (either socially, at work or school, or sexually) or psychomotor agitation

(7) excessive involvement in pleasurable activities that have high potential for painful consequences (e.g., engaging in unrestrained buying sprees, sexual indiscretions, or foolish business investments)

When a client experiences a manic phase or shows signs of approaching a manic phase, symptoms that interfere with his or her normal level of functioning need to be addressed and minimized in a safe and effective manner.

Manic clients may become difficult to work with for several reasons:

- Their behavior may be problematic.
- They may be rude, argumentative, unreasonable, grandiose, and impatient.
- Clients who experience mania also experience alternating moods of deep, protracted, and even suicidal depression.

This is so painful and debilitating that the signs of mania often are seen as a welcome relief from the depressive period. Those who experience these extreme mood cycles may be resistant to or avoid using strategies that might help alleviate symptoms; they may become angry and defensive when confronted about behaviors that might indicate the onset of an episode.

- Many early warning signs of mania are quite normal, acceptable, and, in fact, desired behaviors in most people.

Examples include feelings of confidence, creativity, enthusiasm, sociability, energy, and productivity. It is difficult to know when intervention strategies are appropriate. Family members, friends, and supporters may alienate or anger the person by suggesting that particular behaviors are inappropriate.

Counselors might prefer to avoid treating clients who experience mania. However, once the counselor learns the necessary skills to help alleviate what are often very painful and debilitating symptoms, the work can be extremely rewarding. This chapter will discuss a number of excellent self-help strategies that can be taught to clients to help minimize the effects of mania.

WORKING WITH CLIENTS BETWEEN EPISODES OF MANIA

Responsibility:

It is important to work with manic clients *between* episodes to help them understand that managing their actions while manic is their responsibility, even though the mania is not their fault. A thorough discussion of what happened during previous manic episodes and the consequences of those behaviors can help enhance the client's resolve to prevent further episodes. However, it is important that the counselor not adopt a blaming or judgmental stance toward the client's actions. Clients need to know that through careful, intensive work, another episode can be avoided or at least dealt with more appropriately. In my clinical study (Copeland, 1992), I found that those who clearly took responsibility for their own wellness, did not expect someone else to fix them, and did not blame their problems on anyone else, are those who experienced the highest levels and longest periods of stability.

Taking responsibility for one's own recovery includes regular contact with health care professionals who provide information and advice on avoiding episodes. Decisions concerning treatment must be made on an individual basis with the manic client and his or her chosen medical care professionals. However, anyone who experiences mania needs to have regular, complete physical examinations to identify any of the medical problems that can cause or worsen mania.

Education:

Participants in the studies I have conducted have emphasized that understanding mania is essential to controlling it. They use the time between episodes to study available educational resources and to attend meetings, seminars, and support groups to increase their understanding of their problem. The counselor should read local newspapers and other periodicals for notices of appropriate meetings and seminars. If no support group exists in your area, assist and support the client in establishing one. An extensive list of resources is available in *The Depression Workbook: A Guide to Living with Depression and Manic Depression* (Copeland, 1992).

Planning:

For clients who have experienced one or more episodes of mania, it is essential to help them make plans and decisions about treatment if they have another episode and become unable to make decisions for themselves. Based on what the person has learned through the educational process, decisions can be made in advance about such issues as the types of treatment that are acceptable, under what conditions acceptable treatments may be used, which health care professionals should be included in the decision-making process, and which health care facilities are appropriate. A trusted person can be given durable power of attorney to make decisions, and a legal document can be drafted that defines the conditions under which that person has the right to make decisions. Sample chart 10.1 (p. 232) presents an example of a statement of intent.

While the manic person is stable, he or she also can make decisions aimed at alleviating the aftereffects of the episode. For example:

> If I am manic, I will avoid
>
> ______________________________
>
> (people, places, activities) that are stimulating and troublesome.
>
> If I am manic, I want
>
> ______________________________
>
> (name of person) to take my credit cards, check book, and car keys.

Establishing a Support System:

A strong, consistent support system of people who are knowledgeable about mood disorders is an absolutely essential component of the recovery process for anyone who experiences mania. A person should have a support system of at least five people (preferably more) who are chosen by the client and are willing to work with the client to monitor symptoms, provide feedback, give assistance in decision making, offer advice, and listen in a nonjudgmental fashion.

Counselors can be of assistance in establishing the client's support team. Explore with the client ideas about those with whom they are most comfortable, whom they consider to be their best friends. This can include family members, friends, and health care providers. These people should be contacted and asked if they are willing to serve in this capacity. The names and phone numbers of supporters should be listed by the telephone for easy access.

The next step is to hold a meeting of the support team with the client. At this meeting, the client explains what he or she wants from the support team, which symptoms indicate that the client might be having an episode, what action the person wants the members of the support team to take, and which treatment strategies are acceptable. Members of the support system should have each others' telephone numbers and the numbers of health care providers so that they can coordinate efforts if necessary. Meetings of the support team should be held on a regular basis, perhaps once a month, and more frequently when the client is having a difficult time.

Clients who have a long history of mood instability often are abandoned by family members and friends. Thus, identifying people who are willing to be supportive may be difficult. In this case, the counselor must be understanding and encourage involvement in support groups and other activities from which their clients can build support. Building and keeping a strong support system is an ongoing process.

Watching for Early Warning Signs:

The manic client must be vigilant in watching for early signs of mania (see Table 10.1), but not so vigilant that this becomes an obsession. It is important to help the client discern his or her own early warning signs that signal an impending manic episode. These early warning signs vary among persons, so this work must be performed on an individual basis.

It is quite useful for clients to develop a daily warning signs

Table 10.1
POSSIBLE EARLY WARNING SIGNS OF MANIA

Insomnia	Noises sound louder than usual	Obsessiveness
Surges of energy	Inappropriate behavior	Unusual outbursts of enthusiasm
Flight of ideas	Thrill seeking	Doing several things at once
Making lots of plans	Increased sexual activity	Anxiety
Inappropriate anger	Negligent driving	Excessive self-involvement
Restlessness	Itching	Disorganization
Loss of appetite	Feeling flushed and hot	Greater sensitivity than usual
Increased appetite	Sleeping much less than usual	Bizarre ideas and thoughts
Feelings of superiority	Others seem to be in slow motion	Poor judgment
Overambition	Irritability	Increased alcohol or tobacco use
Assuming too much responsibility	Spending too much money	Tingly feelings
Nervousness	Hyperactivity	
Inability to concentrate	Euphoria	
Outbursts of temper		
Feelings of being unreal		

chart (Sample chart 10.2, p. 233) so that they can identify impending signs of a manic episode. Such record-keeping activity also provides a daily record of clients' emotions. If a symptom recurs over several days, they will be able to take preventive actions. Sample chart 10.3 (p. 234) illustrates a blank daily warning signs chart that can be photocopied for clients. Before the blank chart has been used, make an ample supply of copies for weekly use. These charts can provide valuable information for physicians and counselors in determining appropriate treatment.

TAKING ACTION

If the client notes that he or she is experiencing signs of mania that are rather intense for one day or milder for several days, he or she may want to take action (Table 10. 2). The first step is for the client to contact health care providers and support-

Table 10.2
WHAT TO DO WHEN YOU ARE BECOMING MANIC

- Obtain help and put protective systems in place before things get out of control.
- Use your support system. Let members of that system know how you are feeling. Talk for as long as needed with supportive friends, expressing all emotions that arise.
- Stay at home or in familiar surroundings. Avoid overstimulating environments such as bars.
- Reduce the stress in your environment. Steer clear of stressful people.
- Write down a list of things to do for the day and stick to it.
- Regulate your activities to avoid overstimulation. Restrict yourself to activities that are quiet and soothing, such as a long, slow walk; a long, warm bath; or a relaxing swim. Sit for a while in a steam room or hot tub; listen to quiet music; read a soothing book; watch a nature show on television.
- Keep a list of things you can do to use up excess energy like washing the floor, weeding the garden, painting, cleaning the closets, etc. But make sure they are not overstimulating.
- Practice relaxation techniques several times a day.
- Avoid sugar, caffeine, and alcohol. Eat regular meals; do not skip meals. Do not eat too much of any one thing.
- Do not make any major decisions until you feel calm.
- Do not commit yourself to extra activities.
- Avoid spending money. Give your credit cards and money to a trusted support person.
- Regularly stop what you are doing, bring your focus to yourself, and ask yourself how you are doing. Keep your mind focused on what you are doing. Don't allow your thoughts to ramble or become excessive.
- If all of your relaxation techniques are not working to put you to sleep, and you are not sleeping, seek help from a physician immediately. Loss of sleep exacerbates mania.
- If you become uncontrollably agitated, see your health care provider immediately.

team members, to let them know what is happening, ask them for advice, and set up appointments. If the person is uncomfortable with what is happening, he or she may request an emergency visit with a health care professional or with members of the support team.

Table 10.3
Techniques To Alleviate Early Warning Signs of Mania

Activities

Mild exercise—a slow walk or any kind of exercise done slowly and thoughtfully

Yoga

Reading that is pleasurable but not overstimulating

Listening to classical or "easy" music

Deliberate, warm baths

Gardening

Various crafts such as needlework, woodworking, pottery, drawing, painting

Relaxing in a meditative natural setting

Playing a musical instrument

Writing in a journal

Support

Talking with an understanding person

Receiving emotional support from a trustworthy person

Talking to a counselor

Attending a support group

Peer counseling

Clients have found a variety of techniques useful in alleviating the early warning signs of mania (Table 10.3). Some of my clients have told me that, by using these techniques, they have avoided an episode.

The following subcategories describe in more detail relaxation and stress reduction techniques, peer counseling, focusing, and journaling. All of these strategies are simple, safe, and inexpensive. Depending on the person and situation, they range from being somewhat effective to completely effective in controlling symptoms of mania.

Relaxation and Stress Reduction Techniques:

Relaxation and stress reduction techniques have been used successfully to interrupt and eliminate early signs of mania. However, they cannot be learned when a person is already experiencing symptoms; they must be learned when a person is feeling well and stable. They need to be practiced at least twice a day for a total of 10–30 minutes daily. When a client is experiencing early warning signs of mania, he or she should increase the number of times a day these techniques are practiced.

Relaxation and stress reduction techniques can be learned at classes that are sponsored by hospitals or health care agencies. If such a course is not available, these techniques can be learned by watching instructional videos that are available at many libraries. There are also many self-help books that include instructions for relaxation and stress reduction, including *The Depression Workbook* (Copeland, 1992), *Living Without Depression and Manic Depression* (Copeland, 1993), and *The Relaxation and Stress Reduction Workbook* (Davis, Eschelman, & McKay, 1988).

Audiotapes designed as guidance for relaxation techniques often can be purchased at a local health food store. Counselors themselves can make these tapes by taping a relaxation exercise from a book or developing an exercise that meets the needs of a specific client. When the client is beginning to experience signs of mania, it may be difficult to do these exercises without such an audiotape as a guide.

Peer Counseling:

Peer counseling, also known as exchange counseling or co-counseling, also can be used successfully to manage symptoms of mania. Again, this is a strategy that needs to be learned and practiced regularly in order to be effective. The dynamics of this method involve two people who trust each other and agree to pay attention for equal time to each others' issues, needs, distress, or whatever is appropriate at that time. (Sessions involving three people or groups have also been found to be effective.) These two people meet for a predetermined length of time. Each person spends a portion of the time as the "counselor"—paying attention, listening, and supporting the client who is sharing information; he or she then spends an equal amount of time as the "client." Criticism, judgments, and negative reactions are not permitted.

The basic assumption of this type of counseling is that distress (which manifests as depression, mania, mood instability, sadness, anxiety, fear, embarrassment, guilt, shame, low self-esteem, and lack of self-confidence, among other things) is caused by past experience, hurtful feelings, trauma, and misinformation. Through the peer counseling process, the distress is explored, tested for reality, and discharged, which puts the information into a much-needed new context.

Peer counseling sessions can be set up on a schedule to meet the needs of those involved. It may be daily, weekly, or on an irregular schedule. Although many sessions last an hour, it is possible to be productive in a session that lasts only 5–10 minutes. Occasionally, clients feel the need for an intensive session in which they co-counsel for a longer period—a day or more—with different counselors, taking turns giving and receiving attention. I recommend that clients try peer counseling—it's free, it can be very beneficial, and each person gets time to talk and listen.

Focusing:

Focusing is an experiential therapy technique that has been found by some to be particularly useful in alleviating symptoms of mania. It helps clients understand why they are feeling manic and discover what they can do about it; this can cause a dramatic change in the way they feel. Focusing should be learned and practiced when the client is feeling well so that it can be helpful when they are experiencing problems. See Gendlin (1988) for examples of focusing exercises. These questions can be read to the client by a counselor or supportive friend, or they can be recorded on a tape and played back as needed.

Journal writing:

Journal writing can be a very powerful tool for dealing with mania and mood instability. According to Adams (1990),

> In moments of ecstasy, in moments of despair, the journal remains an impassive, silent friend, forever ready to coach, to confront, to critique, to console. Its potential as a tool for holistic mental health is unsurpassed.

The kind of deep inner exploration and evaluation that the journal-writing process encourages is an invaluable asset to a person who is trying to maintain stability while having symptoms of mania. The process of recording feelings on paper is relaxing in itself.

Journal writing is as easy as buying an inexpensive notebook and starting to write. The client can write whatever he or she wants; it does not necessarily have to be logical. Those who write in a journal do not have to worry about punctuation, grammar, spelling, or neatness. Whatever is written is for the value of the writer. Choosing to share writings is a personal choice, and the privacy of the journal should not be violated. It helps to set aside a time every day for journal writing. A person can spend as little or as much time journaling as he or she wants.

STRESS AND TRAUMA

The onset of a manic episode often is preceded by periods of stress or trauma. Counselors must be vigilant, helping the client implement self-help strategies, support, and stress reduction techniques when he or she is experiencing excessive stress or has had a traumatic experience. At these times, the counselor or members of the support system may need to play more active roles, advocating for the client, helping him or her make necessary life changes, assisting in the decision-making process, and providing understanding and companionship.

Some clients have found working through a wellness program specifically designed for those with posttraumatic stress disorder (PTSD) or working with a counselor who specializes in PTSD treatment to be helpful. An outline of such a wellness program can be found in *I Can't Get Over It* (Mastsakis, 1992).

WORKING WITH A PERSON WHO IS EXPERIENCING MANIA

When a client is clearly in the throes of a manic episode, counselors need to help him or her use the strategies that were planned for use in such an event.

- Refer to the planning section in this chapter on acceptable strategies and treatments.

- In consultation with other members of the support system, assist the person in implementing these strategies.

This is usually very difficult and will take a lot of time, great patience, and perseverance. But the reward of a person successfully working through an episode with little aftereffects is well worth the effort.

- Set up a system so that support team members can spend time with the person on a rotating basis, listening and sharing activities.

- One person on the support team should be responsible for scheduling this time. Listening, even when what the person is saying is not true or does not make sense, helps to diffuse difficult situations. It is not necessary to correct information or inconsistencies. Just stay with them, listen to them, and let them talk it through. Allow them to express as much emotion as they need.

- Emphasize to support-team members that during a manic episode, they will have to meet more often to coordinate efforts.

- Help the manic client avoid overstimulating situations, places and activities, and substances such as drugs and alcohol. Remind him or her that this is not an appropriate time to make major life decisions such as leaving a spouse, moving, or leaving a job.

Planning the Day:

It can help manic clients stay focused and in control if, in the morning, the counselor or a member of the support team helps them make a plan for the day or that part of the day that is most difficult. For instance, a person may work from 9 a.m.–5 p.m. (Because mania usually accelerates later in the day, working is often possible.) From 5 p.m.–6 p.m., they might take a walk with a member of the support team. From 6 p.m.–7 p.m., they might have dinner with another member of the support team followed by a 1-hour peer counseling session from 7 p.m.–8 p.m. From 8 p.m.–10 p.m., they might watch a video with a member of the support team. From 10 p.m.–11 p.m., they might work on a creative project such as writing or art. From 11 p.m.–midnight, they might read a novel. This would be followed by a session of relaxation exercises for 30 minutes to help them get to sleep. If the person is not working, the day's schedule could be filled with a variety of activities such as sports, writing, art or craft activities, household chores, and/or gardening.

The client probably will not be able to adhere to the plan in its entirety, and should not be chastised if this is the case. However, the plan will still prove useful as a guideline.

HOW CLIENTS WANT TO BE TREATED DURING A MANIC EPISODE

When a client is manic and his or her behavior is considered to be inappropriate, others tend to react by being angry, overbearing, overpowering, patronizing, and/or condescending. In fact, this kind of treatment exacerbates the mania. When clients are experiencing mania, it is common to have others tell them to "slow down," "relax," "stop moving," or "take it easy." They cannot. Forcing them to do so would be very painful and detrimental to the healing process. Try and provide them with an appropriate place where they can move as much as they need to.

Manic clients should be treated with respect, understanding, and compassion; they respond best when treated in this fashion. Through my research with manic clients, I found that they did *not* want to feel abandoned, avoided, blamed, teased, patronized, rebuffed, and/or stigmatized. They stressed that they also disliked being treated with fear, anger, disgust, exasperation, terse behavior, hatred, and/or impatience.

Counselors need to be aware that they can make manic clients unproductively rebellious by:

- Using the terms *compliance* and *noncompliance,* which can be disempowering, as they imply that someone else has control over the decision-making process

- Making long-term projections—telling manic clients that they will have to deal with (and undergo treatments for) mania for the rest of their lives can make them actually deny that the problem exists and impedes working toward stability

Often, clients who experience severe symptoms of mania are forcibly restrained. The justification for this is that it is for their safety or because they are unmanageable. However, restraining a person in this condition is very punitive and painful. Clients who have been forcibly restrained say that the damage to one's sense of self is irreparable. The alternative to restraint is providing a safe space where clients can pace, talk, laugh, cry, get angry, work on projects, listen to music, etc., with compassionate supervision until the episode subsides. Unfortunately, few safe spaces exist. Supporters may have to be innovative to provide this kind of care.

THE VARIOUS FACETS OF MANIA

Psychosis:

The clients who participated in my study often reported that they experienced psychosis when they were manic. If a person is psychotic, they are out of touch with reality and out of their own control. Someone or several people need to be with the person at all times in a safe place. Reassurance, compassion, and protection are essential at this time. Health care providers must be contacted. Hospitalization may be required if the person presents a danger to self or others.

Increased Clarity:

Many clients who experience mania report an increased clarity as one of the symptoms. Some clients have found ways to use this clarity to their advantage without exacerbating the mania. They may catch up on chores and projects that they have previously found to be very difficult. They may write or express themselves through various artistic media.

Increase in Intensity of Mania Relative to the Time of Day:

Most manic clients experience an increase in the intensity of mania as the day progresses. People may work from 9 a.m.–5 p.m. or may be involved in their usual activities during the day. As evening approaches, the mania often becomes more intense, interfering with activities and sleep. They learn to plan their activities accordingly; in the evening, it is best to spend time with supporters or become involved in activities such as peer counseling, art work, woodworking, journal writing, and so on.

Seasonal Patterns:

Some clients note a seasonal pattern to their manic episodes. Spring was the season in which the majority of the clients in my study reported that they are most likely to experience episodes of mania; summer was the second most common season, and autumn was the third. Only a few said they experienced mania mainly in the winter. Obviously, those who notice a seasonal pattern to mania should be more vigilant in self-management at those times of the year.

Embarrassment and Guilt:

Many manic clients have an extremely difficult time dealing with the embarrassment and guilt that often follows an acute manic attack. It takes extensive counseling (including peer counseling) and support to work through these issues. Once the mania subsides and the person becomes aware of things he or she has done, he or she often withdraws, becomes very reclusive, and may even lapse into a major depressive episode. Others in his or her life, especially members of the support team, are so glad the client is no longer manic that they ignore the depression. Those who are committed to being part of another person's support system need to maintain this relationship after the mania subsides, encouraging and supporting the person in the process of recovery and letting go of the negative aspects of mania. Suicide can be a real danger at this time.

Medication Issues:

Many people who experience recurring episodes of mania use mood-stabilizing medications (e.g., lithium [Eskalith, Lithane], carbamazepine [Tegretol], or valproic acid [Depakene, Depakote]) prescribed by a physician to help avoid or reduce symptoms of mania. Clients who educate themselves about their medication (and thus can be more knowledgeable about and involved in the decision-making process) tend to take their medication as prescribed and consult their physician for instructions and advice about medication changes, especially if these decisions are made before a manic episode.

Counselors should be informed about medications taken by their clients. Indeed, the more counselors know about the medications and their side effects, the more helpful and supportive they can be to their clients. Counselors can be instrumental in encouraging clients to educate themselves about their medications, follow medication protocol, and take medications as prescribed. Sample chart 10.4 (p. 235) presents a form that clients can use to guide them in asking their physician questions about medication.

Clients may decide not to take medications because they are experiencing or fear experiencing short- and long-term side effects. Such fears should be respected; however, they can be reduced through self-education and other measures. Persons who take medications report that side effects can be minimized by a healthy daily routine that includes three nutritious high-complex carbohydrate meals, plenty of fluids, 30 minutes of exercise (preferably outdoors), adequate sleep, and daily use of relaxation techniques. This type of routine also can prevent weight gain associated with some medications. In addition, taking a fiber supplement can help to alleviate constipation, a side effect associated with certain medications, especially tricyclic antidepressants; however, it is always wise to consult the prescribing physician if such side effects occur.

Believe it or not, some clients may decide not to take their medication because they enjoy manic episodes. In such cases, the counselor should be available to discuss all aspects of the medication issue(s) and should consider clients' views objectively. Advise clients to always consult the prescribing physician before making any medication changes. Reminding clients of any disastrous results of previous manic episodes—without being judgmental—is also a helpful method for encouraging them to take prescribed medications.

CONCLUSION

Counselors play a key role in helping clients who experience episodes of mania to achieve long-term stability by:

- Giving them a safe place to discuss issues in a nonadversarial way
- Helping them understand that long-term stability—and their actions while they are manic—are *their* responsibility
- Encouraging them to educate themselves about the disorder
- Helping them plan and use strategies that can prevent manic episodes and/or reduce symptoms
- Assisting them in developing a strong support system
- Providing support and advice regarding medical treatment and healthy living habits

In short, the counselor is an essential, valuable part of the manic client's overall wellness program.

REFERENCES

Adams, K. (1990). *Journal to the self.* New York: Warner Books.

American Psychiatric Association. (1994). *Diagnostic and statistical manual of mental disorders* (4th ed.). Washington, DC: Author.

Copeland, M. E. (1992). *The depression workbook: A guide to living with depression and manic depression.* Oakland, CA: New Harbinger Publications.

Copeland, M. E. (1993). *Living without depression and manic depression.* Oakland, CA: New Harbinger Publications.

Davis, M., Eschelman, E. R., & McKay, M. (1988). *The relaxation and stress reduction workbook.* Oakland, CA: New Harbinger Publications.

Gendlin, E. (1988). *Focusing.* New York: Bantam.

Mastsakis, A. (1992). *I can't get over it.* Oakland, CA: New Harbinger Publications.

FOR FURTHER READING

Belmaker, R. & van Praag, H. M. (1980). *Mania: An evolving concept.* New York: Spectrum Publications.

Davis, L. (1990). *The courage to heal workbook.* New York: Harper & Row.

Goodwin, F., & Jamison, K. R. (1980). *Manic-depressive illness.* New York: Oxford University Press.

Jamison, K. R. (1995). *An unquiet mind.* New York: Knopf.

Sample Chart 10.1
Statement of Intent

I, ________________________________ (name) give the following people permission to make decisions on my behalf when I am not able to make decisions for myself.

1) ____

2) ____

3) ____

The following paragraph describes those behaviors that would indicate that I am not able to make decisions for myself:

Acceptable treatment options:

Unacceptable treatment options:

Acceptable facilities if hospitalization is necessary:

Unacceptable hospital facilities:

Signed ______________________________ Date ______________

Witness ______________________________ Date ______________

Witness ______________________________ Date ______________

Sample Chart 10.2
Daily Warning Signs Chart for Mania

I will be honest with myself in this assessment. If I note that I am showing signs of mania, I will contact my support system. I will take corrective action that I have learned or that is recommended by others.

Week of _______	*Sun*	*Mon*	*Tues*	*Wed*	*Thurs*	*Fri*	*Sat*
Symptoms							
Insomnia							
Restlessness							
Hyperactivity							
Obsessiveness							
Irritability							
Tingly feelings							
Disorganization							
Poor judgment							
Loss of appetite							
Thrill-seeking							
Overspending							
Anxiety							
Racing thoughts							

This chart may also record information such as:

I ate well
(High-carbohydrate,
low protein and fat diet)

I exercised

I took good care of myself

I spent time with supportive persons

I checked in with my support system

Medications taken:

Appointments with health care professionals:

Sample Chart 10.3
PERSONAL DAILY WARNING SIGNS CHART FOR MANIA

This is a blank chart that can be photocopied for clients. Before it has been used for the first time, make an ample supply of copies for weekly use.

Week of________	*Sun*	*Mon*	*Tues*	*Wed*	*Thurs*	*Fri*	*Sat*
Symptoms							
Daily activities							
Medications taken							
Appointments with health care providers							
Necessary actions							

Sample Chart 10.4
Questions to Ask Physicians About Medication

Drug name (generic):

Proprietary/brand name:

Class of drug:

Suggested dosage level:

How does this medication work?

What do you expect it to do?

How long will it take to achieve the result(s)?

What risks are associated with this medication?

How effective is this medication?

What are its short-term side effects?

What are its long-term side effects?

Can side effects be minimized? If so, how?

Are there any dietary or lifestyle changes or restrictions that should be implemented while taking this drug?

Why do you recommend this particular medication?

Have you had other patients that have used this medication? If so, how have they done?

How is this medication monitored?

What tests are required prior to taking this medication?

What symptoms indicate that the dosage should be altered or the medication stopped altogether?

Do you have any printed information on this medication that I can review?

Where can I obtain more information about this medication?

11

Self-Management Approaches for Seriously Mentally Ill Persons

Alex Kopelowicz, MD, and Robert Paul Liberman, MD

Dr. Kopelowicz, a NIMH Postdoctoral Research Fellow at UCLA School of Medicine, is Medical Director of the San Fernando Mental Health Center. Dr. Liberman is Professor of Psychiatry at UCLA School of Medicine, Director of the Clinical Research Center for Schizophrenia & Psychiatric Rehabilitation, and Director of the Clinical Research Unit at Camarillo State Hospital.

KEY POINTS

- The technology for training seriously mentally ill patients to assume self-management of their mental disorders is in its infancy, but progress has already been made that needs to be disseminated and used by other practitioners.
- This drive for patient self-management is rooted in consumerism and the self-help movement; the primary goal is to find ways to make patients more active participants in their own treatment.
- Skills training is an integral component of self-management.
- This chapter describes two modules, Medication Management and Symptom Management, that are designed to compensate for the cognitive and symptomatic obstacles to learning that are frequently experienced by patients with schizophrenia.
- The key to broadening recovery to more persons with schizophrenia is early intervention to engage the patient and family in a comprehensive program of treatment and rehabilitation within the first years of illness.

INTRODUCTION

Although advances in the neurosciences and the prospect of new and more effective psychotropic drugs have captured the attention of psychiatrists and psychiatric training programs, these developments have also inadvertently promoted a biological perspective on schizophrenia and other serious mental disorders, thereby ignoring contributions from psychosocial research and practice. Clearly, judicious use of pharmacotherapy remains the *sine qua non* for building a foundation for treatment and rehabilitation. By employing the biopsychosocial approach to comprehensive care—with social and independent living-skills training, family psychoeducation, self-management of medication and symptoms, assertive clinical case management, and supported housing and employment—psychiatric rehabilitation often can amplify the impact of medication in fostering higher functioning and even symptomatic and social recovery from schizophrenia and other disabling mental disorders.

The biopsychosocial approach to treatment and rehabilitation offers opportunities to patients, clients, or consumers who wish to be active participants in their own treatment. Being a responsible consumer of maintenance antipsychotic medication requires lengthy, repeated education of patients about the effectiveness, value, side effects, and self-administration of medication, as well as learning the negotiation skills necessary to effectively communicate with a physician. The technology for training patients to assume self-management of their mental disabilities is in its infancy, but already progress has been made that needs to be disseminated to and used by other practitioners (Liberman et al., 1993).

THE ZEITGEIST IS CHANGING

Patients with major mental disorders no longer are content to remain in a passive role with their physicians and other service providers. They prefer to see themselves as clients, survivors, or consumers with an active interest in learning about their disorders, setting their goals, and selecting their treatments. From a role of passive compliance with treatments prescribed for them, more patients now insist upon an informed collaboration with their professional treaters.

The growing consumerism movement has converged with other developments to make the potential for illness self-management feasible and successful. Aside from the high rate of symptomatic remission among cases of recent onset, these developments include: destigmatization of mental illness; improved symptom relief from newer antipsychotic drugs; optimistic follow-up data regarding the course of schizophrenia; the emergence of skills-training technology that overcomes the cognitive deficits associated with schizophrenia; the active coping role that helps limit the intrusion of symptoms into everyday life; and the demonstrated effectiveness of integrated, comprehensive, and coordinated systems of mental health delivery. The additive benefits that accrue from interweaving these factors have led us to question whether, *together with our patients,* we can improve the course and outcome of schizophrenia and enhance the potential for recovery to many more people who have a serious mental disorder.

CONSUMERISM AND THE SELF-HELP MOVEMENT

Unlike other mutual aid self-help groups (such as Alcoholics Anonymous) that emphasize individual reform and cooperation with the medical profession, the mental patient self-help or consumerism movement originated in the early 1970s with a distinctly antipsychiatry focus (Zinman, Budd, & Harp, 1987). The emphasis of these early "grass roots" self-help groups was to challenge or reject social norms and values, to question the need for medications and involuntary admissions, and, generally, to serve as an alternative to the mental health system (Emerick, 1989).

Several recent developments have improved rapport between consumer activists and professionals. In 1987, the U.S. Surgeon General-sponsored Workshop on Self-Help and Public Health recommended the establishment of formal systems of care to build egalitarian links with member-governed voluntary associations (HRSA Bureau of Maternal and Child Health and Resource Development, 1988). This led to the formation of a National Council on Self-Help and Public Health, which encouraged numerous public health agencies to interact with ongoing and fledgling self-help groups (Borkman, 1990). One recent example was the establishment of an Office of Consumer Affairs in the California Department of Mental Health.

A parallel event has been the rise of self-help organizations and clearinghouses that provide information and referral services to individuals and groups (Wollert, 1987). The broad dissemination of material made possible by these clearinghouses has contributed to the development of a "self-help ethos," (Reissman & Gartner, 1987) a value system that includes empowerment and self-determination but does not promote a radical antipsychiatry philosophy. The self-help ethos encourages clinicians to provide more active educational services in an interactive, respectful fashion.

Consumers also educate each other and organize group activities and advocacy efforts, such as the Project Return Clubs in California and Florida, The Recovery, Inc. nationwide, and the Network of Mental Health Clients. The shift of the mental health consumer movement from radicalism to a more constructive partnership with professionals—combined with clinicians' recognition that hierarchical, authoritarian relationships with patients are frequently destructive to the therapeutic alliance (Frank & Gunderson, 1990; Stark, Corrigan, & Liberman, 1992)—has created a window of opportunity for galvanizing truly cooperative working relationships.

THE GROWTH OF COLLABORATION IN TREATMENT

A key goal of the self-help movement is to supplant the passive recipient of mental health services with an active participant in the treatment endeavor. Thus, instead of noncompliance being viewed as the patient's failure to comply, it is seen as a lack of collaboration between patient and clinician or a deficiency in the accessibility (or outreach efforts) of the mental health delivery system. For example, a patient's failure to continue on maintenance antipsychotic medication does not necessarily derive from a lack of motivation by the patient but from inadequate education of the patient about medication benefits and side effects, a rupture in the therapeutic alliance, or failures in the mental health service delivery system. The task for the treater becomes mobilization of the patient's assets and resources (including the family) to cooperate in a treatment partnership, sharing responsibilities for adherence to mutually agreed upon treatment prescriptions.

Because of the chronic and relapsing nature of schizophrenia, the patient and his or her family members must understand the stress-related, neurobiological nature of the disorder and must develop a close working alliance or collaborative empiricism with the treaters. Failure to educate and engage patients and their caregivers in a long-term collaborative and informed therapeutic alliance results in noncompliance with essential antipsychotic medication, psychosocial treatments, and supportive services (Morrison & Bellack, 1984; Van Putten, 1974).

Noncompliance is a serious problem, and the clinician must be sensitive to the obstacles or barriers that lie in the pathway of a therapeutic partnership. The most common barriers to this alliance in treatment can be divided into five domains (Table 11.1) (Corrigan, Liberman, & Engel, 1990). An example of a "patient characteristic" barrier is cognitive disorganization—deficits in short-term memory and sustained attention. Circumventing this problem might require minimizing the complexity of treatment regimens; using telephone calls, compartmentalized pill boxes, and reminders for patients to take their medications; using cognitive rehabilitation techniques to improve the patient's memory and attention (Green & Kinsbourne, 1990); teaching the patient self-monitoring techniques; and enlisting caregivers' assistance in monitoring compliance. When the clinician assumes responsibility for improving collaboration with the patient by imparting needed information and skills, patients become more satisfied, more responsible, and more reliable consumers of services (Hall, Roter, & Katz, 1988).

Table 11.1
Barriers to Patient Collaboration in Treatment and Examples of Corrective Measures

Barrier	***Corrective Measure***
Treatment techniques (side effects)	Educate patients about side effects and their management
Patient characteristics (cognitive disorganization)	Teach self-monitoring techniques to patient
Family characteristics (unrealistic expectations)	Encourage family participation in psychoeducation and support groups
Clinician-patient relationship (clinician's nihilism)	Help patient and family members to set and attain realistic, incremental goals; offer lavish reinforcement when they are achieved and even for effort
Treatment delivery system (lack of coordination)	Use case managers and continuous treatment teams with capability for assertive outreach to coordinate services

POSITIVE OUTCOMES FOR THOSE WITH A SERIOUS MENTAL ILLNESS

Most mental health professionals have viewed the treatment

of the seriously mentally ill as an unrewarding and often frustrating experience (Meyerson, 1978). However, several long-term outcome studies from the United States, Europe, and Japan demonstrate that when people with severe forms of schizophrenia are interviewed 20–40 years after the most disabling period of their illness, more than half are functioning in a reasonably normal way (Bleuler, 1968; Ciompi, 1980; Harding, 1988; Huber, 1973). In their study of patients with serious symptoms of schizophrenia, Harding and colleagues (1987) found that 30 years after deinstitutionalization, 82% of these patients had not been hospitalized in the previous year; two thirds were functioning in the normal range of the Global Assessment Scale, had close friends, and reported living full lives. Furthermore, only 25% required daily maintenance antipsychotic medication to keep them well.

Considering these data, the outlook for people diagnosed with schizophrenia is not bleak; rather, it illustrates that recovery from the illness is possible if continuous access to treatment and rehabilitation is provided. This hopeful attitude has contributed to the growth of biobehavioral technology that uses new and better medications as well as improved psychosocial and behavioral treatments for schizophrenia to accelerate remission of symptoms, recovery of social and vocational functioning, and improvement in quality of life.

INTEGRATED AND COMPREHENSIVE ASSERTIVE COMMUNITY TREATMENT

During the late 1960s and early 1970s, mental health experts realized that office- or clinic-based treatments based on psychotherapeutic models had little relevance for persons with persisting mental disabilities. As a result, they designed a variety of experimental, creative methods of service delivery for community-based treatment of persons with schizophrenia and other chronic disorders (Beard, Malamud, & Rossman, 1978; Fairweather, Sanders, Cressler, & Maynard, 1969; Falloon, Boyd, & McGill, 1984; Liberman, 1977; Paul & Lentz, 1977).

cally mentally disabled patients could be rehabilitated and reintegrated into community life without having to wait 20–40 years for symptoms to "burn out." Despite differences in orientation, structure, and organization, these programs succeeded because they shared basic strategies for effective intervention with the seriously mentally ill. Bachrach (1980) identified nine common principles (Table 11.2) that are credited with the success of these model programs. Preeminent among them are administrative endorsement for a rehabilitation philosophy and the use of practical, learning-based, educational methods that transformed the traditional therapeutic relationships between staff and patients into "teacher-student" roles.

SKILLS TRAINING

Specific learning-based techniques that facilitate collaboration in treatment and focus on the capacity for adaptation, coping, and wellness of the individual have been developed and experimentally validated (Lieberman, Jody, & Geisler, 1993). Skills training provides a technology for galvanizing patients and their families (or significant other caregivers) into both responsible consumers of mental health services and active advocates for their needs in the realm of community support services. Moreover, skills training can equip patients and caregivers with the capacity to cope with ambient biopsychosocial stressors, such as drugs of abuse, family stress and burden, and major life events.

Educating the Family:

One of the most important areas for skills training involves educating the family. Most patients either return to live with their families or continue to have substantial contact with them (Carpentier, Lesage, Goulet, Lalonde, & Renaud, 1992). Families are the main source of enduring financial and social support for patients with schizophrenia. In times of crisis, most often it is the family that offers assistance, so it is not

Table 11.2
PRINCIPLES FOR SUCCESSFUL COMPREHENSIVE ASSERTIVE COMMUNITY TREATMENT

1. Priority given to the persistently mentally disabled population with an optimistic, "can-do" rehabilitation philosophy
2. Linkage with other resources in the community, including liaison with partial hospitalization and inpatient care when indicated
3. Functional integrity in which provision is made for patients to receive the full range of services formerly associated with institutional care (e.g., medical, psychiatric, housing, financial, recreational, vocational)
4. Individually tailored treatment with outreach as needed and least amount of supervision and restrictiveness to encourage empowerment, autonomy, and illness self-management by patients
5. Cultural relevance and specificity
6. Staff trained to engage difficult clients, conduct symptomatic and functional assessment, and provide empirically validated biobehavioral treatment (e.g., social-skills training) and rehabilitation modalities
7. Systematic, written set of policies and procedures, including treatment manuals
8. Educational thrust with patients viewed as "students," "members," or "clients" who can acquire greater self-help and self-reliance through learning-based procedures
9. Ongoing internal assessment and quality assurance mechanisms that permit the program to monitor itself continually and improve its functions, processes, goals, and outcomes

most often it is the family that offers assistance, so it is not surprising that a high level of stress exists in families of psychiatric persons. Nor is it surprising that patients who live with families who exhibit high "expressed emotion" (which can be defined as excessively critical, hostile, or emotionally overinvolved attitudes and behavior) are three to four times more likely to relapse within a year following discharge from the hospital than patients in low expressed emotion families (Kavanagh, 1992). These internationally replicated findings have led to the development of training techniques and educational programs designed to teach patients and families about schizophrenia and its management.

Behavioral Family Management:

Another skills-training method, behavioral family management, is based on behavioral skills training (Falloon & Liberman, 1983; Mueser, Glynn, & Liberman, 1994). Training occurs in five stages, with considerable recycling of each stage throughout the therapy: (a) behavioral assessment, (b) education about schizophrenia and its care, (c) communication skills training, (d) problem solving, and (e) coping with special problems.

The clinical efficacy of this model has been systematically evaluated and replicated in Los Angeles at the Clinical Research Center for Schizophrenia as well as in England (Falloon et al., 1985; Randolph et al., 1994; Strachan, 1992). Results showed that patients who received the family treatment had fewer hospitalization episodes, spent less time in the hospital, experienced fewer major exacerbations in psychotic symptoms, had more sustained remissions, and required fewer emergency crisis sessions than patients who received supportive individual therapy. Patients who received the family intervention also improved more in their social and vocational adjustment and were actually prescribed *lower* doses of neuroleptics to control their symptoms than their counterparts who received individual supportive therapy. Through provision of behavioral family therapy in an educational format, families can be trained to detect and resolve stresses that arise from the persisting vulnerability associated with schizophrenia.

Multidimensional Approach:

In another effort to equip patients and their relatives with knowledge and skills for dealing with schizophrenia, Hogarty and colleagues (1986) developed a psychoeducational family treatment program for patients and their families; patients also received individually oriented social skills training in conjunction with pharmacotherapy. Acutely hospitalized patients with schizophrenia who had been living with high expressed emotion relatives were randomly assigned to one of four treatment protocols: medication only; medication with either of the two modalities alone; and medication with both social-skills training and family treatment.

At 1-year follow-up, the medication-only group had a relapse rate of 41%, whereas the group receiving medication, social-skills training, and family therapy had no relapses. The group receiving medication combined with family therapy alone or social-skills training alone had relapse rates of 19% and 20%, respectively. Most significantly, this study demonstrates that the effects of these therapies are additive, suggesting that a multidimensional approach is most likely to be translated into greater resilience against stress-induced relapse.

These practical, educational, and family management approaches have been replicated in London (Leff, Kuipers, Berkowitz, Eberlein-Vries, & Sturgeon, 1982), Manchester (Tarrier et al., 1988), and New York (MacFarlane, Stasny, & Deakins, 1992). A recent meta-analysis of 27 studies incorporating social-skills training on patients with schizophrenia found significant effect-sizes for this modality's impact on discharge rates from hospitals; relapse rates; acquisition, durability, and generalization of skills; and social adjustment (Benton & Schroeder, 1990).

MODULES FOR SOCIAL AND INDEPENDENT LIVING SKILLS TRAINING

Unfortunately, techniques for teaching social skills are not easily learned by professionals. At least 3–6 months of apprenticeship are required to prepare a psychologist, counselor, nurse, social worker, or psychiatrist to use these methods confidently and competently. To overcome this obstacle, a step-by-step multimedia program for training social and independent living skills was designed for easier use by a wider array of mental health professionals and paraprofessionals

(Wallace, Boone, Donahoe, & Foy, 1985). Several "user friendly" modules are now available in the UCLA Social and Independent Living Skills Program. Together, the modules form a comprehensive rehabilitation program, but they also can be used selectively in combination with existing programs in a wide variety of hospital and community settings.

The techniques described in the trainer's manual for each component include all of the behavioral learning principles known to help people with schizophrenia overcome their learning disabilities: behavioral rehearsal, repetition and over-learning, coaching, shaping and fading, modeling, video feedback, and positive reinforcement. Each module is divided into separate skill areas that have specific educational objectives. The patients proceed through each skill area by employing eight learning activities (Table 11.3).

Module Specifics:

The Medication Management Module of the multimedia program has five skill areas: obtaining information about antipsychotic medication; correctly self-administering and evaluating the medication; identifying the side effects of the medication and distinguishing between benign and serious side effects; negotiating medication issues with health care providers; and understanding the value and benefits of using long-acting neuroleptics.

In the Symptom Management Module, patients learn: how to identify the warning signs of relapse; how to intervene early to prevent relapse once these signs appear; how to cope with persistent psychotic symptoms that continue despite medications; and how to avoid alcohol and other drugs of abuse. Each skill area can be further divided into target behaviors. For example, in the skill area of "Identifying Warning Signs of Relapse," patients learn how to discuss warning signs with their relatives and physician so that there is agreement on the symptoms that predict relapse (e.g., insomnia, irritability, social withdrawal, ideas of reference). Patients are also taught to keep a checklist of warning signs to monitor themselves over time. This is designed to help patients understand the benefits of early intervention and realize when to request help.

Table 11.3
LEARNING ACTIVITIES FOR EACH SKILL AREA IN SKILLS TRAINING MODULES

Learning Activity	*Role of Trainer*
1. Introduction to skill area	Tell participants the skills that will be taught and the benefits of learning them
2. Videotape questions/answers	Show participants a videotaped demonstration of the skills, and ask questions to be sure the material is understood
3. Role play	Help participants practice the skills
4. Resource management	Teach participants to identify the resources needed to perform the skills and methods of obtaining these resources
5. Outcome problems	Teach participants to solve problems that might occur when the skills are used in new situations
6. In vivo exercises	Supervise participants as they perform the skills in new situations
7. Homework assignments	Encourage participants to perform the skills independently in new situations
8. Booster sessions	Provide participants with "refresher" courses on an as-needed basis

These modules were designed to compensate for the cognitive and symptomatic obstacles to learning that are regularly experienced by many patients with schizophrenia. The two modules outlined above, Symptom Management and Medication Management, have been used to train patients in illness self-management (Wallace et al., 1985; Eckman et al., 1992; Eckman, Liberman, Phipps, & Blair, 1990). In one controlled

Figure 11.1
DURABILITY OF SKILLS

Skills were learned in two modules, Symptom Management and Medication Management. The contrast group is Supportive Group Therapy.

Medication Management

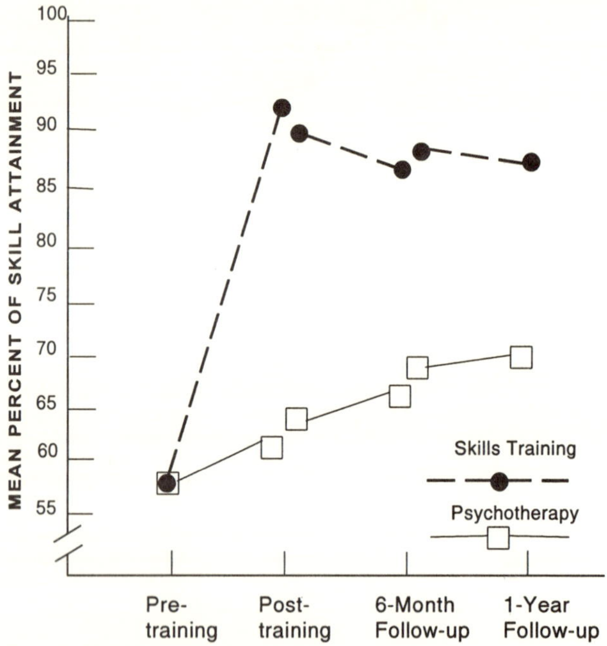

Eckman, Liberman, Phipps, & Blair, 1990). In one controlled study, 41 patients with schizophrenia who received constant maintenance neuroleptic therapy were randomly assigned either to supportive group therapy or to structured, modularized skills training. The skills training comprised training in medication and symptom self-management using the UCLA modules. Patients in group therapy engaged in an insight-oriented and supportive group process that included less-formally structured education about schizophrenia as an illness and the importance of medication. Both treatment conditions involved twice-weekly, 90-minute sessions over the course of 6 months.

After 6 months, the patients who received skills training

Symptom Management

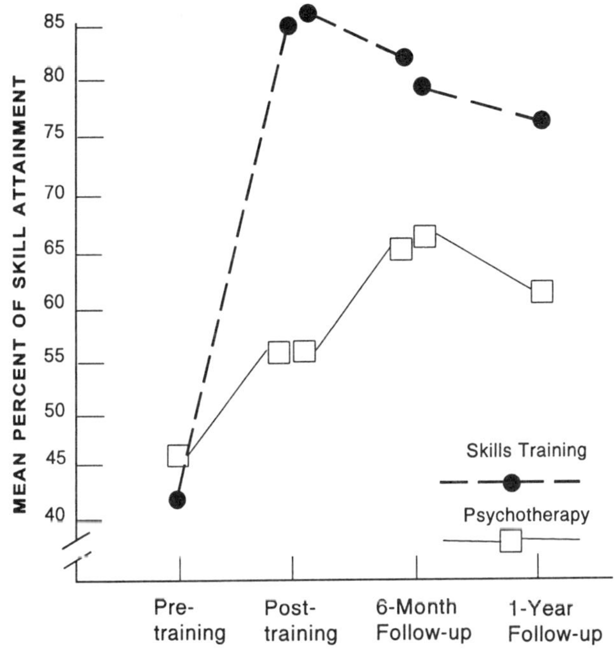

those in group therapy did not. As shown in Figure 11.1, these skills were largely retained 1 year after training was completed. Even patients with moderately severe levels of psychopathology showed significant learning effects. Although the data used to compare groups for improvements in psychopathology and relapse were inconclusive, nearly all of the patients who participated in the skills modules systematically and regularly monitored their warning signs throughout the 6-month training period, indicating an increase in the collaborative relationship with the prescribing clinician. Moreover, the patients who received skills training showed significantly improved utilization of their illness self-management skills and social adjustment 2 years after they entered the study.

EVALUATING SKILLS TRAINING

Controlled studies have tested for the efficacy and replicability of skills training for patients with schizophrenia. One study (Wallace, Liberman, MacKain, Blackwell, & Eckman, 1992) randomly assigned patients at seven facilities (one state hospital, five residential care homes, and one day treatment program) to a control group, which consisted of customary social rehabilitation therapy, or to a modular program, in which they received specific training on how to develop independent recreational activities, improve their grooming skills, and learn medication self-management. Patients and trainers were evaluated on their ability to learn and teach these skills, respectively. Over a period of 30–40 hours of training per module, the patients who received skills training acquired and retained significantly more than the patients who received the customary form of social rehabilitation across all facilities. More germane to the question of disseminability, the effectiveness of the intervention depended on the trainers' adherence to the instructional techniques specified in the modules—not on their level of education or professional degree. Thus, the techniques showed great utility in the hands of professional and nonprofessional trainers alike.

FIRST PERSON ACCOUNTS

It has become increasingly clear that many persons with schizophrenia have learned coping strategies to deal effectively with their illness. The *Schizophrenia Bulletin* has published the "First Person Accounts" section continuously since 1979. Besides letting patients and families know that they are not alone in confronting the problems associated with schizophrenia, this section has frequently included anecdotes that provide insight into the coping techniques people have used to combat their illness successfully.

More recently, individuals have come forward to tell their

stories of relapse and recovery. Fred Frese, a practicing psychologist from Ohio, described the personal coping techniques he developed for dealing with his symptoms of schizophrenia in a series of articles and lectures, and in a videocassette (Frese, 1991). The autobiography *Welcome, Silence* documents one woman's odyssey from acute schizophrenia to practicing psychiatrist (North, 1987). Many others, unfortunately, fear "coming out of the closet," believing that the stigma of mental illness endangers their jobs, social positions, and families (Frese, 1991).

Many case reports confirm the benefit of cognitive and behavioral coping methods. A retrospective study of 10 fully recovered persons with schizophrenia identified various "curing elements" critical to effective management of the disorder (Rund, 1990). Another report focused on how mental health consumers who have learned to cope with symptoms have been trained and employed as case management aides (Sherman & Porter, 1991). It was found that coping techniques not only benefited the consumer but also the "prosumer" (i.e., the one who both performs and consumes mental health services).

In the past decade, researchers have used semistructured interviews with open-ended probes to learn patients' techniques for controlling their symptoms of psychosis. One study found that patients' self-monitoring of internal states and their evaluation of such states were prerequisites for effective self-control of symptoms (Breier & Strauss, 1982). In another study, many patients with schizophrenia were found to monitor symptoms of incipient decompensation and alter their behavior effectively when symptoms of decompensation were present (McCandless-Glimcher et al., 1986). A third investigation revealed that the formation of a "disease consciousness" — that is, an awareness of the existence of psychotic behavior — was the most crucial step in attaining self-control (Dittmann & Schuttler, 1990).

These studies, along with the Symptom Management Module (in which patients are successfully taught coping strategies for dealing with psychotic symptoms) (Falloon & Talbott, 1981; Green & Kinsbourne, 1990) demonstrate that the key question is not whether it is time yet for cognitive remediation in the treatment of schizophrenia (Green, 1993), but rather, "When will clinicians use the patient's own adaptive strivings or coping strategies as an essential part of treatment?"

CASE EXAMPLE

Mr. S is 27 years old and has suffered from paranoid schizophrenia since age 17. His first psychotic break occurred at a rock concert, and use of lysergic acid diethylamide (LSD) was suspected as the triggering event. He was hospitalized for treatment of delusions and hallucinations 2 weeks later and three more times before graduating from high school.

During the first few years of his illness, he had the good fortune of being treated by a psychiatrist who believed in the value of patient education. Using the Medication Management Module, the psychiatrist and Mr. S spent 45 minutes weekly for 3 months exploring the learning activities of this module. At many of the sessions, the psychiatrist and Mr. S invited his parents to attend so that they would be able to reinforce and support his self-management and use of medication without being overly involved or nagging. Mr. S learned about schizophrenia, the medications used to treat the disorder, and their side effects. He learned and applied effective coping mechanisms for dealing with dry mouth and supersensitivity to sun exposure.

He was engaged in a social-skills training group of outpatients that featured an individualized approach to learning how to achieve one's needs (Liberman, Mueser, & DeRisi, 1989). Led by a behaviorally oriented psychologist, the group enabled Mr. S to learn relationship-building skills (i.e., the correct response to social cues such as facial expression, tone of voice, and body language). This enabled him to judge other people's responses to his actions and helped him make subtle behavioral adjustments to mask his sometimes-severe thought disorder. He was accepted to a prestigious university to which he applied while an inpatient in a psychiatric hospital.

Feeling overconfident because he was attending a university and was clinically stable, he discontinued his medication. Within 3 months, he suffered another psychotic break, necessitating a psychiatric hospitalization and retitration of his neuroleptic medication. He recovered several weeks later but felt the need to enroll in a different university "where people don't know me" back in his home state. At this time, he resumed treatment with his original psychiatrist, who persuaded Mr. S to participate in the Symptom Management Module, which taught Mr. S how to identify his prodromal symptoms of impending relapse. For Mr. S, psychotic decompensation was heralded on each occasion by several weeks of ideas of reference, suspiciousness, difficulty concentrating, and arduousness in expressing himself. With Mr. S's permission, the psychiatrist invited his parents to participate in the framing of Mr. S's "relapse prevention plan," which involved asking his parents for assistance with making a phone call to the psychiatrist and driving him to the psychiatrist's office.

Mr. S and his therapist worked together to develop a self-monitoring system that identified early warning signs of stress and relapse. Each night, Mr. S would rate his daily symptoms and adjust his medication accordingly. For example, if Mr. S felt he had no problems concentrating, no difficulty expressing his thoughts, or no feelings of suspiciousness, he would take the baseline level of 5 mg of fluphenazine (Prolixin). If he had experienced ideas of reference but no speaking problems that day, he would take 10 mg. The presence of both cognitive and loose associations when speaking to others would warrant 15 mg.

Another crucial factor in Mr. S's self-management was his ability to form trusting relationships. His several close and loyal friends allowed him to gather feedback on his cognitive and behavioral processes as well as empirically validate his perception of symptoms. This was an important element in building self-esteem that increased his confidence in his capacity for self-assessment.

Mr. S's psychiatrist, with help from a social worker, engaged Mr. S, his parents, and his girlfriend in 25 sessions of behavioral family management (Falloon, Boyd, & McGill, 1984), during which they learned basic communication skills (e.g., giving positive feedback to each other, making a positive request instead of a "demand" from others, and expressing angry or frustrated feelings directly and non-accusingly). After 10 sessions of systematic training in communication skills, Mr. S and his parents were taught how to use these skills in coping with and solving day-to-day problems. The problems could arise in the family relationships (e.g., Mr. S secluding himself for long periods of time in his room) or in the community (e.g., Mr. S experiencing difficulty using the new computerized index catalogue at the local library).

Mr. S continued successfully in college and graduated with honors in psychology. He applied and was accepted for graduate school in clinical psychology in another state. One year later, he married his girlfriend of 3 years.

Graduate school went very well for nearly 2 years. He had been on the same medication regimen, but for practical reasons, he switched to a local psychiatrist who did not concur with the diagnosis of schizophrenia, principally because Mr. S was functioning at such a high level. Soon thereafter, the psychiatrist thought he saw early signs of tardive dyskinesia, and persuaded Mr. S to stop his medication and begin taking lithium (Eskalith, Lithane). Within 6 weeks, he decompensated and was admitted to a psychiatric facility. He was restarted on fluphenazine, and although his psychotic symptoms abated rapidly, his return to baseline functioning was delayed by the heavy-handed and stressful workload of his graduate program. He was forced to resign from the program; he was allowed to finish his master's degree but was not permitted to pursue a doctorate or a clinical certificate.

Despondent but not defeated, he returned to his home state

permitted to pursue a doctorate or a clinical certificate.

Despondent but not defeated, he returned to his home state and began working as an administrator in a mental health advocacy program. He has been successfully employed for the past several years; at the time of this writing, he is the assistant director of the program. Although his original goal was to be a clinician, he has channeled his desire to help others avoid the torment he experienced by becoming active in the political arena, believing that by working to influence the attitudes of legislators, he can most effectively fight discrimination against the mentally ill.

Although he acknowledges the importance of medication, social support, his own intelligence, and good premorbid adjustment as protective factors in his ongoing efforts to cope with schizophrenia, he believes the key to his wellness is self-discipline. His ability to sacrifice comfort for psychiatric stability is partially a result of his stoic personality, but he ascribes most of his self-management ability to the skills training he had received. It is this inner strength that is tested daily: at home, by taking extra fluphenazine; at work, by trying to appear objective when supervising co-workers who talk disparagingly about clients; at political gatherings, where he tries to remain the professional advocate but wishes to scream out his personal anguish. His biggest disappointment is that he cannot tell his story for fear of losing his job, social position, and credibility. He says there are many people with schizophrenia like him in the community. If so, these people have much to teach us about self-management of schizophrenia.

FROM ILLNESS SELF-MANAGEMENT TO RECOVERY

What are the prospects for broadening symptomatic and social recovery to a larger number of persons with schizophrenia? The key to succeeding in this endeavor lies in early intervention that engages the patient and family in a comprehensive program of treatment and rehabilitation within the first years of the illness. When persons who have a recent onset of schizophrenia are involved in an integrated biobehavioral treatment program, they show rapid and substantial remission of their positive and negative symptoms (Liberman et al., 1993).

For example, at the UCLA Aftercare Clinic, persons with recent-onset schizophrenia who received 12.5 mg of fluphenazine for 2 weeks, family education, individual case management, and psychoeducational group treatment were in complete remission of clinically significant levels of positive psychotic symptoms for 82% of their first year in treatment and in remission of clinically significant levels of negative symptoms for 78% of the first year (Nuechterlein et al., 1993). These lengthy periods of remission of psychopathology offer clinicians a window of opportunity to intervene with psychosocial services and skills training when patients have the cognitive capacity to benefit from learning experiences. If treatment and rehabilitation is sustained and flexibly linked to the phase and type of an individual's schizophrenic disorder for many years, then the prospects rise considerably for sustained symptomatic remission and normal psychosocial functioning (e.g., living independently, working or studying, having friendships, and pursuing recreational activities).

The elements of service described herein are not "pie in the sky"—they have been assembled and delivered in real programs. For example, a community mental health system in the County of Buckingham in England implemented an integrated system of care for the seriously mentally ill in the mid-1980s. Services such as those cited in this lesson were delivered *in vivo*, especially in the patients' homes and workplaces, by a team of specialized psychiatrists, psychologists, social workers, and psychiatric nurses. Epidemiologic surveys in this county indicate that the incidence of new cases of chronic schizophrenia decreased tenfold during a 5-year period (Falloon & Fadden, 1993).

Scientist-practitioners working at the UCLA Clinical Research Center for Schizophrenia & Psychiatric Rehabilitation nia. Working with a private agency of specially trained case managers, the "life adjustment team," psychiatrists and psychologists from the Clinical Research Center are integrating many of these principles to accelerate the process of symptomatic and social recovery in these patients, who range in age from 17 to 40.

Case managers, under the supervision of psychologists and psychiatrists, teach clients medication and symptom self-management skills, basic conversational skills, and recreational skills. Behavioral family management is employed for achieving a partnership with family members who, along with the client, become educated and empowered to participate as full members of the "team." Personalized goals are formulated by each client with the astute assistance and coaching by the case managers, and these goals are monitored weekly and reported monthly and quarterly to the client, family, and treating psychiatrist.

Vocational rehabilitation, in the form of transitional and supported work, is facilitated by the case managers when clients' symptoms have stabilized and their goal setting reaches the domain of work. The therapeutic alliance between the clients and their case managers is developed and strengthened through frequent interactions in natural, community-based recreational and social settings, as well as through home visits. Even though a formal research study is still being planned to evaluate this integrated mental health treatment and rehabilitation program, 10 clients already have achieved stable and prolonged remission of psychotic symptoms and reintegration into full-time work or university study.

SUMMARY

Community-based care of persons with serious mental disorders has become infused with greater optimism in recent years because efforts are increasingly guided by empirically validated and treatment-specific interventions. These treatments include a new generation of antipsychotic and antidepressant medications, use of existing and customary antipsychotic drugs with higher benefit/risk ratios, social-skills training, supported employment, assertive case management, and psychoeducational family management. The clinical and economic effectiveness of treatment systems marked by comprehensiveness, accessibility, and coordination of services is now generally recognized.

Psychopharmacologic and psychosocial treatments appear to be additive in their efficacy. For example, adding psychoeducational or behavioral family management to maintenance antipsychotic medication reduces relapse rates by half. Combining social-skills training with maintenance pharmacotherapy yields better social functioning while minimizing relapse. If comprehensive and coordinated treatment and rehabilitation services are accessible on a continuous basis for those in the early phases of their psychotic disorders, the goal of recovery (i.e., sustained remission of psychotic symptoms and normal instrumental role functioning) is a legitimate aim of any clinical program.

REFERENCES

Bachrach, L. L. (1980). Overview: Model programs for chronic mental patients. *American Journal of Psychiatry, 137,* 1023–1031.

Beard, J. H., Malamud, T. J., & Rossman, E. (1978). Psychiatric rehabilitation and long-term rehospitalization rates. *Schizophrenia Bulletin, 4,* 622–635.

Benton, M. K., & Schroeder, H. E. (1990). Social skills training with schizophrenics: a meta-analytic evaluation. *Journal of Consulting and Clinical Psychology, 58,* 741–747.

Bleuler, M. (1968). A 23-year longitudinal study of 208 schizophrenics and impressions in regard to the nature of schizophrenia. In D. Rosenthal & S. S. Kety (Eds.), *The transmission of schizophrenia*. New York, NY: Oxford University Press.

Breier, A., & Strauss, J. S. (1982). Self-control in psychotic disorders. *Archives of General Psychiatry, 40,* 1141–1145.

Carpentier, N., Lesage, A., Goulet, J., Lalonde, P., & Renaud, M. (1992). Burden of care of families not living with young schizophrenic relatives. *Hospital and Community Psychiatry, 43,* 38–43.

Ciompi, L. (1980). Catamnestic long-term study on the course of life and aging of schizophrenics. *Schizophrenia Bulletin, 6,* 606–618.

Corrigan, P. W., Liberman, R. P., & Engel, J. (1990). From noncompliance to adherence in psychiatric treatment: Strategies that facilitate collaboration between practitioner and patient. *Hospital and Community Psychiatry, 41,* 1203–1211.

Dittmann, J., & Schuttler, R. (1990). Disease consciousness and coping strategies of patients with schizophrenic psychosis. *Acta Psychiatrica Scandinavica, 82,* 318–322.

Eckman, T. A., et al. (1992). Technique for training schizophrenic patients in illness self-management: A controlled trial. *American Journal of Psychiatry, 149,* 1549–1555.

Eckman, T. A., Liberman, R. P., Phipps, C. C., & Blair, K. (1990). Teaching medication management skills to schizophrenic patients. *Journal of Clinical Psychopharmacology, 10,* 33–38.

Emerick, R. E. (1989). Group demographics in the mental patient movement: group location, age and size as structural factors. *Community Mental Health, 25* (Winter), 277–300.

Fairweather, G. W., Sanders, D. H., Cressler, D. L., & Maynard, H. (1969). *Community life for the mentally ill*. Chicago, IL: Aldine.

Falloon, I. R. H., Boyd, J., McGill, C. (1984). *Family care of schizophrenia*. New York, NY: Guilford Press.

Falloon, I. R. H., Boyd, J. L., & McGill, C. W. (1984). *Family care of schizophrenia*. New York, NY: Guilford Press.

Falloon, I. R. H., et al. (1985). Family management in the prevention of morbidity of schizophrenia. *Archives of General Psychiatry, 42,* 887–896.

Falloon, I. R. H., & Fadden, G. (1993). *Integrated mental health care.* London, UK: Cambridge University Press.

Falloon, I. R. H., & Liberman, R. P. (1983). Interactions between drug and psychosocial therapy in schizophrenia. *Schizophrenia Bulletin, 9,* 44–55.

Falloon, I. R. H., & Talbott, R. E. (1981). Persistent auditory hallucinations: Coping mechanisms and implications for management. *Psychological Medicine, 11,* 329–339.

Frank, A. F., & Gunderson, J. G. (1990). The role of the therapeutic alliance in the treatment of schizophrenia: relationship to course and outcome. *Archives of General Psychiatry, 47,* 228–236.

Frese, F. J. (1991). *Schizophrenia: Surviving in the world of normals.* Videocassette produced by Wellness Reproductions Inc., 23945 Mercantile Road, Beachwood, Ohio 44122.

Green, M. F. (1993). Cognitive remediation in schizophrenia: Is it time yet? *American Journal of Psychiatry, 150,* 178–187.

Green, M. F., & Kinsbourne M. (1990) Subvocal activity and auditory hallucinations. *Schizophrenia Bulletin, 16,* 617–626.

Hall, J. A., Roter, D. L., & Katz, N. R. (1988). Meta-analysis of correlates of provider behavior in medical encounters. *Medical Care, 26,* 657-675.

Harding, C. M. (1988). Course types in schizophrenia. *Schizophrenia Bulletin, 14,* 633–644.

Harding, C., Brooks, G., Ashikaga, T., Strauss, J. S., & Breier, A. (1987). The Vermont longitudinal study of schizophrenia. *American Journal of Psychiatry, 144,* 949–955.

Hogarty, G., et al. (1986). Family psychoeducation, social skills training and maintenance chemotherapy in the aftercare treatment of schizophrenia. *Archives of General Psychiatry, 43,* 633–642.

Huber, G. (1973). *Verlauf und Ausgang Schizophrener Erkrankungen.* Stuttgart, Germany: Schattauer.

HRSA Bureau of Maternal and Child Health and Resource Development. (1988). *Surgeon General's workshop on self-help and public health.* (DHHS Public Health Service Publication No. 224-250). Washington, DC: US Government Printing Office.

Kavanagh, D. J. (1992). Recent developments in expressed emotion and schizophrenia. *British Journal of Psychiatry, 160,* 601–620.

Leff, J., Kuipers, L., Berkowitz, R., Eberlein-Vries, R., & Sturgeon D. A. (1982). A controlled trial of social intervention in the families of schizophrenic patients: two-year follow-up. *British Journal of Psychiatry, 146,* 594–600.

Liberman, R. (1977). Behavior therapy in a community mental health center. *American Journal of Psychiatry, 134,* 401–406.

Liberman, R. P., Mueser, K., & DeRisi, W. J. (1989). *Social skills training for psychiatric patients.* New York, NY: Pergamon Press.

Liberman, R. P., Wallace, C. J., Blackwell, G., Eckman, T. A., Vaccaro, J. V., & Kuehnel, T. G. (1993). Innovations in skills training for the seriously mentally ill: The UCLA Social & Independent Living Skills Modules. *Innovations Research, 2,* 43–60.

Lieberman, J., Jody, & Geisler (1993). Time course and biological correlates of treatment response in first episode schizophrenia. *Archives of General Psychiatry, 50,* 369–376.

MacFarlane, W. R., Stastny, P., & Deakins, S. (1992). Family-aided assertive community treatment. In R. P. Liberman (Ed.). *Effective psychiatric rehabilitation: New directions for mental health services.* San Francisco, CA: Jossey-Bass.

McCandless-Glimcher, L., McKnight, S., Hamera, E., Smith, B. L., Peterson, K. A., & Plumlee, A. A. (1986). Use of symptoms by schizophrenics to monitor and regulate their illness. *Hospital and Community Psychiatry, 37,* 929–933.

Meyerson, A. T. (1978). What are the barriers or obstacles to treatment and care of the chronically disabled mentally ill? In J. A. Talbott (Ed.), *The chronic mental patient: Problems, solutions, and recommendations for public policy.* Washington, DC: American Psychiatric Press.

Morrison, R. L., Bellack, A. S. (1984). Social skills training. In A. S. Bellack (Ed.), *Schizophrenia: Treatment, management, and rehabilitation*. New York, NY: Grune & Stratton Inc.

Mueser, K. T., Glynn, S. M., & Liberman, R. P. (1994). Behavioral family management for serious psychiatric illness. In A. B. Hatfield & H. Lefley (Eds.), *Models of interventions with families of mentally ill relatives – New directions for mental health services*. San Francisco, CA: Jossey-Bass.

North, C. S. (1987). *Welcome, silence*. New York, NY: Simon & Schuster.

Nuechterlein, K. H., et al. (1993, October). *Symptomatic recovery in recent onset persons with schizophrenia*. Paper presented at Annual Institute on Hospital & Community Psychiatry of the American Psychiatric Association, Baltimore, MD.

Paul, G. L., & Lentz, R. (1977). *Psychosocial treatment of chronic mental patients*. Cambridge, MA: Harvard University Press.

Randolph, E., Eth, S., Glynn, S. M., Liberman, R. P., Shaner, A., Leong G., & Escobar, J. (1994). Replication of behavioral family management in schizophrenia: Outcome from a clinic-based intervention. *British Journal of Psychiatry, 164*, 501-506.

Reissman, F., Gartner, A. (1987). The surgeon general and the self-help ethos. *Social Policy, 18* (Fall), 23–25.

Rund, B. R. (1990). Fully recovered schizophrenics: A retrospective study of some premorbid and treatment factors. *Psychiatry, 53*, 127–139.

Sherman, P. S., & Porter, R. (1991). Mental health consumers as case management aides. *Hospital and Community Psychiatry, 42*, 494–498.

Stark, M., Corrigan, P. W ., Liberman, R. P. (1992). Schizophrenic patients' attitudes to therapists using behavioral and humanistic techniques. *Journal of Psychotherapy Practice Research, 1*, 80–85.

Stein, L. I., Test, M. A. (1978). *Alternatives to mental hospital treatment*. New York, NY: Plenum Press.

Strachan, A. (1992). Family management. In R. P. Liberman (Ed.). *Handbook of psychiatric rehabilitation*. New York, NY: Macmillan Publishing Co.

Tarrier, N., et al. (1988). Community management of schizophrenia: A controlled trial of behavioral intervention with families to reduce relapse. *British Journal of Psychiatry, 153,* 532–542.

Van Putten, T. (1974). Why do schizophrenic patients refuse to take their drugs? *Archives of General Psychiatry, 31,* 67–72.

Wallace, C. J., Boone, S. E., Donahoe, C. P., Foy, D. W. (1985). Psychosocial rehabilitation for the chronic mentally disabled: Social and independent living skills training. In D. Barlow (Ed.), *Behavioral treatment of adult disorders.* New York, NY: Guilford Press.

Wallace, C. J., Liberman, R. P., MacKain, S. J., Blackwell, G., Eckman, T. A. (1992). Effectiveness and replicability of modules for teaching social and instrumental skills to the severely mentally ill. *American Journal of Psychiatry, 149,* 654–658.

Wollert, R. (1987). *A survey of self-help clearinghouses in North America: special report for the U.S. Surgeon General's workshop on self-help and public health.* (DHHS publication No. 224-250). Washington, DC: US Government Printing Office.

Zinman, S., Budd, S. U., Harp, H. (1987). *Reaching across: Mental health clients helping each other.* Riverside, CA: California Network of Mental Health Clients.

Name Index

A

B

C

D

E

F

N

O

P

R

S

T

U

V

W

Y

Z

Subject Index

A

B

G

H

I

N

O

P

Q

R

S

T

U

V

W

X

Z

Contributors

Mary Ellen Copeland, MS, MA
Mental health counselor and educator based in Brattleboro, VT.

Robert L. DuPont, MD
President, Institute for Behavior and Health, Inc., Rockville, MD, and Clinical Professor of Psychiatry, Georgetown University School of Medicine, Washington, DC.

Frederic Flach, MD
Adjunct Associate Professor of Psychiatry, Cornell University Medical College, New York; Attending Psychiatrist at Payne Whitney Clinic of The New York Hospital and St. Vincent's Hospital and Medical Center, New York.

Glen O. Gabbard, MD
Bessie Walker Callaway Distinguished Professor at the Menninger Clinic, Training and Supervising Analyst, Topeka Institute for Psychoanalysis; and Clinical Professor of Psychiatry, University of Kansas School of Medicine, Topeka, KS.

Sam Goldstein, PhD
Clinical instructor and psychologist at the Developmental Disabilities and Mental Retardation Clinic, Department of Psychiatry, University of Utah School of Medicine, Salt Lake City, UT.

Thomas R. Insel, MD
Director, Yerkes Primate Center, and Professor of Psychiatry, Emory University School of Medicine, Atlanta, GA.

Richard P. Kluft, PhD, MD, FAPA
Clinical Professor of Psychiatry, Temple University School of Medicine, and Senior Attending Psychiatrist and Director of the Dissociative Disorders Program, The Institute of Pennsylvania Hospital, Philadelphia.

Alex Kopelowicz, MD
NIMH Postdoctoral Research Fellow at UCLA School of Medicine, and Medical Director of the San Fernando Mental Health Center.

Robert Paul Liberman, MD
Professor of Psychiatry at UCLA School of Medicine, Director of the Clinical Research Center for Schizophrenia & Psychiatric Rehabilitation, and Director of the Clinical Research Unit at Camarillo State Hospital.

Richard A. McCormick, PhD
Chief, Psychology Service at the Cleveland V.A. Medical Center, and Assistant Clinical Professor of Psychology, Case Western Reserve University, Cleveland, OH.

Thomas W. Miller, PhD, ABPP
Chief of Psychology Services at the Department of Psychiatry, University of Kentucky Medical Center, Lexington, KY.

Robert F. Newby, PhD, ABPP
Child neuropsychologist and Associate Professor of Neurology, Medical College of Wisconsin, Milwaukee, WI.

Stanton E. Samenow, PhD
Clinical Psychologist and Consultant in Alexandria, VA.